African American Literature of the Twenty-First Century and the Black Arts

African American Literature of the Twenty-First Century and the Black Arts

The Case of John Edgar Wideman

Stephen Casmier

LEXINGTON BOOKS
Lanham • Boulder • New York • London

Published by Lexington Books
An imprint of The Rowman & Littlefield Publishing Group, Inc.
4501 Forbes Boulevard, Suite 200, Lanham, Maryland 20706
www.rowman.com

6 Tinworth Street, London SE11 5AL, United Kingdom

Copyright © 2021 The Rowman & Littlefield Publishing Group, Inc.

All rights reserved. No part of this book may be reproduced in any form or by any electronic or mechanical means, including information storage and retrieval systems, without written permission from the publisher, except by a reviewer who may quote passages in a review.

British Library Cataloguing in Publication Information Available

Library of Congress Cataloging-in-Publication Data on File

ISBN 978-1-7936-1460-5 (cloth)
ISBN 978-1-7936-1462-9 (pbk)
ISBN 978-1-7936-1461-2 (electronic)

To Camille and Ida

Contents

Preface: What Comes Before in Wideman Scholarship		ix
Acknowledgments		xxvii
Introduction: Wideman, Contemporary Writers, and the Black Arts		1
1	*Reuben* and the Sorcerer	23
2	*Philadelphia Fire* and the Art of Bundling the Inchoate	43
3	*The Cattle Killing* and the Art of the Slavery Narrative Conjure	67
4	*Two Cities* and the Art of Breaking Writing's "Spell"	89
5	*Fanon* and the Art of Spiritualizing Narrative	111
6	*Writing to Save a Life* and the Art of Hagiography as Possessed Text (*Texto Montado*)	133
Conclusion: A "Very Igbo Understanding"		159
Works Cited		165
Appendix: Keeping the Language of Fiction Alive: Interview with John Edgar Wideman, June 2019		175
Index		191
About the Author		201

Preface
What Comes Before in Wideman Scholarship

My nearly 40-year engagement with the work of John Edgar Wideman almost began in Nice, France, where I spent my junior year of college as an exchange student. Back then, I had never heard of Wideman and was more concerned with better-known African American writers and perhaps tracking down James Baldwin, who lived in the region and whose work I intensively read that year. While I was studying at the University of Nice, an expatriate American instructor, Jacqueline Berben (later Berben-Masi), tracked me down and recruited me to make an improvised English comprehension tape on which I youthfully held forth on the topic of the status of race relations in the United States, unrest in Miami, and Grand Master Flash and The Furious Five. I first heard about Wideman from Berben-Masi. She discussed her French dissertation on his work under the direction of the influential French African Americanist Michel Fabre, who was a Richard Wright Scholar. They felt he might be Wright's literary heir—the next Black American star writer. Still, I recalcitrantly didn't read any of Wideman's work, but I instantly recognized his name in 1984 when I saw an intriguing piece in a popular news magazine about his book, *Brothers and Keepers*. At a time when African American novels such as Alice Walker's Pulitzer Prize-winning *The Color Purple* and Gloria Naylor's *The Women of Brewster Place* (which I had enthusiastically read) seemed to have little positive to say about Black men and everything written or shown about us in the establishment media described murderous gang bangers, crack addicts, thieves, irresponsible fathers, violent husbands, cheats, and lazy slackers who did not represent the aspirations of the growing Black middle class, *Brothers and Keepers* resonated with what I experienced and knew about some of my amazing friends who didn't make it to college, who were increasingly ending up in prison, and who weren't living with me in university housing. It struck a resonant chord.

Still, my engagement with Wideman did not begin in earnest until 1989, when I was working upriver from New Orleans as a newspaper reporter for *The Times-Picayune*. One day, I received an unexpected telephone call from Margaret Porter Troupe, the wife of poet and writer Quincy Troupe. She was working as a press agent for a publisher and had been looking for someone to write a review of a new novel by Wideman called *Philadelphia Fire*. Someone routed the call to me, one of the few Black reporters working at the paper. I thought reviewing the novel would give me a chance to exercise another type of more personal journalistic voice, one anchored in the real world of the news as it explored the distinct imaginary world of fiction. Instead, I found a work that upended the difference and cast a disruptive pallor over my budding journalistic career. Still, I wrote the review. And then, I got another call from Porter Troupe, which put me in contact with her husband, Quincy, who had worked with Miles Davis on his autobiography and was touring the country promoting the book, standing in for Miles, and often speaking in the musician's distinctive voice. Troupe came to New Orleans for his last stop on the book tour. I interviewed him and wrote an article for the paper. At that moment, it all came together for me in what a character from Nathaniel Mackey's novel, *Bedouin Hornbook*, might call a "mixtery" (39): my New Orleans life dancing as a straggler in second line jazz parades, while also listening to the experimental music of local tenor saxophonist Edward "Kidd" Jordan and trumpeter Michael Ray, a member of the myth science arkestras of Sun Ra who took to the stage in New Orleans on his own amid various glowing neon lights as he played colors instead of scripted music; my experiences as an African American who grew up as a teenager listening to Richard Pryor and watching the unearthly performances of athletes such as boxer Muhammad Ali and more recently of basketball player Michael Jordan; my exposure to Troupe's then channeling of Miles' voice, a musician who wielded the power of silence and had the ability (in the words of jazz pianist Herbie Hancock) to make even the most wrong of notes sound right; and my reading first of Toni Morrison's mind-blowing work, *Beloved*, and then of *Philadelphia Fire*—a work that somehow figured out a way to make a book dance, play music, float like a butterfly, slam dunk, and conjure an aspect of the real, lived experience of a people whose blackness did not signify a lack, but the presence of "bad" black "mixtery." Not long afterward, I left journalism and began the more serious study of literature in France at the Université de Nice-Sophia Antipolis, where I wrote a dissertation on Wideman and jazz, which I defended in 1998.

THE FIGURE OF A NEGLECTED WRITER IN WIDEMAN CRITICISM

When I wrote that work on *Reuben, Philadelphia Fire and The Cattle Killing*, scholars had not previously devoted substantial attention to Wideman. In fact, over the ensuing years, many have continued to lament the lack of critical and widespread public interest in Wideman's work. This has remained an enduring *leitmotif* of Wideman scholarship. In fact, even in 2011, Tracie Church Guzzio noted that scholars had "largely neglected" Wideman in comparison to writers such as "Toni Morrison, Zora Neale Hurston, Alice Walker and Ralph Ellison" (4). I even begin this work with similar observations. Still, beginning in the late 1990s, I had been involved in a circulating and generative critical discussion of the author's work beginning with a dissertation defense before a panel that included influential figures in the field such as Berben-Masi, Fabre, and Claude Julien. I presented a paper on Wideman at the American Literature Association in 1999 and nearly every year afterward for the next twenty years. In fact, the chapters that make up this work began as some of those papers. Most significantly, I participated in early international conferences on the author where Wideman was in attendance, including one on Law and Literature at the University of Nice in 2001, a celebration of Wideman's work sponsored by the literary journal *Callaloo* and held at the University of Virginia in 2000, and another gathering held in Wideman's honor at the University of Pennsylvania in 2003. Through these events, an international nexus of Wideman scholars and scholarship had emerged. Among others, these events brought together European and American scholars such as Berben-Masi, Julien, Jean-Pierre Richard, Yves-Charles Grandjeat, Fritz Gysin, Claudine Raynaud, Michel Feith, Charles Rowell, Brent Edwards, James Coleman, Roland Murray, and the core of scholars who began forming the John Edgar Wideman Society of the American Literature Association: Wilfred Samuels, Raymond E. Janifer, Keith Byerman, Bonnie TuSmith, Karen Jahn, Tracie Church Guzzio, and, among others, myself.

Still, before these events, Coleman, who never actively participated in the society, but had been at the Callaloo celebration, wrote the first monograph on Wideman in 1989, *Blackness and Modernism: The Literary Career of John Edgar Wideman*. He later published another book in 2010 with the title, *Writing Blackness: John Edgar Wideman's Art and Experimentation*. Also, in 1995, Doreatha Drummond Mbalia published the second book, *John Edgar Wideman: Reclaiming the African Personality*, which was shortly followed by Byerman's 1998, *John Edgar Wideman: A Study of the Short Fiction* and Bonnie TuSmith's 1998 collection of interviews, *Conversations with John Edgar Wideman*. Then, following the international conferences, Byerman, one of the central facilitators of Wideman scholarship and his chief critical biographer, worked with TuSmith to edit a 2006 collection of critical essays on Wideman: *Critical Essays on John Edgar Wideman*. In 2013, Byerman also published *The Life and Work of John Edgar Wideman*. In the meantime, *Callaloo* united many of the papers presented at its 2000 celebration into the first major collection of critical essays: *John Edgar Wideman: The European Response*. In 2011, Guzzio, a founding member of the Wideman Society published an encompassing monograph with the title, *All Stories Are True: History, Myth, and Trauma in the Work of John Edgar Wideman*. Quintin Miller followed this work with his 2018 book *Understanding John Edgar Wideman*. Finally, in 2019, Michel Feith, who was at the 2003 event in Pennsylvania, published another fairly expansive and critically rigorous 2019 monograph titled, *John Edgar Wideman and Modernity: A Critical Dialogue*. So, in all, the lack of critical attention to Wideman's work involves a plethora of articles scattered among the most prestigious literary journals (a 2021 search of the *Jstor* and *Project Muse* databases using the name "Wideman" in the title field generated about 100 articles—the name "Morrison" generated over 2,500), a society established to study his work, two books of critical essays, a critical biography, a collection of interviews, and seven monographs.

A major characteristic of Wideman criticism is that many of the scholars present themselves as crucial mediators or interpreters of a complicated, significant, and underappreciated writer that they desperately want, in the words of James Coleman, "to reach a broad audience of general readers" (Coleman, *Writing* ix). Wideman's work, nevertheless, seems to push against this critical desire. Something about the dawning of understanding that comes with reading and "getting" Wideman's work produces an all but closed-off sense of deep and confessional intimacy with the writer and his family that one rarely ever experiences in the most cherished personal relationships. This brings to mind an observation by Claude Julien, who quotes a Nabokov scholar and one of my professors from the Université de Nice who states: "one does not read just books, but authors" (quoted in Julien 540). Perhaps "reading" Wideman becomes more like experiencing a visual artwork or "a nonrepresentational, abstract expressionist painting, savoring its ineffable significance," as described by Walter Ong in his book on poet Gerard Manley Hopkins, *Hopkins, the Self, and God*. Through such savoring, Ong says, "we all are enabled to be intimately alone together" (Ong, Hopkins 131). Trying to convey such intimate isolation in the language of literary criticism and render the experience of reading his work less (in the words of Ishmael Reed) "reader-unfriendly" (quoted in Guzzio 4) may inevitably lead to a certain paradox of Wideman criticism that captures the aporia induced by a writer who imbeds autobiographical details in his work, but also broadcasts "telling stories" and "lies" in deference to the Igbo proverb that he endlessly references and which can be found in Chinua Achebe's novel *Things Fall Apart*, in which a character asserts that "There is no story that is not true" (130). Ultimately, criticism cannot work the way a novel does the way that written fiction cannot do what music, a film, a painting, a collage, a sculpture, a traditional Igbo mask, or a voodoo charm does. This is a central tension to Wideman's work and writing about it. This leads to the paradox of critical desire that the Wideman scholar experiences. Why would those who have had the experience of such radical intimacy want to witness the type of insidious and artless appropriation of Wideman's work—such as the Hollywood industry appropriation of Morrison's *Beloved*—which would render the writer a popular figure in a society that suffers from the type of disease that he tirelessly works to diagnose and fight against?

A TENSION BETWEEN THE "REAL" WIDEMAN AND THE IMAGINED WIDEMAN IN THE SCHOLARSHIP

Within the scholarship, a "figure" of the author emerges which seems to induce paradox and the tensions of a critical aporia. These tensions largely emerge from what Brent Edwards describes as Wideman's "self-inscription" in the texts (Edwards, Wideman's 203). This practice provides a certain opening to the author himself, exposing his work, perhaps, to reductive readings dependent upon the type of critical license once denied serious literary criticism of the mid- to late-twentieth century by Roland Barthes who proclaimed the author dead and rendered superfluous efforts to understand a text through acts of her or his resuscitation. In his introduction to the 1999 *Callaloo* collection of essays, *John Edgar Wideman: The European Response*, French scholar Claude Julien tries to pin down this feature of Wideman's writing. Julien first confesses that to him, Barthes' prohibition never usefully applied to African American texts. He then confesses something else: all of the scholars in *The European Response* "bear the author in mind . . . it is clear that no Wideman text can flow from another author's pen" (540). Wideman criticism thus enjoys a license that allows scholars access to what Julien refers to as the "figure of the author" (539). This includes his personal history; his psychology; his emergent relationship to the Black community; his communal and historic context; and his struggle as a Black man against the racism of the dominant society. Wideman scholarship thus testifies to a movement in criticism, says Julien, "that reinstates interpersonal relationships between an author and his readers in critical discourse" (546). In 2011, Guzzio summarizes the meaning of this "interpersonal" relationship to Wideman scholarship. In order "to heal the violent and brutal history of African Americans," asserts Guzzio, Wideman infuses his fiction with his own "personal tragedies, his family background, and the legacy of slavery and racism" (13). Unfortunately, such blending, she asserts, often leads many Wideman scholars to be "more concerned with connections to his biography than with a critical and serious consideration of his writing" (5). Early scholars, she argues, often relied too heavily on "apocryphal" stories about the alienated Black artist trying to work his way back home who experienced: an incubation period, a latent discovery of his "Homewood ear," and transformation by "going home" for his grandmother's funeral and learning to value the Black "voice" through family stories (8). In interviews, Wideman lavishly supports such stories, but also renders them suspect by one where he says, "I don't think I ever ran away from the Black world in a kind of blind acceptance of something else" (quoted in Guzzio 11).

Still, in early Wideman scholarship, perhaps the most significant and implicitly structuring of such porous readings are the more Afrocentric works by Coleman and Mbalia. Much of the scholarship largely ignores the latter work, though Mbalia largely accepts the figure of Wideman as elaborated by Coleman in his 1989 book. Coleman's notion that Wideman's work went through distinct phases marked by the author's alienation from and rapprochement with the Black community and its "voices" remains as a given of Wideman scholarship. Indeed, I also explore this characterization in the present work. Mbalia, also working in this vein, explores the writer's "evolution from one who is dominated by the history, culture, and language of Europe to one who accepts and appreciates African history, culture and language" (15). For its methodology, her work emphatically embraces Afrocentricity, African socialism, and pan-Africanism. And largely for that, it received one of the most scathing critiques of a work of criticism that I have ever read. In his review of the book for a 1998 volume of *Amerikastudien/American Studies*, German scholar Klaus Schmidt treats Mbalia's book as more of an archaic artifact of Black Cultural Nationalism than as serious academic criticism. Schmidt scathingly characterizes Mbalia and her work as "oversimplistic" (539), "presumptuous" (540), "didactic in tone" (541), "inappropriate" (540), "polarizing" (541), and even labels it with the coded word "arrogant" (541). Schmidt's review encapsulates a dominant practice in Wideman criticism and of a certain strain of African American literary history. In the context of the late 1990s, Mbalia's work with its emphasis on the author and his biography, personal history, psychology, feelings, desires, sense of self-awareness, identity, rapport with family, relationship to the Black community, and leadership role in society reads as a holdover from a particular caricature of the Black Aesthetic Movement of the 1960s and 1970s.

This is an aspect of the aporia—the recurrent tension between the imagined Wideman and the "real" Wideman—embodied by the author figure that emerges from the criticism. This shape-shifting figure seems to induce a desire in the scholarship and impel it toward acts of critical recovery that depend on a stabilizing foil— a strawman. To provide the integrity and distinction for the Wideman figure that would enable his inclusion within the incipient category of Contemporary African American literature of a new era, he had to be distanced from the Black Arts. For such acts of recovery, critical anthologies began to tell a dubious story of the movement as they narrowed and began leaving out the full range of works produced during the Black arts era. From "roughly the mid-1970s through the late 1980s," observes Aldon Lynn Nielsen in his 1997 book, *Black Chant: The Languages of African-American Postmodernism,* "there was a general attenuating of critical attention to the fuller spectrum" of works produced during the "Black Arts period" (160). During the burgeoning neoliberal period, the Black Arts Movement suffered from the same type of reductions, conversions, summaries, translations, and transformations that the narrator of *Writing to Save a Life* unmasks in the military file of Louis Till. Although Nielsen had put many of these critical mischaracterizations of the movement to rest in his rigorous 1997 work, they seem to re-emerge within Wideman scholarship and African American literary history as an inexorably useful strawman. For instance, in his 2019 monograph on Wideman, French scholar Michel Feith, in an otherwise illuminating and theoretically engaging study of Wideman's work, imbeds many of these reductions into his arguments. For his portrait of the artist, Feith produces a caricature of the movement against which he pits the Wideman figure. He positions what he calls the "cultural immobility" (178) of the Black Arts movement against Wideman's "aesthetic experimentation" and "radical questioning of the epistemology of modernity" (8). He casts Wideman as above the fray of that movement as Feith cavalierly blends his reading of the Afrocentrism of Molefi Kete Asante with the work of Black Arts writers, excoriating what he calls a "reactive, essentialist epistemology" founded on "a separate aesthetic based on an irreducible black vernacular culture" (178). This description takes in a great deal as it even seems to blend into the blackening mix the vernacular criticism that had begun to emerge in the 1980s under the guiding hands of Henry Louis Gates (who edited the *Norton Anthology* along with Valerie Smith) and Houston Baker.

AN APORIA IN THE SCHOLARSHIP THAT PIVOTS ON THE NOTION OF FUNCTIONAL ART

This sets the stage for an aporia in Wideman criticism which largely pivots on an understanding of the Black Arts Movement's notion of "functional art." During the "attenuating" period described above by Nielsen, both Gates and Baker struggled to normalize and mainstream African American literary criticism, self-consciously rendering it more acceptably rigorous and freeing it from the grip of Black Cultural Nationalists and what influential African Americanist Arnold Rampersad calls their "propaganda and defensiveness" (498). Literary critics themselves thus emerge as doubles of the alienated, and Europeanized Black intellectual and the figure of Wideman etched into early scholarship. Being "outed" or labeled as elitist and inauthentic (an anxiety that Wideman discuses in the interview at the end of this book) consumed them. Winston Napier draws such a portrait of Houston Baker in his 1994 article "From the Shadows: Houston Baker's Move Toward a Postnationalist Appraisal of the Black Aesthetic." He describes a Black intellectual's struggle to overcome the divide between the elite white academic world and restrictive definitions of Black authenticity. Baker, he says, "wanted to reinvigorate the role of the black scholar/critic too often dismissed by black nationalists as a tool of the white academy and its discursive universe" (170). He adds that many scholars had compromised their work in fear of "nationalists criticizing academic rigor as indicative of intellectual elitism, an elitism which, some claimed, precluded one's ability to be 'truly' black" (170). This test of Black authenticity for the writer arrives in the form of privileging "functional" or Black art over art dedicated to effete aesthetic experimentation, argues Cheryl Wall in her "Introduction" to the "Contemporary Period" of the *Norton Anthology of African American Literature*. Contemporary writers such as Wideman, she attests, had "discarded" "Manifestoes of the Black Arts movement" which insisted on "art that was functional, collective, and committed to revolution and change" (Wall 914).

This structures the aporia in much of Wideman scholarship. In one way or another most Wideman scholarship describes works that may exhibit the aesthetically experimental, anti-Black arts, "inward turn" that the *Norton* uses to characterize Contemporary African American Literature, but Wideman scholars also inherently embrace the more Afrocentric early readings of Coleman and Mbalia, which particularly regards Wideman's later texts as outwardly directed, political, and didactic works. For Coleman, Wideman writes "political fictions intended to help black people" (165), draws readers into "critical process" (166), encourages them (165), and shakes them "into examining unquestioned assumptions" (166). For Mbalia, his work reeducates, raises consciousness, decolonizes and Africanizes. His texts exhort Black writers and intellectuals to turn outward and resume their engagement with the Black community. For Guzzio, his work imparts ultimate messages (247), dismantles "master plots" (247), illustrates "possibilities" (247), attempts "healing" (243), and recovers "the self and [. . .] the community (246). Wideman, she asserts, "believes, unflinchingly, in the power of the story to save us, himself, his family, the world" (247). In a cornerstone article of Wideman scholarship, Heather Russell Andrade asserts that Wideman's work functions to expose and critique (50) as it operates similar to "African American and African Caribbean feminist models" that explore "alternatives to the postmodern as a way of understanding" (44). Through their "ateleological, achronological, and multinarrated design" (51), Andrade argues, these works deploy a functional "freeing praxis" (53) that breaks, displaces, replaces, and ruptures (51) the "quintessential linear narratives" of "enlightenment rationalism [. . .] and civilization [that had chronicled] the necessary movement from an apocryphal darkness to transcendent light, from unknowingness to certain knowledge" (49). Feith largely agrees and reads Wideman's work as a "critical dialogue" with modernity. On one level, Wideman's inexorably hybrid texts "attempt to perform a liberation" and extend "the Enlightenment project of the pursuit of liberty and tolerance" (243). On the other hand, he produces counterhegemonic texts that denounce, unveil, provide alternatives to, and deconstruct instrumental reason as they "suggest a cure for the evils of modernity" (180). In summary, most of the criticism accepts that Wideman produces art that functions in a political way and is largely in accord with the "Manifestoes of the Black Arts movement" that contemporary writers had "discarded." Indeed, in the present work, I read Wideman's texts as responding to their moments of production including "his experiences of personal tragedy" (Coleman, *Writing* x) the incipient mass incarceration epidemic of the neoliberal era, the merciless policing and taking of Black life, and the prosecution of the War on Terror. He produces charms and weapons directed against the white supremacist fetishes of the larger society.

THE TENSION BETWEEN "IDEAL POETIC TRUTH" AND "REALITY" IN WIDEMAN SCHOLARSHIP

This returns to the recurrent tension between the imagined Wideman and the real Wideman which seems to produce a type of porous, semipermeable membrane that perhaps admits too much of the biographical, too much of the "real," and too much of the functional into aesthetically experimental texts. Indeed, in 2010 Guzzio felt it necessary to deemphasize or refute "more biographical considerations of Wideman's work" (10) and emphatically argue that "critical discussion of Wideman's art does not fully investigate the urgent philosophy behind the words 'all stories are true'" (11). This suggests another, very early way of distancing Wideman's work from that of Black Arts Movement writers. This difference concerns how writers respond to the supposed boundary between the imaginary and the real. For many critics, Wideman's work exalts the imaginary while that of Black Aesthetic movement writers wallows in a prosaic and concrete notion of the real. According to the early 1987 work of Jaqueline Berben-Masi, the philosophy Guzzio later emphasizes positions Wideman fully against Black Arts Movement writers such as Amiri Baraka. One of the most prolific and influential early scholars of Wideman, Berben-Masi highlights the importance of the imaginary in the author's work in her French dissertation, *La communauté et la communication dans l'univers fictif de John Edgar Wideman* (*Community and Communication in the Fictive Universe of John Edgar Wideman*). In this thesis, Berben-Masi aptly proclaims that what "Paul Ricoeur calls the aporia between the real and the imaginary lies at the very heart of the philosophy and aesthetic of Wideman's entire body of work" (11) [my translation]. Berben-Masi then positions this "philosophy and aesthetic" against those governing Baraka, whom she paints as an apocalyptic persona and a militant poet/priest, who endorsed a politics of flamboyant revolution, Black separatism, and political engagement through exhortations and lamentations that sing a swelling "opera" to victimization (9–10). Berben-Masi underscores Baraka's rebuke of "subjective mystification" as producing a signal distinction between Wideman's literary preoccupations and those of the Black poet. She asserts that Baraka condemned a lot of Black writers for this "crime [which] distanced them from reality [my translation]" (11). Baraka's stance, Berben-Masi argues, defies the "ideal of poetic truth that Wideman pursues because this ideal exists in large part within illusion and mystery [my translation]" (11).

Tellingly, this struggle seems opposite to the one waged by Baker and the emergent tools of African American literary criticism with which he grapples. In his portrait of Baker, Napier presents the literary theorist pursuing "advanced scholarship" as he struggles with the reductions and mystical speech acts of Black Arts Movement writers who sought to transubstantiate words into the material of functional weapons. As a reaction, Baker, privileges "theoretical insights" over performatives and "'speech acts' which 'fail as analytical statements because their speakers substitute will for reason, volition for analysis, and desire for systematic observation'" (quoted in Napier 165). Meanwhile, an actual reading of Baraka's work from the mid-1960s to late 1960s unmasks a critical aporia in Wideman scholarship when it comes to distancing Wideman's philosophy from Baraka's understanding of certain aspects of African and African American cosmology. The structuring power of Wideman's version of the Igbo proverb "all stories are true" and of the Frantz Fanon quote that Wideman uses in the epilogue to *Fanon*, which asserts that "imaginary life cannot be isolated from the real life" actually deploys a driving spirt of the Black arts and of Baraka's work. According to Baraka: "It's all there. We are exact (even in our lies)" (Baraka, Changing 187).

Moreover, the notion that experimentalism and accepting European influences is unique to Wideman and was somehow anathema to folk Black culture and to Black Aesthetic writers is another strawman. As Nielsen notes in *Black*

Chant: "Scholars truly conversant with folk tradition will know that there is no contradiction between an interest in folkways and an interest in intellectually rigorous literary works" (61). Baraka takes the observation a step further in his remarkable 1966 essay on the Black aesthetic, "The Changing Same (R&B and New Black Music)." He asserts that the "Black artist is most often hip to European arts" (Baraka, Changing 199). Baraka uses Black pianist and experimental musician Cecil Taylor as an example. "One hears Europe and the influence of French poets on America and the world of 'pure art' in Cecil's total approach [. . .] but his music is moving because he is still Black, still has imposed an emotional sensibility on the music that knows of actual beauty beyond 'what is given' [. . .] he is always *hotter, sassier* and newer than the music" (198–9).

THE TENSION BETWEEN WORDS AS REPRESENTATION AND WORDS AS THINGS IN WIDEMAN SCHOLARSHIP

The effort to recover Wideman from the grip of the Black arts leads to one final and crucial tension involving functional art found in Wideman's work. The scholarship takes up this tension and guides much of what I explore and elaborate within this work. In the 1960s, the relentlessly discredited and distanced Black Cultural Nationalists circulated a notion they derived from their understanding of Black cosmology which held that words could actually function in the same manner as African fetishes and Black Atlantic charms. Such a notion is integral to the Black Aesthetic, argues Ron Karenga, in his 1968 essay "Black Cultural Nationalism" (1968) which first appeared in *Negro Digest* and was then anthologized in Addison Gayle's seminal work, *The Black Aesthetic*. Karenga openly embraces Baraka's call for words that "kill and shoot guns and 'wrassle cops into alleys taking their weapons" (34). He responds to Baraka's 1965 poem, "Black Art," and his conjuring of "live words of the hip world live flesh &/coursing blood" (Baraka 219). Indeed, the term "black arts" deliberately summons African spirituality and supernatural practice. Meanwhile, Wideman seems to invoke that legacy (that power) in his 2016 work, *Writing to Save a Life: The Louis Till File*, as his narrator figure recalls receiving a powerful talisman of Dominican Santeria from a member of the Chicago Black Panther Party and utters the words: "Found and lost, found again, lost again" (192).

Throughout the six works I discuss here, one finds "figures," "characters," doubles of narrators, or perhaps *loas*, who relentlessly confront art in other media often with the same "ungenerous envy of any arts success while my [. . .] project falters" as expressed by the narrator figure of *Writing to Save a*

Life (176). These works often view as successful other media such as photography, sculpture, film, and music while they also constantly struggle to take writing beyond the act of merely representing a world that it seems to have no power to actually change. They openly struggle against their very form, and manifest an aspect of a writer figure's continuing effort to transform his medium from an act of representation while delving into the Black Atlantic space of the crossroads which could tie the written word to the concrete matter of functional art. Can words function as something other than themselves; as fetishes, charms and weapons? Can they work against the Medusa-like "stare that freezes and kills" of written representation, and, in the words of a character from *Two Cities* (describing the sculpture of Alberto Giacometti, the music of Thelonious Monk, and the collages of Romare Beard), "turn things loose"? Must words only act as representation? Can they put on masks, become charms, effect healing, and deploy as weapons? Can written work function as what Robert Farris Thompson calls, "secular *nzo a nkisi*, a charm for the denial of hurt" (158)? Can it perform a Black American-style ritual akin to traditional Igbo mourning rites that clear the way for ancestral spirits to actively participate in the world? Can they extract and redeploy the spirit of human life? In his chapter on "African Tropism," Feith observes that *Reuben* poses such questions: "How to convey in writing the performances of music, dance, vernacular speech, so as to imbibe the literature with these influences instead of dividing the live from the printed word" (190).

POETICS, EFFECT, ARCHITECTONICS, AND AN "AESTHETICS OF DISPOSAL" AS STRUCTURING SCHOLARSHIP

Unlike the other monographs on Wideman, this work exclusively discusses *Reuben, Philadelphia Fire, The Cattle Killing, Two Cities, Fanon,* and *Writing to Save a Life* and presents them as successful works of discredited Black Atlantic craft. Most of the antecedent scholarship remains faithful to the discipline of contemporary literary study and critical theory as it explores how reading and writing work within systems of discourse and signification. Wideman scholars elaborate the urgent and didactic qualities of texts that self-consciously struggle to alleviate suffering within this world, and lavishly use words such as magical, mysterious, ritual, spiritual, materialize, actualize, jazz-like, the blues, the crossroads, talisman, fetish, ghosts, haunting, conjuring, and voodoo. Still, most of them pull back and shy away from a practice that would first rigorously decode and intensively read the words of a text and then denounce writing, signs, signification, and representation as if spirit capturing or spiritualizing stories could exist like materialized matter that functions on its own without being dragged into the realms of signs and symbols. Still, I owe a great debt to scholars such as Brent Hayes Edwards, Yves-Charles Grandjeat, Heather Russell Andrade, and Michel Feith who lay some of the theoretical foundations for my study.

At the 2000 *Callaloo* celebration, Edwards and Grandjeat presented work that engages aspects of Wideman's writing that resonate with some of the critical methodology that I have found useful. Edwards later published his work, "Wideman's Breadth," in a 2003 French collection of essays destined to pay tribute to Michel Fabre. Grandjeat published, "'These strange dizzy pauses': Silence as Common Ground in J.E. Wideman's Texts," in the 2000 Callaloo collection of essays, *John Edgar Wideman: The European Response.* Both elegantly use critical theory to explore Wideman's poetics and focus on how his work struggles against systems of signification and functions to produce certain aesthetic effects. Meanwhile, Andrade targets Wideman's architectonics and their relationship to African cosmology and Black Atlantic craft and Feith produces an extensive study of African cosmology in Wideman's work.

Grandjeat images the author as a figure in search of a "liberated form—a freeing and freed form" that refuses "to perform any type of rhetorical capture or discursive framing" (692). The text, he asserts, assumes "an appropriate aesthetic form for a meditation leading to a poetics, an ethics, and a metaphysics of silence" (687). He references the recurrent "discourse on plastic and visual arts" in addition to the notions of "weaving" (689), the assembling of "bits and pieces of material" (689); and the poetics of texts that perform like "variations on a jazz score" and execute "moves like a basketball game" (692). Edwards locates Wideman's work within an African American literary tradition beginning with the slavery narrative that struggles "with literary form (an attention to and extraordinary pressure on the frame of a text) [and] the generic framing of black subjectivity" (200–1). He invokes a spirit of vernacular theory, describing the "emulation of black music" by the texts and their movement "away from signification and towards the openness of the musical" (202). Similar to Grandjeat, he focuses on poetics and effect. The texts scat, conjure the "'cut'" of Black music (204), jostle speaking "out of notation [and] into motion" (203), and quilt, producing a "musical weave" that juggles "buoyant fabric" (204). Like most Wideman scholars, Edwards responds to the author as a figure whose biography and personal history openly infiltrate his texts and give license to a certain way of reading the author. Yet, he also implies that such "self-inscription" leads to a sense of transubstantiated presence or "face-to-face encounter" (203). Indeed, the texts engage in what Edwards terms "a complexly prolix physicality" that underscores "the body's ingenuity" and ultimately leads him to experience the performance of "'the body'" of the novel *itself*" (203). In my chapter on *Writing to Save a Life,* I relate this notion to saintly hagiography through which the writing "affirms the "interchangeability between text and saintly body. . . . Text becomes body, body text" (Rachel Smith 155). In *Writing Blackness*, James Coleman also seizes on this aspect of Wideman's work in his analysis of *Fanon*. In this work, the writer figure, Coleman argues, pushes "the narrative beyond the normal boundaries of writing to suggest the human *living* that it cannot represent, and to intimate that the novel itself is a *living* book" (166).

In his later, 2017 book, *Epistrophies: Jazz and the Literary Imagination*, Edwards also presents a critically rigorous exploration that complicates the distancing of the Black Arts from Wideman's work and the line, for instance, drawn by Feith who ridicules the "roots-oriented onomastics" imbedded in what he calls "the Black Arts inspired celebration" of Kwansa (196) and the "essentialist myth of group identity" (226) grounded in a nationalist longing for African roots and nostalgic ideas about cultural retention. Feith proposes using Gerald Vizenor's theory of "survivance" as a way of exploring the notion of cultural retention and Wideman's "African Tropisms." He locates a "similar vision" in the idea of the "changing same" that he finds in a quote from Paul Gilroy's The *Black Atlantic*. "Following the lead established long ago by Leroi [sic] Jones [Amiri Baraka], I believe it is possible to approach the music as a *changing same* rather than an unchanging same" (quoted in Feith 226). This characterizes a great deal of the criticism of African American literature of the neoliberal era and of Wideman's work. Through a secondary source, it paradoxically uses the inexorably fluid ideas of Baraka, a major Black Aesthetic movement writer, to erect a strawman and denounce the movement's cultural immobility. Even so, "survivance" does not fully register what Baraka may have intend by the "changing same." Perhaps the "historiographic sensibility" of the Black Arts aligns more with that of experimental jazz pianist, Cecil Tayler, as elaborated by Edwards. Taylor's transformative playing, Edwards asserts, is "primed to take the testimony—one might even call it the haunting—of a "spirit" or "passion" that "informs" the methodological approaches of the black aesthetic tradition" (168). Taylor's experimental and inventive approach, Edwards argues, resounds with "a certain violence that characterizes that unearthing or haunting, a force that not only founds but simultaneously 'deposes'—overthrows or sublates" (Edwards, Epistrophies 168). Edwards, through his reading of Baraka's 1965 work, *The System of Dante's Hell*, proposes another nomenclature for this approach, calling it "an aesthetics of disposal" (161), which "approaches the past as a *deposit* [where] prior stylistic practice contains elements of 'deposition'" (168).

In addition to internalizing these notions of poetics, effect, and an "aesthetics of disposal," this work also tacitly embraces the critical notion of architectonics as it applies to Wideman's work. Indeed, one of the most useful works about Wideman explores this notion through the use of African cosmology and first appeared in *Critical Essays on John Edgar Wideman*, edited by Bonnie TuSmith and Keith Byerman in 2006. In "Race, Representation and Intersubjectivity in the Works of John Edgar Wideman," Heather Russell Andrade poses a question similar to that asked above by Feith. "But can one, in fact, quilt so magically?" she asks. "Wideman would suggest that one can" (47). Her study of Wideman's architectonics, ties some of Wideman's works to the Black arts in the form of African Great Time, *àshe* and the *orishas* of traditional Yoruba religion, and the cultural retentions of the Black Atlantic craft of quilting. In this work, Andrade seems to witnesses the possibility of such magical quilting in the "crafting hand" (52) of a spirit of African and Black Atlantic cosmology—of the black arts—as a "force within the text" (52) that guides their "revolutionary"(53) and "potentially emancipatory architectonics" (55). "Wideman's writing" she observes, "is unequivocally informed by a self-consciously assimilated African worldview" (52).

DECULTURATION AND THE CEREMONIAL ACUMEN OF THE BLACK ARTS IN WIDEMAN SCHOLARSHIP

This study emphatically departs, however, from some observations made by Feith in perhaps one of the most extensive treatments of African cosmology in Wideman scholarship. In his chapter on "African Tropism," Feith presents an engaging elucidation of *The Cattle Killing*. This work, he argues, through its themes and use of African tropes, struggles to escape its bonds as writing to effect a cure, and conjure a healing ritual. Yet, Feith argues, the work itself is an "ill-adapted medium for a traditional shamanistic cure." He then positions *The Cattle Killing* against what he presents as the more successful efforts of "Native American texts." He argues that in "spite of its strong ritual and spiritual dimension, the novel cannot claim ceremonial status and full performative use of language." He surmises that whatever "the writers' individual strategic choices, we may venture the hypothesis that, due to the partial deculturation of the diaspora, attempts by an African American author to endow a fictional work with full ceremonial and curative potency is bound to read more contrived than similar endeavors by Amerindians" (214).

Such a position not only fails to grasp the naked power of African American ceremony, but it exposes the hidden essentialism of supposedly anti-essentialist readings which revel in the theoretical notion of hybridity anchored in postcolonialism. The hybrid, like race itself has no meaning. It still assumes that somewhere in time and space lies the pure unadulterated origin. Everything is always already deracinated. The Black arts celebrate and cermonialize such deracination through a wanton "aesthetics of disposal" that takes the "testimony" of a spirit as it violently "overthrows or sublates" it (Edwards, Epistrophies 168). In his introduction to *Flash of the Spirit*, Thompson describes the infectious and relentlessly improvisatory power of the decultured black arts as he elucidates the African "deposits" safeguarded in Black Atlantic expression. "Listening to rock jazz, blues, reggae, salsa, samba, bossa nova, juju, highlife, and mambo, one might conclude that much of the popular music of the world is informed by the flash of the spirit of a certain people specially armed with improvisatory brilliance" (xiii).

According to Baraka in the "The Changing Same," the Black arts practitioners he describes dig everything (193), explore the unknown and the mystical (192), expand consciousness (192), do not accede to givens (192), and seek God in the form of energy (192). They engage in "mixtery" and summon the transformative and sublating guidance of *misterios* (*loas*). Like James Brown, or the women who gather to sing and exorcise a spirt in Toni Morrison's *Beloved*, they wield the power to break "the back of words" (Morrison 261). They "pass on" and thus deploy the power of the griots of Sahelian Africa, the *nyamakala*, who know how take *nyama*, the primordial force of sound, and work it like a blacksmith forges metal to produce words that function as concrete tools, weapons, charms, fetishes, and things in and of themselves. Through this power, they tell stories (even lies) that capture, save and redeploy spiritualizing force. To those outside the circle, their practice may seem imperfect, irregular, asymmetrical, ragged, funky, be-bopped, jagged, offbeat, atonal, hoarse, out of tune, unfinished, ostentatious, ignorant, hot, sassy, uncultured, decultured, over-cultured, deracinated, nostalgic, essentialist, or contrived. But the black arts practitioner works dexterously and expertly like James Brown, Cecil Taylor, John Edgar Wideman, and the cowboy hero, Loop Garoo, of Ishmael Reed's work, *Yellow Back Radio Broke-Down* as he calls upon the right and most powerful *loas* to help craft a charm:

I the Father which wert in heaven conjure and command thee O Legba master of the crossroads to connect this cowboy's circuit to Guinea and summon forth: [. . .]

O Jack Johnson give me the power to rise for the bell until Yellow Back Radio is down for the count

O Doc John, Doc Yah Yah and Zozo Labrique Marie Laveau the Grand Improvisers if I am not performing these rites correctly send the Loa anyways and allow my imagination to fill the gaps [. . .]

Marinette of the dry arm send the dead swiftly to make my vengeance so complete and artsy craftsy that I though an amateur will be admired by houngans the world over [. . .]

O Black Hawk America Indian houngan of Hoo-Doo please do open up some of these prissy orthodox minds so that they will no longer call Black People's American experience "corrupt" "perverse" and "decadent." Please show them that Booker T and the MG's, Etta James and Johnny Ace and Bojangles tapdancing is just as beautiful as anything that happened anywhere else in the world. Teach them that anywhere people go they have experience and that all experience is art. (63–4)

Although Wideman's ceremonial acumen is superficially different from Reed's; it is "radically" the same—the changing same. It functions. It captures, saves and deploys the "flash of the spirit" as it expands consciousness, halts enemies, and performs healing.

Acknowledgments

The Royal Street Circle: filmmaker Christopher J. Harris at the University of Iowa and comparative literature scholar Kevin Bell at Pennsylvania State University.

The former members of the BGF: Tukufu Zuberi now at the University of Pennsylvania, J. Lorand Matory now at Duke University, independent scholar, William Balan-Gaubert, and the brilliant "homeless professor," Donald H. Matthews.

The African American Studies Program at Saint Louis University including Christopher Tinson, Olubukola Gbadegesin, Katrina Thompson, Jonathan Smith, and affiliated faculty, Karla Scott, Eddie Clark, Nathan Grant, George O. Ndege, Emmanuel Uwalaka, and Joya F. Uraizee.

My colleagues in the Department of English in addition to the Mellon Fund, the Stolle Fund, and the Provost's Faculty Research Leave program at Saint Louis University.

Members of the John Edgar Wideman Society including Wilfred Samuels, Raymond E. Janifer, Keith Byerman, Bonnie TuSmith, Karen Jahn, and Tracie Church Guzzio

Introduction
Wideman, Contemporary Writers, and the Black Arts

> *One reason people are scared by art—the idea that the artist is connected with demons or some sort of separate power—is because effective art can take your breath away [. . .] [S]uddenly as a spectator, or hearer, or watching a dance, you realize, you know, that you don't have it all figured out. That whatever protective covering this society or this village or this race gives you; there is other shit going on. Woah! And if you don't attend to that, you're going to pay. Something tells you you're going to pay. And so, you get that sort of mystery. Mystery.* —John Edgar Wideman

John Edgar Wideman is one of the most significant, innovative, critically acclaimed, yet in many ways underappreciated writers of the last fifty years. Since the late 1960s, he has published eleven novels, three book-length memoirs or collections of essays, seven collections of short stories, a travel book, and an untold number of works scattered among a plethora of prestigious magazines and periodicals. Still, at a recent conference, members of the American Literature Association's John Edgar Wideman Society wondered why he isn't better known; why, for instance, Hollywood hadn't made one of his books into a film, as it had done for Toni Morrison or his contemporary Alice Walker. Indeed, in the early days, he and Walker even shared the same editor.

Wideman came of age as a writer toward the end of one literary period, where writers of the Black Aesthetic movement dominated the scene, and at the beginning of another, where writing by African American women blossomed. This new period seemed to take off with Walker's 1982 novel, *The Color Purple*. In its wake, scores of African American writers won America's and the world's most prestigious literary awards, culminating with the Noble Prize for Literature won by Toni Morrison in 1993. Meanwhile, the literature seemed to withdraw from the strident politics of the Black Cultural Nationalism of the 1960s. To many critics, it appeared to move away from the idea of committed and functional art while taking an "inward turn" toward more personal, intimate, and aesthetic concerns (Wall 914). African American writing seemed to come in from the streets and assume the same timeless aesthetic qualities possessed by great works of Western writing and worthy of consideration by scholars of elite literature departments. Through it, African Americans now seemed able to make a legitimate and indisputable claim to their own culture, language, and literary tradition.

In the 1980s, things had changed since the1960s and 1970s, when African American intellectuals had embraced the racialized and inexorably alienating term "Black" in an effort to transform the system and the Western ways of knowing in which, asserts poet Amiri Baraka, "everything Black was bad." But, he adds, "we was Bad" (Baraka, Movement 499). This changed with activist Jesse Jackson's two influential runs for president during the 1980s. He openly attempted to alter the public discourse and rejected the Black identity as he embraced the more ethnically resonant and historically accurate term African American, which described just one identity among others of his multicultural Rainbow Coalition. Yet, this name for a coalition had actually existed before as a revolutionary vision of the Chicago Chairman of the Black Panther Party for Self Defense, Fred Hampton, who was murdered by police in 1969. Hampton wanted to bring together the oppressed lumpen proletariat and working-class groups in a coalition that would overthrow the capitalist system. He stirred crowds with the chant, "I am a revolutionary" and concluded his speeches with the words, "Black Power." After Hampton's death, Jackson became a major reformist and civil rights leader in Chicago. And he altered Hampton's words. Instead of saying, "I am a Revolutionary," he roused the crowds with "I am Somebody." Instead of closing with the words "Black Power," he often ended with the less antagonistic phrase "Soul Power." Meanwhile, he helped convert the desire to transform society at its foundations through tearing down oppressive ways of thinking into a practice of interest group politics with African Americans vying for their piece of the pie along with everyone else in country. Overall, the Civil Rights community in the emergent neoliberal era of the 1980s concentrated most of its energy on issues of diversity, jobs, and affirmative action. Meanwhile, something horrific was happening to the Black Americans still locked in separate communities.

Displacements, migrations, and the deindustrialization of bourgeoning global capitalism had transformed once isolated but stable "ghettos" into vulnerable, disorganized, dislocated, and primarily young concentrations of the "underclass," which was beleaguered by massive unemployment, crime, drugs, and failing schools. Meanwhile, Ronald Reagan, who was president from 1980 to 1988, demonized the Black people who lived in these areas. Under Reagan, the "tough on crime" war waged by U.S. law enforcement against seemingly lawless groups like the Black Panthers in the 1960s and early 1970s became the War on Drugs in the 1980s. This resulted in an explosion in the incarceration rate of African Americans males. At the same time, many of the culture workers, writers, educated elite, and members of the Black middle class seemed to distance themselves from previous notions of solidarity with the poor still living in these communities. African Americanist and profoundly influential public intellectual Henry Louis Gates famously pushed such distancing in both his pronouncements and to some extent in his literary scholarship. In his 1996 article, "The Two Nations of Black America: The Best of Times, the Worst of Times," Gates takes issue with the "vanguard of black cultural nationalist political consciousness" of the 1960s and positions that dictated what it meant to be "to be 'authentically' black" (Gates, "Two Nations" 6). He denounced the new manifestation of their ideas in the incipient valorization of ghetto culture and "gangersterism." He further rejected the Black middle class ethos of feeling connected to and making excuses for "the pathological behavior that results from extended impoverishment"—"black-on-black homicide, gang members violating the sanctity of the church, unprotected sexual activity, [. . .] teenage pregnancies, [and] the spread of AIDS from drug abuse and unprotected sexual relations" (7). He asserts: "We have the largest black middle class in our history and the largest black underclass." He then cites the statistics: "In 1990, 2,280,000 black men were in prison, or probation, or parole, while 23,000 earned a college degree. That's a ratio of 99 to 1, compared with a ratio of 6 to 1 for white men." Still, he argues, "we have to stop feeling guilty about our success," realize that "we don't have to fail in order to be black," and understand that "we don't have to pretend any longer that 35 million people can ever possibly be members of the same economic class" (7). In many ways, Gates further validates this turn away from a sense of racial solidarity with the underclass in his scholarly work, which locates an idea of African American identity in a distinct culture and not in the unyielding practices of institutionalized racism and a ravaging system of oppression. Indeed, it can be found to some extent in the literary canon-producing *Norton Anthology of African American Literature*, which he coedited with Valerie Smith. Its ideological distancing of the "fight the power" and functional writing of the Black Arts Movement from the self-consciously aesthetic, personal, and intimate writing of "The Contemporary Era" firmly demonstrates that African American literature doesn't have to engage with gangbangers, drug addicts, or the 2,280,000 people all but re-enslaved by mass incarceration to offer the world a unique and valued voice.

What to make, then, of John Edgar Wideman, whom the *Norton* locates in the "Contemporary Period," and whose most popular work, *Brother's and Keepers* (1984), defies the distance Gates extols? Instead, this work presents the image of an Ivy-educated, Rhodes scholar and middle class professor who openly embraces an intimate and inseverable connection to his once drug-addicted, petty-criminal brother who is a convicted murderer languishing in prison—the type of person that an entire society has hunted, caged, killed, sentenced to "death by incarceration" (Robert Wideman), and then struggled to erase from its consciousness. How can one critically appraise the ensuing six novels by Wideman—*Reuben* (1987*)*, *Philadelphia Fire* (1990), *The Cattle Killing* (1996), *Two Cities* (1998), *Fanon* (2008) and *Writing to Save a Life* (2017)—which overflow with the criminal element, including accused rapists and murderers; sham lawyers; the bombed out and indecent members of a funky, archaic cult; shunned carriers of madness, sickness, and plague; gangbangers and orphaned children who worship money, power, and things; victims of unsanctioned lynchings and sanctioned executions; and generally bad men who batter women and seem to embrace proudly some of the worst aspects of toxic masculinity? Meanwhile, these works aesthetically distance themselves from the task of representing these figures, engaging in reasoned didactic argument, devolving into agitprop formulas, or offering a journalistic status report on the state of African Americans under the somewhat hidden but systemic racism of the late twentieth and early twenty-first centuries. To experience these works feels more like listening to a magical, detoxifying work of the best free jazz than like reading a fictionalized account of a series of documentary moments. They don't use words merely to represent something. Instead these works enter the world on their own terms, producing their own reality, and changing the order things. They are functional works of the discredited black arts that demand a critical approach that responds to them as things in and of themselves.

The six somewhat distinct but deeply connected essays that follow are such an attempt. They explore the later works of Wideman which embrace a continuity with the "functional" writing of the Black Aesthetic movement through structures that openly deploy particular forms of African and Black Atlantic cosmology—the black arts. These works function as charms anchored in a magical tradition where words become more than mere representations. They delve into the "other shit going on" of an ancient, powerful, and revolutionary practice. They deploy words as matter—as weapons—when all other rational means of redemption and protection offered by the dominant society seem to have failed. Within these six works, Black spirits dance as the novels open themselves to the type of knowledge demeaned by the West but circulated by African American music, traditional African cosmologies, magical Black

Atlantic craft, and other forms of Black art. These works put on masks, carve charms from words and imaginatively use writing to craft weapons for healing and protection from the relentless and hostile fetishes of the dominant culture. This practice begins with *Reuben* (1987) and *Philadelphia Fire* (1990); works structurally guided by Haitian Vodun and Kongo cosmology as elaborated by anthropologist Robert Farris Thompson in his book, *Flash of the Spirit* (1983). Their eclectic and seemingly postmodern structure deploys voices and stories as "spirit-embodying material," which enable them to function as what Thompson calls, "secular *nzo a nkisi,* a charm for the denial of hurt" (158). In *The Cattle Killing* (1996), dystopian tales of mass indifference to the oppressed, the murdered, the forgotten, and the dead structure a text which employs the urgent and tactical spirit of the slavery narrative against the harmful fetishes and false prophecies driving contemporary society. *The Cattle Killing* rekindles the urgency of the early Black narratives as a response to the new form of slavery and violence against Black people that had taken hold at the turn of the twenty-first century in the form of institutionalized racism and mass incarceration. *Two Cities* (1998) works as bridge novel; a mystical work of the crossroads that conjures the transformative power of Papa Legba of Haitian cosmology. It continues the project of Black Arts writers to make their work matter and transform writing into a usable, physical force. It performs as a work of connection that transcends literary representation and links purpose with art in other media such as sculpture, collage, and African American music. *Fanon* (2008), a post-September 11 work, pits itself against the dialectic of torture and despair driving America's prosecution of the war on terror. It displaces such despair with a Black American-style ritual akin to traditional Igbo mourning rites that clear the way for ancestral spirits to actively participate in and penetrate through the boundaries erected around the sick imagination of a closed-off world desperately in need of their transformative power. Finally, *Writing to Save a Life: The Louis Till File* (2016) performs as a "possessed text," hagiography, icon, Black Atlantic talisman or literary charm that preserves and safeguards living spirits. As it extracts the spirit of a man hanged on charges of rape and murder, it works backward toward the discarded "protest fiction" of an earlier era. These works, therefore, function as Black American-style written charms destined to give hope, save life, heal, and interfere with the wanton destructiveness of a world where the blues of the crossroads "rule." They work against the Medusa-like "stare that freezes and kills" of written representation, and, in the words of a character from *Two Cities*, describing the sculpture of Alberto Giacometti, the music of Thelonious Monk, and the collages of Romare Beard, "turn things loose." They sound "notes played so they can dance away, make room for others. Free others to free themselves" (118–19).

CANON-PRODUCING ANTHOLOGIES

In a 2014 documentary about World War I, the narrator, David Reynolds, describes the way poetry anthologies transformed how the history of that war is both taught and remembered (Reynolds). The same can be said about African American literature anthologies presenting works of the late 1960s and early 1970s, a period that had a history which, according to one media scholar, was already being rewritten while it was happening (Staub 54). Such anthologies have had a major impact on creating, fomenting, and disseminating the dominating caricature of the Black Power and Black Arts and movements. Indeed, the memory-structuring power of two authoritative Norton Anthologies reify such histories as they ideologically locate the work of writers such as John Edgar Wideman (which spans the decades between the late 1960s and the late 2010s) and distance it from that of the Black Arts Movement. This is an important discussion to have, as there are fewer and fewer people who have an active memory of this period, and perhaps of one of its most brilliant architects (and likely one of its most relentless bullies, and without a doubt one of its most infamous whipping boys): Amiri Baraka. Just months before his death in 2014, Baraka vehemently reacted to what he saw as the compartmentalization of the Black Arts era by the *Norton Anthology of Contemporary African American Poetry*. Furthermore, in the 2nd volume of the *Norton Anthology of African American Literature* scholar Cheryl A. Wall, erects similar boundaries as she draws a distinct line between "The Black Arts Era, 1960–1975," and "The Contemporary Period," which she says produced a "true African American renaissance," remarking that: "Never before had so much distinguished writing been produced by black Americans" (913). Within the "Contemporary Period" are Wideman (born in 1941) and Toni Morrison (born in 1931), while Baraka (born in 1934), Ishmael Reed (born in 1938), and Toni Cade Bambara (born in 1939), remain confined to the other side. It is as much an ideological as it is a historical divide; one which scholars are still struggling to understand. For Wall, and for Charles Rowell, who edited the *Norton Anthology of Contemporary African American Poetry*, the political and aesthetic concerns of writers on either side of the divide are singularly different. On the one side, says Wall, lies "Black Cultural Nationalism." She notes: "Manifestoes of the Black Arts movement, the designation assumed by cultural workers allied with Black Power activists, insisted on art that was functional, collective, and committed to revolution and change. The prescriptiveness that resulted proved too constricting, and the dictates of the Black Arts movement were soon discarded" (914). Meanwhile, Baraka in his 2013 review of the poetry anthology, "A Post-Racial Anthology?," asserts that Rowell makes similar, disparaging observations.

Charles Henry Rowell's introduction and many of the quotes he gleans are aimed at rendering the Black Arts Movement as old school, backward, fundamentally artless. He calls his poets "literary." [. . .] What is distinctive about Rowell's introduction is that just about every page mentions the "Black Arts Movement," "the Black Aesthetic poets," "the Black Power Movement"—all like some menacing political institutions. (166–68)

Such caricatures of the Black Arts Movement, the Black Power Movement and Black Cultural Nationalism with agitprop aesthetics and a laughable political agenda have silted into cultural memory. Indeed, by 1981, the urgent calls of 1960s poetry, for instance, had morphed into a memory-structuring skit by Eddie Murphy on *Saturday Night Live*. Described in the script as a "psychotic young African-American male" and "occupant of [a] maximum security cell," his character, Tyrone Green, recites a poem that has won a prison "poetry festival." "Dark and lonely on the summer night. / Kill my landlord, kill my landlord. / Watchdog barking—*Do he bite?* / Kill my landlord, kill my landlord" (King). Meanwhile, in film (from *Forrest Gump* in 1994 to *The Butler* in 2013) the image of beret-wearing, Black Panther-style radicals also morphed into artless, jargon spewing tropes inducing minstrel-comedy style slapstick abuse and condescending laughter. Forrest Gump raucously believes he has unintentionally crashed a "Black Panther party." In *The Butler*, the character played by Oprah Winfrey slaps the face of her radical, beret-wearing son for disrespecting his obsequious White-House-butler father and daring to call actor Sidney Poitier an "Uncle Tom." At the same time, the works of Black Arts writers were represented as the literary counterpart to these images. Critics disparaged them as stridently "timely"—lodged in a fading era of protest—and not aesthetically "timeless" or capable of withstanding the test of time. Meanwhile, the output of the Contemporary era, through the eyes of critics such as Rowell, seemed to have sprouted in a vacuum, bypassing the Black Arts era and (in the words of James Weldon Johnson as quoted in Ishmael Reed's *Mumbo Jumbo*) were "like *Topsy*, [they] '*jes' grew*." (Reed, Mumbo 11).

THE DIVIDE

So, the efforts to place Wideman clearly on one side of the divide not only commits a historic and ideological injustice to the critical memory of the Black Arts movement; they prevent a more rigorous and layered assessment of Wideman's work. The project of containing or quarantining the Black Arts Movement and thus presenting certain artists as safe—meaning more aesthetic and apolitical—while academically mainstreaming the study of African

American literature seems to have begun in earnest in the 1980s, at the dawn of the Reagan and neoliberal era. Few popular Black writers after Toni Cade Bambara openly embraced the communist, socialist, or Black internationalist label and political agenda.

Such a distancing of Wideman's work was attempted in a 1989 interview between Wideman and Rowell, who edits *Callaloo,* an influential academic journal and literary magazine that has published creative writing, artwork, and critical essays on the African Diaspora since 1976. In the interview, Rowell asks several questions ("without provoking any people out there in our age group who were the architects and advocates of the Movement") seemingly intended to maneuver Wideman away from the shadow of the Black Arts Movement, though he "entered the literary scene in 1967 with the publication of *A Glance Away* his first novel. That was during the height of the Black Arts Movement." Rowell then asks: "Why were you never part of the Black Arts Movement? *Hurry Home, The Lynchers*, and your first novel suggest that you did not at all subscribe to the tenets of the Black Arts movement?" (91). Although Wideman does admit being a "loner" and having a large ego, he rejects the bait. He tells Rowell:

> Black Arts theorists—and we must remember there are many points of view—shouldn't be dismissed. They deserve study and reconsideration [. . .] It's not a simple question of repudiating certain figures and certain attitudes of the sixties. For instance, the notion that black people had to tell their own stories, that black people needed to investigate the language, that black people are on the edge of a kind of precipice and that, as a people, we might very well disappear if we didn't start to, number one, demand equality in the political sense, if we didn't begin to investigate our past, if we didn't begin to see ourselves as part of a world, a Third World—all of these ideological and philosophical breakthroughs were crucial to reorienting us, and they still provide a basis for much of the thinking and the writing that is significant today [. . .] And so, those of us who are still writing now, I hope, really are beneficiaries of what was going on at all levels in the sixties [. . .] I see continuities, rather than a simple break with or repudiation of the Black Arts Movement of the sixties. (Wideman, Rowell 90–91)

Yet, caricatures of slogan shouting, misogynist, mindless, Black Arts zealots and strident, seemingly oxymoronic Black nationalists more interested in propaganda than art, truth or nuance persist and perhaps even taint the way later generations of activists and scholars process their message. For instance, the brilliant scholar and Black Power activist Angela Davis had filmed a documentary and written two books about prisons more than a decade before Michelle Alexander wrote *The New Jim Crow* in 2010. It took direct contact with the racist horrors of the American criminal justice system for Alexander to realize that the "radical groups" who seemed to make absurd comparisons linking the criminal justice system to Jim Crow weren't crazy, deluded, and mindlessly ideological.

At first glance, it seems that direct contact with the prison system may have worked similar magic on Wideman, driving him to check his ego and rendering him less of a loner in relationship to what Wall called the movement's constrictive insistence on functional art. The Movement did indeed emphasize functional art, which the writers themselves self-consciously placed in what they viewed as the magical tradition of the black arts of Africa. In his introduction to his 1972 book, *Understanding the New Black Poetry*, Stephen Henderson discusses the early 1960s context of "the emergence of the new Black Consciousness and Black Arts Movements" (xiii). During this period, African American artists took a decisive turn away from "narcissistic" art, rooting or linking themselves to their own traditions as they "rediscovered Africa and Pan-Africanism" (17). Such an engaged role for the artist stems from an understanding of traditional African practice and is thus an integral part of the Black Aesthetic, argues Ron Karenga, in his 1968 essay "Black Cultural Nationalism" (1968) which first appeared in *Negro Digest* and was then anthologized in Addison Gayle's seminal work, *The Black Aesthetic*.

> Tradition teaches us, [Senegalese poet] Leopold Senghor tells us, that all African art has at least three characteristics: that is, it is functional, collective and committing or committed [. . .] It must be functional, that is useful, as we cannot accept the false doctrine of "art for art's sake." For, in fact, there is no such thing as "art for art's sake." All art reflects the value system from which it comes. (33)

Yet, this emphasis on both African cosmology and functional art seemed absent in Wideman's work before the mid-1980s.

According to critical biographer, Keith Byerman, this earlier work demonstrates that "Wideman wanted nothing to do with" Black Aesthetic writers, "precisely because they wanted literature to serve political rather than artistic goals" (147). In *The Life and Work of John Edgar Wideman,* Byerman observes that Wideman's early work was "about the private lives of its characters, not their social concerns" (147). Yet, Byerman observes, Wideman also "admits that his ambitions changed over time." Indeed, the passage of time reveals that the dogmatically "timely" writing of the 1960s and early 1970s—functionally addressed to the political concerns of a particular people at a specific historical moment—began to evince a terrifying "timeless" quality; an idea that Western critics use as a standard to separate great works of art (which withstand the test of time) from the trendy "agitprop" that many disparaged in the work of Black Arts Movement writers. Despite the promise of the 1960s, the fact that, according to Wideman, "black people are on the edge of a kind of precipice and that, as a people, we might very well disappear" (Wideman, Rowell 90) remained and took on a disturbingly timeless, immemorial quality during the last quarter of the twentieth century and the first decades of the twenty-first century.

BECOMING A SORCERER

Still, in the 1970s and 1980s, the figure of John Wideman produced by interviews and biographical writing seemed hopelessly deprived of the urgent and necessary tools that a Black man needs to avert devastation. He cut an isolated figure; cut off from community. Representations of his life and work, projected a man hopelessly aloof from a nurturing community, arrogantly standing above the fray and far from the madding crowd of the engaged, stridently political writers who were his agemates. According to Byerman:

> [His] initial set of books tended to reflect Wideman's training in the great tradition of Western literature, with its emphasis on sophisticated techniques in writing and a pessimistic view of life. They located that negativity in the African American community and can therefore indicate why he spent the early part of his career away from places such as Homewood. [. . .] It was, as much as possible, a place to be from, not in. (15–16)

He thus appeared cloaked in the mantle of a Black Stephen Dedalus, emerging from James Joyce's modernist masterpiece *A Portrait of the Artist as a Young Man*; a dedicated artist "invisible, refined out of existence, indifferent, paring his fingernails" (215). Though born in 1941, he embodied the proud loner, whose literary output gave little truck to "functional" art. Indeed, in 1975, he even retreated into exile, living in Laramie, Wyoming, away from the inner-city problems ravaging his family and childhood neighborhood of Homewood, in Pittsburgh Pennsylvania.

Meanwhile, disastrous things were happening there and in the country at large following the heady days of the 1960s and the activism of the Civil Rights and Black liberation movements. In his once controversial 1987 book, *The Truly Disadvantaged*, sociologist William Julius Wilson attempts to chart the unflattering evolution of communities such as the Homewood. Wilson first describers the Great Migration of families such as Wideman's (which during the early part of the twentieth century migrated from Washington, DC, Virginia, and South Carolina), as "one of the most important social transformations in recent United States History" (7). Yet, from the 1940s through the 1980s, observes Wilson, relentless displacements ravaged what were once segregated, but stable African American communities. During this time, isolated communities with their diverse mixture of lower "class, working class, and middle class black families"; "stable working class" (7); "extended family networks"; "sense of community, positive neighborhood identification, and explicit norms and sanctions against aberrant behavior" (3) were destabilized by deindustrialization and the movement of the Black middle class away from segregated ghettos and into more affluent communities. According to Wilson, they left behind disorganized, dislocated, and primarily young concentrations of the "underclass" which were "plagued by massive joblessness, flagrant and open lawlessness, and low achieving schools" (58). All of this produced "a disproportionate concentration of the most disadvantage segments of the black urban population, creating a social milieu significantly different from the environment that existed in these communities several decades ago" (58). For Wilson, spaces like Homewood were no longer communities, but economic wastelands, circled around and picked clean by incipient global capitalism. They were no longer just ghettos, but dense concentrations of "the truly disadvantaged" of American society.

At the same time, observes Michelle Alexander, in her 2010 book, *The New Jim Crow*, what was once the promised land for Southern migrants, had devolved into the same horrific system organized by the logic of slavery and Jim Crow that the hopeful migrants had fled. The same period witnessed an exponential rise in the incarceration rates of African Americans, producing what she describes as a "civil rights nightmare" (15) that resulted in a "racial caste system" (11) and a "system of social control unparalleled in world history" (8). "No other country in the world," she observes "imprisons so many of its racial or ethnic minorities" (6).

> More than 2 million people found themselves behind bars at the turn of the twenty-first century, and millions more were relegated to the margins of mainstream society, banished to a political space not unlike Jim Crow, where discrimination in employment, housing, and access to education was perfectly legal, and where they could be denied the right to vote. The system functioned relatively automatically and the prevailing system of racial meanings, identities, and ideologies already seemed natural. Ninety percent of those admitted to prison for drug offenses in many states were black or Latino, yet the mass incarceration of communities of color was explained in race-neutral terms, and adaptation to the needs and demands of the current political climate. The New Jim Crow was born. (58)

The prison industrial complex, before it had that name, was careening out of control, relentlessly snatching up and shoving Black life into cages. "In less than thirty years, the U.S. penal population exploded from around 300,000 to more than 2 million," observes Alexander.

Things had become worse in the 1980s under President Reagan. In 1982, the president declared a war on drugs. According to Alexander: "By waging a war on drug users and dealers, Reagan made good on the promise to crack down on the racially defined 'others'—the undeserving" (63). Meanwhile, she says, Reagan relentlessly deployed "coded antiblack rhetoric" (56) blaming liberal policies for nurturing crime and the culture of Black pathology. By 1986, his offensive had transformed American consciousness and become the banal common sense of American society as broadcast by the media. Says Alexander,

> articles typically featured black "crack whores," "crack babies," and "gangbangers," reinforcing already prevalent racial stereotypes of black women as irresponsible, selfish "welfare queens," and black men as "predators"—part of an inferior and criminal subculture. (52)

All of this occurred, says Alexander, with relatively little protest and with the "civil rights community oddly quiet" (9) if not acquiescent as it focused primarily on issues of diversity and affirmative action. Indeed, many African American leaders became part of the problem as they begged for relief for communities where the once economically balancing Black middle class had largely fled to tony neighborhoods and the suburbs following desegregation. Meanwhile, activist and openly Marxist Black writers such as Angela Davis, Toni Cade Bambara, and Amiri Baraka, seemingly still under the quixotic spell of the Black liberation movement of the 1960s, continued to denounce the effects of ongoing intuitional racism and found themselves and their message increasingly marginalized. African American creative writing itself seemed to take a turn away from its defined role as a functional tool of resistance to oppression and disarmed itself, undertaking the less confrontational more politically viable task of representing largely aesthetic and personal concerns. Wideman's early work—the novels *A Glance Away*, *Hurry Home*, and *The Lynchers*—seemed to represent this state of unilateral disarmament in African American letters.

Indeed, *The Lynchers* can even be read as a critique of the functional art of Black Cultural Nationalism. A highly stylized modernist or somewhat postmodernist novel, *The Lynchers* alienates itself from the highly popular model of conventionalized racial realism often seen as characteristic of protest fiction and African American writing since Richard Wright's *Native Son*. It denounces the conventions of closure, the easy plot-centered narrative, and the dead-end thinking many saw in Black Cultural Nationalism. In this novel, narrative "plot" itself becomes the antagonist. In this work, a group of friends plots to contest racism by publicly lynching a White man. The work thus serves as an early 1970s, African American "novel of disillusion" (a label applied to some postcolonial African novels after Ghanaian writer Ayi Kwei Armah published, *The Beautiful Ones Are Not Yet Born* in 1968), expressing an open pessimism toward the promises of Black liberation. The men in *The Lynchers* mostly end up murdering each other.

Yet, the problems of Homewood famously followed Wideman to his Laramie exile in the person of his brother, Robert. On a February afternoon in 1976, Robert telephoned his brother from a nearby bowling alley in Laramie (7). Wideman chronicles the moment in perhaps his most widely read work, *Brothers and Keepers* (1984). Robby was on the run from the law. He had been involved in a murder; a hold-up gone bad. Soon afterward, the law caught up with Robert, sentenced him to life in prison, and shoved his Black life for the next forty years into a "cage"—an organizing word that Wideman uses for prison after his daughter innocently asks in *Brothers and Keepers*, "How long will Robby be in a cage?" Wideman then observes: "Jamila knew what she was talking about. We said 'jail' and she heard 'cage'" (34).

Wideman's work thus changed and refused to remain "quiet" or "acquiescent" on the issues facing the Black community. *Brothers and Keepers* first captures the spirit of the forces ransacking Homewood in the 1960s and 1970s as experienced by Robert and described by Wilson and Alexander. His community experiences the radicalization, street protests, and riots of the late 1960s; the drugs that began drowning the community; economic collapse; deindustrialization; the militarization of the police; the demonizing of African Americans; the callousness of the legal system; and the widespread lack of empathy for the bourgeoning Black prison population. *Brothers and Keepers* conveys the aporias and roots of what has become known in the twenty-first century as Afropessimism through the thoughts of Wideman's mother, whom the dehumanizing lack of fairness in the legal system morally damages.

> when she realized fairness was not forthcoming, she began to hate. In the lack of reciprocity, in the failure to grant that Robby was first a man, then a man who had done wrong, the institutions and individuals who took over control of his life denied not only his humanity but the very existence of the world that had nurtured him and nurtured her—the world of touching, laughing, suffering black people that established Robby's claim to something more than a number. (72)

The work ends with a letter from Robby in prison, who offers a pessimistic, 1984 look into the future outlined by Alexander. Things, he says "are bleaker than they've ever been."

the joint is busting at the seams with cons and they're sending more every day. Two men to a cell for most of the newcomers, and they don't have enough jobs for men and then they're cutting back on the school programs. Big time, no rehabilitation, lock em up like animals—then let them out on society crazed and angry. Shit don't make no sense but the people cry for punishment and the politicians abide them—can they really be so blind? (243)

He thus describes the early ravages of the mass incarceration epidemic that accelerated in the 1980s.

Then, in 1986, the same system that had snatched up his brother and was gobbling up Black life throughout the United States, struck even closer to home and turned its attention on his youngest son. Critical biographer Byerman writes that Widemam's son, "Jake, apparently suffered a psychotic break and stabbed to death" a friend while attending a summer camp (vii). The writer's efforts to rescue his mentally ill, teenage son from death or life in the cage mostly resulted in helpless frustration after frustration. They fought back the death penalty for Jake, but the system convicted the teenager and all but sentenced him to what Robert later calls "death by incarceration" (Robert Wideman).

At that point, Wideman's writing took an urgent and political turn, though it had not yet embraced the full functionality of the Black Arts. Even so, in his own statements, Wideman reveals that by the late 1960s, he had already "immersed" himself in knowledge of the Black Arts and its traditions. He had come of age as a writer in the turbulent context of the Black Aesthetic era though his early work seems stridently resistant to it. Yet, he intimately knew the production of Black writers. He had to. An Ivy League college athlete and Rhodes scholar who grew up in Pittsburgh and had lived in Europe, Wideman was asked in the late 1960s to "integrate" the *Norton Anthology of American Literature* as well as create the first Black Literature course at the University of Pennsylvania, where he then worked as a professor. Over one summer, he tells Wilfred Samuels in a 1983 interview: "I went from a very superficial acquaintance to an absolute immersion in Black Literature [. . .] I read fast and I concentrated, even spent time in the Schomburg [. . .] African American writing was a serious academic concern" (Wideman, Samuels, 18). In a later, 1988 interview with literary scholar James Coleman, he relates that his concentrated study helped him "to understand how [to use] Afro-American folklore and language" (Wideman, Coleman 67). He thus embraced "black influences" and began to plumb the literature for distinct devices to color his writing. He assembled a toolkit of African American literary tropes and conventions that he deployed in works about his hometown, which critics call *The Homewood Trilogy*. These works consist of *Hiding Place* (1981), *Sent for You Yesterday* (1983), and a collection of short stories titled *Damballah*

(1984). In the latter, he displays a familiarity with Haitian and Black Atlantic cosmology, yet he mostly uses their folkloric themes to generate figures that place it within a Black literary tradition. In 1984, he uses many of these same literary techniques to write *Brothers and Keepers*. The latter, which treats the urgent and political issue of his brother's incarceration, stands as one of the few early scathing critiques of the burgeoning prison industrial system not written by holdover radicals from the 1960s, marginalized members of a "radical group" (4), a "smattering of lawyers and advocates" (5), and people with conspiracy theories about systematic racism that were "initially dismissed as far-fetched, if not downright loony" (7) that Alexander describes in *The New Jim Crow*.

After the imprisonment of Jake, the form of Wideman's work changed. The functional African art embraced by writers of the Black Arts movement no longer just provided tropes and figures that merely influenced this work; it deeply structured it. It was as if, as an artist, Wideman's own experience paradoxically mirrored that of modernist master Pablo Picasso, who became transformed when he first encountered African masks into a practitioner of the black arts or into what he called a *sorcier* or "sorcerer" (Malraux, *Tête* 19). Picasso speaks about this experience to André Malraux, who captures it in his 1974 book, *La Tête d'obsidienne* (*Picasso's Mask*). The day he saw the African sculptures, Picasso says, something changed. He suddenly understood that the forms were "were magical things" (Malraux, *Head* 10). He adds: "all the fetishes were used for the same thing. They were weapons. To help people avoid coming under the influence of spirits again, to help them become independent" (10). That day, Picasso says he conceptualized his first "exorcism-painting" (Malraux, *Head,* 10): the cubist masterpiece, *Les Demoiselles d'Avignon*.

In 1987, Wideman's art makes a similar decisive turn as manifested by his work, *Reuben*. Written in the wake of his son's 25-years-to-life sentence for murder, this work presents the eponymous figure of the novel (a jackleg lawyer) who fails to unravel the life-sucking hold of unyielding legal processes legitimately. So, he resorts to what Wideman calls in a 1988 interview with James Coleman, "a principle of word magic [. . .] to untangle people from the negative effects of the dominant culture, to protect people from one another and also from those invidious forces that are all around them" (Wideman, Coleman 68–9). Not only does the figure of Reuben thematically embrace this "principle of word magic," but the novel itself presents a stylistic rupture with Wideman's earlier work much as Picasso's first "exorcism painting," *Les Demoiselles d'Avignon*, seems to involve a similar break with his earlier work in particular and with Western traditions of artistic representation in general. As critics came to view Picasso's work as an early model of modernism in painting, some early critics of Wideman understood *Reuben* as a primordial candidate for a new, trendy label. In 1989, critic James Coleman imposes the term "black postmodernism" on the work in his book, *Blackness and Modernism: The Literary Career of John Edgar Wideman*. A few years later, Klaus Schmidt, affirms the validity of the term in his in 1995 article, "Reading Black Postmodernism: John Edgar Wideman's *Reuben*."

For both critics, the fissure begun by *Reuben* has more to do with style and literary representation than with a magical struggle to transform the written word into the substance of Black Atlantic craft. In his essay, Schmidt describes literary Black postmodernism as Widemam's way of mimetically representing the apocalyptic landscape of Homewood and the African American community and using *Reuben* as a distorted, but instructive mirror of contemporary society. "Analogous to the disintegration of the dominant postmodern society, the black microcosm delineated in the novel emerges to be an incoherent imaginary space" (96). Such a mirror, he argues, offers a "counterversion of the reality as propagated by the dominant white society" (84). He then suggests that representing Reuben's "magic abilities" in addition to using techniques drawn from an emergent Black postmodernist toolkit equipped with metanarrative devices involving fragmentation, ambiguity, imaginary opposites, unresolved plots, indeterminacy, the demythologizing of canonical texts, polyphony, divergent voices, Black orality, call and response, and marginal witnesses enable the work to dissolve "ontological boundaries" (82) and subvert the "epistemological interests of the readership" (84). For Schmidt, Black postmodernism thus works to destabilize and subvert the reader's sense of the real and even their sense of themselves as beings. In other words, *Reuben* uses its representations to undermine the very structures of Western knowing, its Cartesian rationality, its concoction of human beings, and its division of the world between the known and the imaginary. This harkens forward to the ensuing works which endlessly repeat their version of a Nigerian proverb, "All Stories are true," and to the author's epigraph to his 2008 work, *Fanon*. Wideman begins this work with a quote from Frantz Fanon, the Martinican psychologist and principal theoretical architect of the Black liberation movement, who argues that "imaginary life cannot be isolated from the real life."

Meanwhile, in *Blackness and Modernism*, Coleman locates *Reuben* within a seemingly linear trajectory of Wideman's literary career as he moves from a self-styled and alienated modernist writer to one more concerned with issues facing the African American community. Under this formulation, African American orality and the various voices emanating from folk tales, stories, songs, and childhood rhymes present a way of finally reconciling Wideman's writing with the strivings of the African American community and bringing it beyond the "dead end pessimism" of modernist fiction. Black postmodernism, Coleman argues, is "optimistic because it sees an opportunity for subjective fulfillment of the reader and self-fulfillment in art" (6). Coleman later states that the "postmodernist approach allows Wideman to write freely and experiment as much as he wants, at the same time, it allows him to be deeply committed to blackness as he wants to be" (135).

Despite such apparent optimism, the figure of Reuben consciously operates in a community of incipient devastation and ruin, and on behalf of doomed clients who face confinement, estrangement, death, and inexorable injustice from an incurably sick society that has entangled them in a twisted web of processes—a "chain"—from which there is no exit. At one point, Reuben elaborates this as he conjures the words of an Aretha Franklin song, "Chain of Fools."

> *Chain, chain, chain* . . .
> *Chain of fools.*
> Aretha's song danced from nowhere into his daydream. Up-tempo, electronic funk, tambourines ringing, sounding brass [. . .] To arrive at this bad dream of Homewood and lost children and mothers grieving you needed a chain of events, one after another, didn't you? [. . .] Chains had to be what people wanted or they would not have happened everywhere, always. (18–19)

Reuben thus seems pessimistic, with no faith in the "chain" of signifiers structuring Western thought that could suddenly renounce its nature and produce a foundation for Black liberation or conjure from the detritus of Homewood the notion of a Black "human being" whose life actually matters. Instead, the figure of Reuben attempts to sunder the chain, working more as a "a shaman or priest" anchored more in a dark discredited tradition than as legitimate lawyer anchored in an enlightened one (Wideman Interview, Coleman 152).

Perhaps this magical turn away from legitimate or rational solutions might suggest substituting the twenty-first century label of Afropessimism for those of Black postmodernism or Contemporary African American literature when it comes to positioning Wideman's work. By seeming to turn toward "superstition," Black magic, and the Black arts, *Reuben* and Wideman's ensuing work openly pit themselves against Western ways of knowing, or what Frank Wilderson in his 2020 book, *Afropessimism* calls the "narrative mode" of European epistemology. Within this system, which dictates the very terms of knowing the world, argues Wilderson, the Black person "(if person, subject, being are appropriate, since Human is not)" (12) becomes the inexorable foil "of humanity" (13). "Blacks are not Human subjects," he asserts, "but are instead structurally inert props, implements for the execution of White and non-Black fantasies and sadomasochistic pleasures" (15). This system, Wilderson asserts, subjects "Black people" to "social death" and forever bars them from any useful "narrative of redemption" (16). Under this lens,

Wideman's ensuing work can be taken as consisting of texts that resist or defy the structures of Western epistemology and ontology that depend upon and produce the nothingness and inexorable aporia of the "black person" as articulated by Frantz Fanon and James Baldwin in the 1950s and then taken up with a vengeance by the Afropessimism in the second decade of the twenty-first century.

Still, like postmodernist literature, Afropessimistic thought, though it has a Black twist, still arrives imbedded with the theoretical dead-ends of postructuralism that dominated the American academy during the later part of the twentieth century with its disavowal of the Enlightenment "Human" as an ethnocentric construction; its emphasis on the structures of writing, narrative, and discourse as the masquerading but inexorably jaded speech of a hidden, self-interested character; and its reduction to linguistic phenomena (to issues of representation) of all attempts at knowing. As the most recent development in Black thought, it perhaps projects a linear trajectory; one that is perhaps charted by works such as the *Norton Anthology of African American Literature* which moves from the eras of slavery, reconstruction, the Harlem Renaissance, modernism and realism, the Black Arts, and Contemporary Writing as if the descendants of enslaved Africans had not relentlessly, and experientially confronted and responded to the exact same aporia, the same endlessly running "script" of expendability and parasitic dependence that inexorably positions White over Black. Meanwhile, Black people had used their own dogmatically discredited knowledge, their own wisdom, their own ordering of life and the cosmos to both survive and even thrive in the West.

Beginning with *Reuben,* Wideman's work openly turns away from the Western "narrative mode" of dogmatically embracing the totalizing structures of a particular idea of language as constituting reality. It thus seems pessimistically to reject the narrative of redemption for Black people as it also dabbles in the Black arts, or in what Toni Morrison has called "discredited knowledge"—the "superstition and magic, which is another way of knowing things." In her 1984 essay, "Rootedness: The Ancestor as Foundation," Morrison argues that such knowledge is discredited "only because Black people were discredited therefore what they knew was 'discredited'" (Morrison, Rootedness 342). Such knowledge does not develop, it repeats in the fashion described by literary critic James Snead in his brilliantly useful essay, "On Repetition in Black Culture." "In black culture, repetition means that the thing *circulates*" Snead asserts. It is "'there for you to pick it up when you come back to get it'" (149–50). This evokes the forms of lived knowledge of African American vernacular culture and of Black Aesthetic practice such as the repetitions of the blues and the motto of the Association for the Advancement of Creative Musicians, a Chicago Black artist collective started in the 1960s. The motto cyclically embraces the performance of "Great Black

Music, Ancient to the Future." This reflects the attitudes of avant-garde and experimental musicians such as Lester Bowie or Sun Ra (who for instance called Louis Armstrong, one of the early twentieth-century progenitors of jazz, his "destiny"). This suggests that the "word magic" that the figure of Reuben practices and which launches the aesthetic principles of the ensuing works may be part of the circulating, "discredited knowledge" described by Toni Morrison. Such a knowledge teaches how to make words do more than merely represent the world like the signifiers, signs, and symbols of Western thought that had subjected "Black people" to the "social death" elaborated by Afropessimism, and which forever barred them "from the narrative of redemption" (16). Indeed, in the 1960s, the relentlessly discredited Black Cultural Nationalists circulated a notion they derived from African cosmology which held that words could function like the African sculptures that Picasso describes as "weapons" (Malraux, *Head* 10). Black Arts theorists such a Karenga adhered to similar descriptions of African art and, for instance, embraced Amiri Baraka's call for words that "kill and shoot guns and 'wrassle cops into alleys taking their weapons'" (34). Such knowledge has a beat, or a recurrent living pulse, as described in *Writing to Save a life*, as the narrator describes the recovered memory of a Black Atlantic talisman he once received that throbs with the mysterious rhythms of Black power— "Found and lost, found again, lost again (192).

Still, it must be admitted that within western society, this circulating knowledge about the role of Black art has suspect origins. Picasso says he stood alone, gaping at an exhibit of African sculptures when he discovered that the people who crafted the objects, hadn't crafted them as representations of reality, but as protective "weapons" (11). Yet, these objects came to France for Picasso's observation at the turn of the twentieth century, divorced from their context and their disparate ethnicities, all but effacing the individuality of their particular African makers. In 2016, a traveling exhibit of the sculptures that influenced Picasso and other European modernists at the turn of the twentieth century (generically titled "*Senufo*") underscores the colonial context that brought them to France in the first place. Europeans came to know the objects as originating from a group they called, the *Senufo*, which was an artificial, colonially constructed identity. "The name *Senufo*," says Tiona Ferdinand Ouattara in the catalog's afterword, "derived from the contraction of a Mande-language phrase, [and] was established and given to this population in the last quarter of the nineteenth century by the French colonial administration" (277).

Moreover, in the 1930s, under a movement they labeled *Negritude*, the African intellectuals who inspired the Black Aesthetic movement along with members of the African diaspora began to give voice to and elaborate the spirt and lived experience of those that created the original masks. One of the architects of that movement, Senegalese poet, writer, and eventual statesman, Léopold Senghor, even wrote a 1945 poem called, "Prayer to the masks," which contains lines that actually seem to embraces the idea of Africans as a foil, or "therapeutic balm" for Western thought that Afropessimism repudiates. In Senghor's poem, "yeast" (*le levain*), takes the place of "balm." "Let us report present at the rebirth of the World/ Like the yeast which the white flour needs" (9). Less than a decade later, Frantz Fanon in his 1952 book, *Black Skin White Masks* (expressing ideas later embraced by Afropessimists), would repudiate this parasitic notion of African peoples as "yeast" or "balm." He excoriates the aporias of negritude and the idea of "the black man [. . .] universalizing himself" within a matrix of Western thought that both relies on and denies their existence. "Beware, reader!" Fanon warns. "There is no question of finding "being" in Bantu thought when Bantus live at the level of nonbeing and the imponderable" (162). He adds, "We know full well that Bantu society no longer exists. And there is nothing ontological about segregation. Enough of this outrage" (163).

Yet, the Negritude movement—its atavism, valorization of African religion as religion and not superstition, ethnological restoration of African culture as a culture, promotion of a shared Black or African consciousness, insistence on a notion of African Authenticity, radical political and social agendas, and imagining of the generic African—had a profound and far reaching influence on the intellectuals of Africa and the African diaspora. Budding writers such as Chinua Achebe (who has had a marked and lasting influence on Wideman) first read translated works of Negritude writers, who "had a degree of sophistication not yet seen in writers in English" in a journal called *Black Orpheus* that "was founded in 1957," asserts James Currey in his article "Literary Publishing After Nigerian Independence: Mbari as Celebration" (9). Still, many African writers came to repudiate Negritude as both constricting and reductive of African reality. Nevertheless, "Negritude probably generated the original inspiration" of "shared cultural and artistic principles in sub-Saharan Africa on the one hand, and the black Diaspora on the other," and thus a "claim to a unifying black literary heritage," argues Africanist Oyeniyi Okunoye in "The Critical Reception of Modern African Poetry" (772). Negritude thus helps establish, Okunoye argues disparagingly "what has almost been taken for granted in the discourse of black art: the essential unity of vision in black expressive culture as evident in an artistic philosophy which privileges functionality and social responsibility" (772). Ron Karenga, says as much in his 1968 manifesto of the Black Aesthetic movement, "Black Cultural Nationalism." "Tradition teaches us, Leopold Senghor tells us, that all African art has at least three characteristics: that is, it is functional, collective and committing or committed" (33).

Yet, in the contemporary era, many writers had come to regard the circulating ideas of both Negritude and the Black Aesthetic movement as reductive, constrictive and founded on sentimental fallacies about cultural retention and an all too sweeping notion of African art. This, too, began to change. Along with other rigorous anthropological work, Robert Farris Thompson's 1983 book *Flash of the Spirit* explored the workings of particular African cosmologies and their expression in the New World revealing that many transatlantic connections were actual and not merely wistful. Wideman's reading of this work before writing *Reuben* seems to have enabled his transformation as a writer the way viewing African sculptures had transformed Picasso. It helped arm him and provided a model for an alternative aesthetic method for structuring his work.

Flash of the Spirit elaborates the nature of the amalgamated "bundle" as a strategic object of Black Atlantic cosmology crafted to "effect healing" and divert, arrest, or undermine power. *Reuben* embraces this craft. Along with *Philadelphia Fire* (1990), *The Cattle Killing* (1996), *Two Cities* (1998), *Fanon* (2008), and *Writing to Save a Life* (2017) it works as a tool to perform acts of protection and healing. What seem like complicated, often inaccessible, fragmented, and postmodern works, can also be experienced as bundles of spirit-saving stories that conjure black magic. In these works, each story, each fragment struggles to arrest or "save" the "flash of the spirit" of victims of the "social death" wrought by a "narrative mode" that places Black life beyond redemption. And while these works might structurally agree with Afropessimists who proclaim that Black people can't be "redeemed" within Western thought; they functionally demonstrate that Black life can be "saved"—if one knows how to do it. So, the work of Wideman, dating from the end of the twentieth century and the first decades of the twenty-first century are both magical and functional. They are indeed Black Art, revealing that Wideman is true to his word when he says in 1989, "I see continuities, rather than a simple break with or repudiation of the Black Arts Movement of the sixties" (Wideman, Rowell 91).

Chapter 1

Reuben and the Sorcerer

Something changed in the work of John Edgar Wideman following the time when he learned that Arizona prosecutors had decided to try his son for murder and were threatening to take the teenager's life. Wideman found himself embroiled in Kafkaesque legal processes he didn't understand and which he couldn't unravel. He was not a lawyer. He was disarmed and without tools. His one tool, writing, seemed at best ineffectual and at worst a hindrance. In 1984, he had written a critically acclaimed, and perhaps his best known and most conventionally accessible work: a memoire about himself and the imprisonment for murder of his brother, Robert Wideman, with the title, *Brothers and Keepers*. "It didn't work. Everything written after that book worked even less," a narrator of his 2016 work, *Fanon*, sadly remembers (52). Even his brother, Robert Wideman, who was finally released in July 2019 after forty-four years in prison speculates that the written work may have damaged his 1998 appeal for a new trial and earlier release. In an op-ed, published online by the *Pittsburgh Post-Gazette* he says: "Unfortunately, the new trial never came to be. Because of the prominence of my case—partly because my brother is a well-known writer who had written a famous book about my case titled "Brothers and Keepers"—political interests intervened and my retrial never happened" (Robert Wideman). As for the 1986 case of the writer's son, the parents of the victim and others attacked the author, asserting "problems with the family" (20), and depicting the sixteen-year-old boy as "a bad seed," asserts Keith Byerman in his critical biography, *The Life and Work of John Edgar Wideman* (22). As a consequence, Wideman seemed to withdraw from openly writing about his son. In his book, Byerman observes that while Wideman overtly writes about his brother Robby, "material about Jake tends to be much more scattered, in *Fatheralong*, *Hoop Roots*,

Briefs, and magazine pieces. This would suggest that, even after 25 years, Wideman cannot quite absorb the meaning of that tragedy" (24–25).

Nevertheless, the title of the 1987 work, *Reuben*, telegraphs a project that is encoded within the Hebrew name of the text. Perhaps on behalf of the writer, the eponymous spirit bearing the name whimsically translates it from a language that has its own cabalistic practices which locate sacred magic in words: "Part of the joke was his name, Reuben. . . . 'Behold, a son, Reuben was his name'" (127). Beginning with a title that means "Behold a son," Wideman seems to set out on a new or perhaps ancient path for the Black artist that would take writing beyond the act of merely representing a world that it seems to have no power to actually change. In a 1988 interview, he explores this path through a description of the spirit of *Reuben* which drives the character and aesthetic structure of the work in addition to that of the five novels that follow.

> Reuben has no choice but to be a servant of the people. He manifests a certain principle of magic. He manifests a principle of word magic that enables us to create our own institutions, our own identities, and he is a figure who will always be in the midst of trouble because the dominant culture resists any attempt to infringe on its power. And Reuben is a power figure. He is an intermediary. He is in the battleground. It's his job to untangle people from the negative effects of the dominant culture, to protect people from one another and also from those invidious forces that are all around them. That's a ritualistic process. It is the same thing that a shaman or priest does in a traditional culture, and so he is a lawyer. Both plots and themes of the fictions I write, and the fictions themselves are an attempt to subvert one notion of reality with others to show that there is not simply one way of seeing things but many ways of seeing things. (151–52)

Reuben thus engages Wideman's effort to transform writing into the type of functional armament once called for by writers of the Black Aesthetic movement. Through this work, Wideman as an artist, equally dons the mantle of "shaman or priest" involving the novel itself in a "ritualistic process" that "manifests a principle of word magic," untangling people and pitting itself against "those invidious forces that are all around them." The text reveals that something had clearly changed in the artist's approach to his work and his response to tragedy and the pessimism inherent to aesthetic disarmament.

Early critics of Wideman's work after *Reuben* had described this transformation as an effort by the writer to embrace postmodernism and emulate the academic trends of the late twentieth century. In a review of one ensuing work for the *New York Times* in 1991, novelist Darryl Pinckney accuses Wideman of deploying "a self-conscious combination of European modernism, the black oral tradition, and, most recently, the atmosphere of deconstruction and canon-bashing closing in on black academic judgments" (19). Others describe *Reuben* as evidence of Wideman's movement from being an avowedly modernist writer to one who embraced what they term Black postmodernism. Meanwhile, another key to the aesthetic transformation of the writer's craft to an ethic of more functional art announces itself on the "Acknowledgments" page that precedes the text: "*Thanks to Robert Farris Thompson for* Flash of the Spirit *and its exposition of Kongo cosmology*." Thompson's landmark, 1983 anthropological work goes beyond what many saw as the nostalgia of Black cultural nationalism or its early-twentieth-century progenitor, Negritude, and their evocation of an essentialist, generalized African essence based on an idea of art forms by anonymous African artists divorced from community and context that seemed at best sentimental and at worst unfounded in the reality of Africans and Africans of the diaspora. Instead, through this work, Thompson explores an actual, Black Atlantic cosmology that elaborates elements of the particular Igbo, Yoruba, and Kongo cultures that crossed the Atlantic and gave rise to the African-based religions of the Americas and the Caribbean. In relationship to *Reuben*, it functions as a guidebook for an aesthetic method that can actually work to save or preserve the essence of a life that inexorably hovers outside of redemption in Western thought. In other words, *Flash of the Spirit* does not merely serve to provide a trendy writer with the tropes, themes, and figures of an insistently postmodern text. Instead it teaches how to transform a written work into another type of magical object, or what Thompson calls "a secular *nzo a nkisi*, a charm for the denial of hurt, for the redirecting of spirit" (158).

Paradoxically, Wideman's reading of Thompson and perceived movement away from modernist writing mirrors the description of a foundational moment in the history of modernist art: Pablo Picasso's initial, 1907 fixation by African sculpture. In an interview published in writer André Malraux's 1974 book, *La Tête d'obsidienne (Picasso's Mask)*, Picasso describes his transformation as an artist when he came upon an exhibition of African masks in Paris. Something, he says "was happening to me, wasn't it?"

> The masks weren't just like any other pieces of sculpture. Not at all. They were magic things. The Negro pieces were *intercessors* [. . .] against everything—against unknown, threatening spirits. I always looked at fetishes [. . .] I understood what the Negroes used their sculpture for [. . .] But all the fetishes were used for the same thing. They were weapons. To help people avoid coming under the influence of spirits again, to help them become independent. They're tools [. . .] I understood why I was a painter. (Malraux, *Head* 10–11).

This response to the aesthetic spirit of African craft mirrors the response described by Black Aesthetic writers of the 1960s who also struggled to make such protective, "magical things" which were not mere representations of reality, but "weapons." Yet, Wideman, who says that he went from "from a very superficial acquaintance to an absolute immersion in Black Literature in the late 1960s" (Wideman, Samuels 18) seems to have initially recoiled from the impetus behind such functional art. Indeed, according to critical biographer Keith Byerman, Wideman, along with other writers categorized within the contemporary era of African American literature, "not only felt that the Black Arts Movement restricted their artistic freedom, but that the Black Power philosophy behind it was socially dangerous" (15). This changed, however, in the late 1980s when Wideman found himself threatened by "unknown threatening spirits" that took the form of the legal processes that had caged his brother and menaced the actual life of his son. So, like Picasso, who claims that understanding African sculpture enabled him to become a "sorcerer" and execute his first work of exorcism, *Les Demoiselles d'Avignon*, Wideman's understanding of Black Atlantic aesthetics through *Flash of the Spirit* launched him on a course of executing similar "weapons" and "tools" that would, in Picasso's words "help people avoid coming under the influence of spirits again, to help them become independent" ((Malraux, *Head* 10) or, as Wideman says about the efforts of Reuben, "untangle people from the negative effects of the dominant culture, to protect people from one another and also from those invidious forces that are all around them" (151).

Reuben thus struggles to move writing beyond the role of representation and transform the novel itself into a charm, or a work of Black Atlantic craft. It may seem to have the qualities of a fragmented, postmodernist text but it also functions as a magical Black Atlantic bundle or container with each story, each fragment of text functioning like the dirt, clay, shards of a mirror, colored glass, seeds, stones, herbs, sticks, animal claws, feathers, shells, bones, and beads that save the "flash of a spirit" and use it, in Thompson's words "to effect healing and other phenomena" (Thompson 117). In exploring these qualities of *Reuben,* this chapter will first describe aspects of *Reuben* that led early critics to understand the work as a postmodernist text. Next, it will go more deeply into the ideas of Thompson embraced and deployed by the work which place it in the aesthetic tradition of functional art and Black Atlantic craft. Finally, this analysis will discuss the various "spiritualizing" or saved elements of the text that make up the magical bundle such as its evocation of Africa as the motherland, its use of ancestral figures, its capturing of communal disintegration, it demystifying and unmasking of the fetishes driving the dominant culture, and its role as what Thompson calls a "secular *nzo a nkisi*" that works to reanimate and save a life that "unknown, threatening spirits" (Malraux, *Head* 10) had place beyond redemption.

REUBEN

Reuben is a work that abounds with lies, half-truths, and unresolved plots that are never securely placed in relationship to a neat, chronologically ordered fictional reality. In *Reuben* readers don't find an obvious, easy-to-read, plot-driven work of conventional literary realism. Instead, it is a text that works against the "law and order" of closure and conventional narrative consciousness, weaving its own spells of protection. The work unmasks and responds to the aesthetic organization of power, subverting "one notion of reality with others" through its distinct aesthetic organization. On one level, it does this by forcing writing to do things that are often more successfully accomplished in other media. Indeed, through a discussion with the almost necromantic work of early photographer Edward Muybridge, who magically reanimated frozen and dead images, the text begins a conversation on representation, time, space, motion, alchemy, resurrection, religious relics, transubstantiation, and life-saving African cosmology. This conversation continues with artists such as anatomical illustrator George Stubbs, in *The Cattle Killing* (1996); the Swiss sculptor Alberto Giacometti, jazz pianist Thelonious Monk, and visual artist Romare Bearden in *Two Cities* (1998); filmmaker Jean-Luc Godard in *Fanon* (2008); and both a Catholic saint and French glass artist in *Writing to Save a Life* (2016).

On one level, *Reuben* works as a status report on what has become of the nurturing Pittsburgh community of Homewood where Wideman actually grew up and that sets his earlier work. It charts the effects of deindustrialization, the flight of the Black middle class, emergent neoliberalism and the conservative law-and-order regime of the 1980s on a Black community in the American rust belt. It is a community in ruins, now served by figures such as the eponymous Reuben, a sham lawyer who struggles to disentangle people form the deadly legal processes that increasingly threaten their lives. The work revolves around Reuben's attempts to reunite Kwansa, a recovering drug addict, former prostitute and teenage mother with her lost son, Cudjoe, who was spirited away by his estranged father. A trickster figure, Reuben dwells at the margins of the community, living in and working from a trailer.

The text is divided into 11 chapters that bear faint traces of a plot and a timeline. In the first chapter, Kwansa visits Reuben's trailer for the first time and asks him to protect Cudjoe. Then, in chapter 3, Cudjoe's father, Waddell, absconds with the boy while Kwansa is out drinking in a bar and flirting with a woman named Toodles. In the second to last chapter, Kwansa and Toodles kill Waddell in a bar fight (with Toodles slitting his throat). Finally, in an unnumbered chapter called "And," the text presents Reuben retrieving Cudjoe from a government institution and bringing him "home." These events, though fragmented and somewhat unresolved, lie at the core of the work. Meanwhile, the text offers several, shorter, and equally unresolved stories told through a variety of narrative styles. Kwansa tells the story of her relationship with Waddell and her expulsion from her grandmother's house after she became pregnant with Cudjoe. Reuben tells iconic "literacy" and "atrocity" stories from his life in Philadelphia. These begin with his work at a fraternity house at the University of Pennsylvania where he has access to books which enable him, autodidactically, to study law. While there he falls in love with the madam of a bordello, Flora. This is short-lived as a jealous group of white fraternity brothers torch the house, killing Flora, though Reuben escapes. There is also a chapter about Reuben's client, Mr. Tucker, who is a handyman that police arrest for demolishing and stealing bricks from vacant Pittsburgh buildings. In an additional story, Wally, a university basketball recruiter, consults Reuben over an entanglement in a budding scandal at work involving the misappropriation of money. He also tells a short version of his life story beginning with his education in Philadelphia and ending with his job at the university; relates a an actual story or fantasy about murdering a white man in a public bathroom stall; and conveys the story of Bimbo, a childhood friend who becomes a singing star before a car accident renders him a paraplegic. In this story, Bimbo begs Wally to help him commit suicide. The rest of the stories of the text occur largely as unresolved fragments, though Reuben does seem to liberate both Mr. Tucker and Cudjoe, bringing them home—wherever or whatever that is.

The text conveys these stories through a ragged sense of focalization with no singular character, no definitive narrative voice or enunciator assuming control. No single consciousness or organizing principle seems in charge. Sometimes, a version of African American orality dominates the "frame," invoking passages from the WPA slave testimonies that Wideman analyzed in academic articles such as "Charles Chesnutt and the WPA Narratives: The Oral and Literate Roots of Afro-American Literature" and "Defining the Black Voice in Fiction." In both essays, Black speakers struggle to elude the dominating grip of standard written English and "free themselves from a frame which a priori devalues black speech" (Wideman, Defining 79). At such times, *Reuben* recalls the earlier works of *The Homewood Trilogy* and seems to become the type of "speakerly text" which concerns "itself with the possibilities of representation of the speaking black voice in writing" described by Henry Louis Gates in his landmark 1988 study of African American literary tropes, *The Signifying Monkey*. Indeed, in several passages, a voice similar to that of the WPA slave testimonies takes over the narration as if responding to unasked questions about Reuben and his trailer. "Don't ax me. Been sitting in that lot all these years but I'll be damned if I know" (6). At other times, the twentieth-century voice of some "brother" sitting in the Velvet Slipper lounge assumes control as he tells the story of the homicidal brawl between

Kwansa, Toodles, and Waddell. "Sheeit. Don't tell me. I was there" (212). Yet, these voices play at the same level of power and dominance and often cede control to others. Indeed, at one point, the narrative ventriloquizes the self-consciously scripted, painstakingly literary, and narrated director's cues of a Rod-Serling type, Twilight Zone voice, instructing readers to "imagine" Reuben as "a short, gimpy, immaculately dressed, bearded, brown man in the piss-colored hall of a public building" (214). The work also overflows with conventional, omniscient, third person and past-tense narration; direct speech; somewhat experimental forms of free indirect discourse; free direct speech; and the voices of documents, newspaper excerpts, poems, lines from nursery rhymes, and songs. Often these have the effect the text describes as Kwansa lays her son down on the couch and repeats a time-worn prayer and discovers that "the words came and said themselves . . she wasn't sure who was speaking the words first, realized that she was following as much as leading" (58). Reuben relentlessly stages this confusion through the scopic tension of "zooming," an idea later encapsulated in *Philadelphia Fire,* by the lyrics of a popular Aretha Franklin song: "Who's Zoomin' Who?"

To some extent, this practice of "zooming" is one in an arsenal of metanarrational techniques that led early critics to label *Reuben* as a Black postmodernist text. It involves using camera cues such as "dissolve to," or "fading in," which temporarily transform sections of the text into a working film script. In his 1995 article "Reading Black Postmodernism: John Edgar Wideman's *Reuben*," Klaus Schmidt argues that zooming "demotes the recipients to passive spectators and, simultaneously, positions them in the center of the narrated action" (91). This, he says, allows the text to subvert the epistemological and ontological status of readers. He further argues that these practices enable the author to incorporate "himself into the postmodern literary text" while "simultaneously [distancing] himself from his personal involvement by fictionalizing himself, i.e. by lowering his real self to the level of a fictional character who has to abide by the rules that dominate the narrative world" (83–84). Yet, transforming the nature of the text in this way—shifting it into the base matter for a film—also performs an additional function. It announces Wideman's preoccupation with escaping the bounds of written representation through the use of techniques garnered from other art forms. Indeed, the ensuing texts in Wideman's oeuvre lavishly deploy similar practices, which reveal a text struggling to move writing beyond the role of representation and transform words into a magical and functional tool of Black Atlantic craft.

Kongo Cosmology

While such techniques give the text a postmodern flavor, the work also functions as a Black Atlantic charm anchored in the cosmology elaborated by

Flash of the Spirit. Indeed, through *Reuben,* Flash *of the Spirit* works as a functional guide on how to "save life" and use it as a force for protection and healing. This is done through the captured stories of the work, which function like the *nkisi* of traditional Bakango religion. According to Thompson "*nkisi* (plural: *minkisi*) is a strategic object said to effect healing and other phenomena" (117). An *nkisi* is a "spirit-embodying" material that captures or saves the essence of a life; the trapped soul of an ancestor or of a "victim of witchcraft" (118). A *nkisi*, mixed and bundled into a *minkisi* container, has the ability to divert the power of a soul and use it for healing, divining, locating, protecting, and binding together loved ones or effectively stopping an enemy in "their tracks" (131). According to Thompson:

> Minkisi containers are various: leaves, shells, packets, sachets, bags, ceramic vessels, wooden images, statuettes, cloth bundles, among other objects [. . .] Spirit-*embodying* materials include cemetery earth—considered at one with the spirit of a buried person—or equivalents such as white clay (*mpemba*), taken from riverbeds [. . .] Spirit-embodying materials are usually wrapped or concealed in a charm, but such objects as mirrors or pieces of porcelain attached to the exterior of the *nkisi* may also signify power—the flash and arrest of the spirit. (117–18)

Thompson specifically follows this eclectic practice of bundling disparate items and its deep spirituality across the Atlantic. He locates it in crazy quilts, collage-like practices of pasting newspaper print and magazine artwork onto cabin walls, the *pacquets congos* of Haitian Vodun, the *punto de segurar* of Cuban Santeria, and the bundles of African American Voodoo.

In literature, this recalls the bundled together, or "eclectic" structures of the early slave narratives described by Robert Burns Stepto in his essay, "I Rose and found My Voice: Narration, Authentication and Authorial Control in Four Slave Narratives," which tactically toyed with the machinery of authentication to undermine the legal processes of enslavement (229). Within *Reuben,* writing performs this same work. Although the text might fundamentally rely on words as representations, it also treats each word, song, prayer, utterance, and saved story as powerful, spirit-embodying material somehow inseparably bound to the original flash of life it captures or saves, like clay, colored shards of glass, or dirt from a cemetery. The work thus struggles with its form, transmutating into a concrete or healing charm of Black Atlantic craft.

With all of its divergent and sometimes rag tag elements, the novel thus has the aesthetic structure of a Black Atlantic bundle. It conjures the *prenda* of Cuban Santeria described in a quote from Lydia Cabrera that Thompson includes in *Flash of the Spirit.*

The *prenda* is like the entire world in miniature, a means of domination. The ritual expert places in the kettle all manner of spiritualizing forces: there he keeps the cemetery and the forest, there he keeps the river and the sea, the lightning-bolt, the whirlwind, the sun, the moon, the stars—forces in concentration. (quoted in Thompson, 123).

Through its stories and voices *Reuben* also overflows with "spiritualizing forces," or *minkisi* in the form of Black cultural nationalist nostalgic notions of an African motherland, unstable ancestral presences, a disintegrating community, and the destructive, written fetishes of the dominant society.

African Motherland

Egypt as an African Kingdom, descending from African royalty, and other nostalgic notions of an African homeland held a special place among the Black Cultural Nationalists influenced by Negritude. *Ruben* captures these notions through the time traveling, disordered memory of Ruben. He remembers this past, but one where he is neither king nor queen. Instead, he is a captive to royalty. Meanwhile, he uses the powerful image of "home" to signify, revise, define, and add resonance to this idea of a mythic past. In one passage, he relentlessly repeats the phrase "home again," as if it were part of an incantation, or a "riff" from a jazz piece. It moves throughout his memories of living in Sub-Saharan Africa and then Egypt as a "dwarf scavenged for Queen Hatshepsut's pleasure. Her tale-telling Moor. Her tribute from the land of the Blacks" (205). He experiences the middle passage and works as an enslaved African in a ship galley, where "Oars fall in unison like the breathing bones of a rib cage" (204). Then, he lands "Home again after all," in a trailer—a moveable home—parked on the Homewood streets. Ultimately, Reuben alights on a homeless self-image of a rootless being that Wally calls a "shit beetle," which magically conjures itself from dung. According to Reuben, "The Egyptians believed the beetle was sacred because it seemed to be creating itself when it emerged from the empty earth" (195).

Ancestral Figures

In an important 1984 essay, novelist Toni Morrison argues that it is "interesting to evaluate Black literature on what the writer does with the presence of an ancestor. Which is to say a grandfather as in Ralph Ellison or a grandmother, as in Toni Cade Bambara, or a healer as in Bambara or Henry Dumas. There is always an elder there" (Morrison, Rootedness 342). Yet, in a world relentlessly under attack by menacing outside forces, attempts at nurturing and protection by these figures often takes unusual and ambiguous forms. Within this world, mothers lose track of daughters, fathers lose track of sons, and the ancient wisdom of the ancestral figures becomes a dangerous, discredited mark of inferiority. In *Beloved,* for instance, the enslaved child Sethe's captive and rebellious mother slaps her during their only encounter. In Wideman's work, fathers and sons often fear contaminating each other with the virus of their discredited being or the contagion stemming from what a character in Wideman's 1996 work, *The Cattle Killing* calls the "madness" besieging a racialized society. "I call the whites' attitude toward us madness" (113), the character of Liam tells another. In the 2016 work, *Writing to Save a Life*, this contagion becomes what the narrator calls "the American darkness" that unravels bonds and "disconnects colored fathers from sons." In this work, the bad, selfish, distant, wife-beating father—an elder—offers corrupt advice to a son facing "death by incarceration" (Robert Wideman) for participating in a holdup-scheme-gone-bad that resulted in a murder. Blindly, controlled by the contagion, the recalcitrant father advises his son, to trust official processes; trust the law. "Don't let them make you say you did that crime they say you did. Tell the truth, Son. Lawyer we got you a good lawyer. No case, he says." The advice backfires and the father unwittingly consigns his son to "All the mean years" he serves in prison. The narrator distressingly asks: "Why did you have to act like you know everything about judges, courts, law, just cause you're black and the cops tossed your belligerent ass in jail overnight a couple of times" (75).

Written nearly thirty years earlier, *Reuben* saves the immemorially agonizing spirit of such moments as one of its bundled *minkisi*. Reuben, an ancestral spirit, actually offers similar legal advice to help Kwansa retrieve her missing son.

> You are the child's mother. That still counts for a lot in these cases [. . .]
> They ain't gon come get Cudjoe?
> No. They can't. Certain steps must be taken. Papers filed, judgments rendered, hearings. There's a process. A routine. There's always a procedure. One thing must be done after another in a certain order, a certain sequence. That's the law. The way it works. So we have time. (11)

He's wrong. Waddell takes Cudjoe, leaving Kwansa to wander the streets of Homewood, desperately searching for her son and channeling the thoughts of all the others who find themselves inexorably enmeshed in vicious processes that they don't understand and whom received bad advice rather than protection from unreliable ancestral sources. "You lied, old man. You was wrong, wrong, wrong old rat faced, slick mouthed man. My son is gone. They took him away" (152).

Kwansa's grandmother, Big Mama, the woman who took her in when nobody else would also saves the spirit of such elders. Big Mama who attends a "Rocking and shaking" sanctified, storefront church (150), first nurtures and cares for Kwansa. But when her granddaughter tells the old woman she is pregnant, Big Mama evicts her from her home after mercilessly beating her.

> The wheezes the old woman gasping to catch her breath, almost dying between blows, worse than the stinging blows themselves. Like an animal behind her back [. . .] it wheezed and grunted and found the strength to strike Kwansa again [. . .] Kwansa had no eyes in the back of her head, so she couldn't believe it was her Big Mama hurting her like that [. . .] Her Big Mama all she had. Big Mama fed her. (147)

Big Mama gives Kwansa all of the love she experiences in her young life, but the old woman also viciously curses Kwansa and the child she carries. Kwansa reflects: "Big Mama ought to known better. God ought to know better" (157).

Wally also expresses simultaneous feeling of tenderness and callousness toward the grandmother who raised him. When she dies, he cavalierly trashes all of "her nice things, the stuff unused, secured in tight bundles wrapped with brown paper and tied with string" (166). Instead of power objects of cultural retention and Black Atlantic craft, he grandmother's "tight bundles" become discredited, embarrassing, and constricting signs of ancestral impotence. Indeed, for him, these things evoke Miss Emily, of William Faulkner's short story, "A Rose for Emily," who poisons her lover and sleeps with his corpse for decades (180). He associates the love of his grandmother with the stale smell of a smothering "blanket [that] trapped and embarrassed him" (106).

Disintegrating Communities

Reuben also collects and saves the spirit of the Homewood of the 1980s, a rustbelt Black community. In 1984, it was "morning again in America." So said President Ronald Reagan in an advertisement of his 1984 reelection campaign. By then, millions of African Americans moving away from the South and the oppressive legacy of slavery had flocked northward toward the jobs and opportunities of what the title of a 1992 book by journalist Nicholas Lemann called, *The Promised Land*. This book describes a Great Migration barely registered before then by the mainstream media. Meanwhile, according to Reagan, the upheavals and "malaise" of the 1960s and 1970s, the disgrace of the Vietnam War, the runaway inflation of an ailing economy, and the denied promises of the Civil Rights era seemed to be rapidly fading into a hermetically sealed past. Yet, during this same period, communities like the mythologized Homewood of Wideman's earlier work, had experienced decline, devastation, and loss of hope later expressed by the Afropessimists of the second decade of the twenty-first century. These communities seemed relentlessly beyond redemption, only inciting a repressed aporia in the imagination of a dominant culture that responded to that anxiety with violent power, containing it through asymmetrical applications of law and order.

Wideman's 1984 memoire, *Brothers and Keepers*, chronicles the plight of a community under siege, which had experienced the radicalization, street protests, and riots of the late 1960s; the drugs that began drowning the community; economic collapse; deindustrialization; the militarization of the police; the demonizing of African Americans; the callousness of the legal system; and the widespread lack of empathy for the bourgeoning prison population. In this work, his mother begins to experience hate for a system that eschews "reciprocity" and fails to recognize her son as "first a man, then a man who had done wrong" and then "denied not only his humanity but the very existence of the world that had nurtured him and nurtured her—the world of touching, laughing, suffering black people that established Robby's claim to something more than a number" (72). *Reuben*, through its capturing of the Homewood community, decodes the banal rhetoric of the dominant society and gives voice to the nurturing world of the "truly disadvantaged" and their "claim to something more" (Brothers 72). Although this world seems beyond redemption, its spirit is saved and magically bundled by the text as an nkisi capturing the living spirit of the community.

Reuben safeguards the spirt of a community in disarray and disintegration, which has become a "bad dream of Homewood and lost children and mothers grieving" (18). Reuben (a fraud), Wally (a thief and possibly a murderer), Kwansa (a former drug addict and prostitute), Cudjoe (a lost child), Toodles (a killer), Flora (a whorehouse madam), Bimbo (a successful and suicidal libertine), Mr. Tucker (an accused thief) face rejection, estrangement, confinement, death, and injustice as they search for intimacy in the rubble of broken homes and burnt bordellos. Everything around them testifies to their marginality and powerlessness. Although sometimes nurturing, the surrounding community also withdraws into selfish survival mode, terrified of the contaminating disorder carried by the "'crack whores', 'crack babies', [. . .] 'gangbangers', [. . .] 'welfare queens', and [. . .] 'predators'" stalking the streets as described by Alexander (52). Big Mama nurtures and then throws Kwansa to the streets where she turns to drugs and prostitution. For Kwansa, the once nurturing voices of the community become sounds of rebuke. "She doesn't want to hear what the voices have to say. Same ole. Same ole. She's heard it all a thousand times before. She believes it. She ain't shit" (59). These voices also haunt Reuben, who gets arrested for impersonating a lawyer: "Mountebank. Charlatan. Fool. Witch Doctor. They say it again. He hears again. ... Their voices taunting him. All of Philadelphia laughing him out of existence again" (71). Yet, the ruins of Homewood are all that these characters have, and conversely, the prostitutes, shysters, predators, crooks, and prisoners are nearly all the Homewood of *Reuben* has.

The community has devolved into a piece of carrion, picked over by the incipient forces of globalization and the bourgeoning neoliberal order. *Reuben* captures this through a familiar story of the 1980s and the saved story of Mr. Tucker. A limping, overall-wearing handyman, who calls work, "woik" (189), Mr. Tucker seeks out Reuben after authorities finger him in a scheme directed by "Somebody in the business of dismantling abandoned houses and selling the copper, brass, and bricks, everything reusable that could be scavenged from ancient row houses" (190). The text preserves the "family dislocations" described by Wilson and the global ransacking of the African American community through a telling play on words performed by its version of a banal headline taken from an American newspaper: "Strip-and-run Home Wreckers At It Again in the City" (191).

It also stores William Julius Wilson's analysis of the burgeoning Black middle class in his book *The Truly Disadvantaged*. According to Wilson, many middle-class Black Americans had abandoned the inner-city for their new version of the Promised Land. Yet, this choice resonates in *Reuben* as a Faustian bargain. Wally, a college-educated recruiter for a university, finds himself embroiled in a scandal. Bimbo, a wealthy music star that Byerman suggests is "modeled on [. . .] Barry White" (56), engages in a hopeless and decadent lifestyle that ultimately leaves him disabled and begging Wally to help him commit suicide.

Dominant Written Fetishes

Michelle Alexander observes that the new Jim Crow "system functioned relatively automatically and the prevailing system of racial meanings, identities, and ideologies already seemed natural" (58). This system depended on the "coded antiblack rhetoric" of ubiquitous stories disseminated by the mainstream American media (56). This wasn't new. Reuben, Wally, Kwansa, and the people of Homewood had hardly ever found their likeness on the pages of the establishment press. An idealized, more reliable, more objective journalistic past has never existed for enslaved Africans and their descendants. Instead, the newspaper largely managed, produced, cobbled together, and disseminated written copies of the script of oppression destroying the lives of Black Americans. According to media scholar David Domke, in his short, 1997 monograph, *Journalists, Framing, and Discourse about Race Relations*: "Many have theorized that the press' selection and framing of language, news, opinion, and perceptions conveys and abets a social reality that legitimates the practices and ideas of the dominant social class, in this case the white majority" (Domke 3). Indeed, in their 2011 book, *News for All the People: The Epic Story of Race and the American Media* Joseph Torres and Juan Gonzalez lavishly detail the history of the American media (largely the press) in nurturing racism:

> They did so by routinely portraying non-white minorities as threats to white society and by reinforcing racial ignorance, group hatred, and discriminatory government policies. The news media thus assumed primary authorship of a deeply flawed national narrative: the creation myth of heroic European settlers battling an array of backward and violent non-white peoples to forge the world's greatest democratic republic. (87)

In other words, Alexander's "prevailing system of racial meanings, identities, and ideologies already seemed natural" (Alexander 58), because American newspapers had spent more than 200 years making them so.

The ideas they propagated ultimately seemed beyond question because they masqueraded as "common sense" and merely confirmed the widely held assumptions about society and human progress of social Darwinism, which the papers presented as natural facts. Thomas Gossett, in his 1963 book *Race: The History of an Idea* describes social Darwinism as a theory that holds that races "represent different stages of the evolutionary scale with the white race—or sometimes a subdivision of the white race—on top" (144). He concludes that the theory "largely survives in the popular mind. Its central idea is that nonwhite races are oppressed, poverty-stricken, and of an inferior social status for no other reason than their innate lack of capacity" (173). Domke further analyzes how newspaper editors in the 1880s and 1890s took "Social Darwinist language" and integrated it "into common usage, supporting a 'scientific' racism that legitimated the rise of segregation and contributed to violence against African Americans" (2). Through such continuing, "coded antiblack rhetoric" (Alexander 56) they thus justified institutionalized oppression and violence against African Americans that extends in time to the mass incarceration and extrajudicial murders of Black people that have ignited the Black Lives Matter movement of the second decade of the twenty-first century.

Newspapers thus engage in sorcery of their own, crafting fetishes—coding, abstracting, and arresting spirits in their stories—and then directing this harvested power against the "non-white people" who inexorably menace white American identity and the country's heroic creation myth. Indeed, to them, non-white people become the "unknown, threatening spirits" described by Picasso (Malraux, *Head* 11). Although American newspapermen would like to think that they produce an item they famously term, the "first rough draft of history" (Shafer), they instead concoct mythology, or what feminist theorists diegetically call *his*-story—with the word story referring to a self-validating fabrication. Throughout the nineteenth and twentieth centuries, newspapers arrived on the streets and in American homes as aesthetically organized, collage-like bundles of stories that magically modeled time, space, history, and what was and wasn't important. Although Kevin Barnhurst and John Nerone, in their 2001 book, *The Form of the News*, argue that modernist newspaper designers "proposed a new way of viewing that took the entire page as a single canvas" (203–4), this aesthetic approach had always been the case with the refinement of the modeling artistic eye demarcating the only difference. Newspaper editors (like web-page designers) work like collage artist, pasting a date here, a place there, a headline on top, and a column below as they produce their own cubist "exorcism-painting" (Malraux, *Head* 10). Like the editors Barnhurst and Nerone describe, they "carved the social world up into separate domains and assigned affairs differential import within those domains [. . .] this form seemed self-evident: it corresponded to the manifest world with the newspaper's latent function in mapping the world taken for granted" (252). In relationship to American identity, the resulting fetish imposes a visualizable order on the American imagination, producing fictions of white identity and supremacy. They tangibly embody a written form of the agenda described in *Reuben*, which asserts that "the man possesses the only program, making it up as he goes along so he's the only one who knows the score. Creating chaos, fear and trembling" (186). As a response, *Reuben* launches a practice taken up by the ensuing works of confronting this fetish of American racism; stealing, saving and redirecting the Black spirts that newspapers arrest. It breaks the enchantment.

As Michelle Alexander underscores, American readers constantly encounter the coded stories that validate racism. *Reuben* saves the codes and grammar of American journalism through snippets from headlines and newspaper stories. This includes the story of Flora, a Philadelphia madam, killed in a bordello fire. Reuben describes to Wally newspaper accounts of the fire that killed the woman he loved. "It was in the papers. The whole sordid story. How a jealous pimp murdered his lady. The demented arsonists caught in his own trap, going up in smoke with his victim" (89). Reuben's story saves a spirit so powerful that it seems to produce prophecy. Three years after *Reuben* was published, a "disgruntled client" lit fire to an infamous bordello in Natchez, Mississippi burning it to the ground and killing the woman who owned it and the arsonist. Even its madam, a woman named Nellie Jackson, resembles Flora. Nellie was a light-skinned African American woman, whose similarly light-skinned prostitutes serviced an all-white clientele. Two newspaper articles in *The Times Picayune* of New Orleans covered the story. Their headlines read: "Two Badly burned in Former Brothel," (*The Times-Picayune*) and "Death of Madam Ends Era in Natchez" (Rose). Nellie had refused to admit a 20-year-old customer "because he was drunk" (*Picayune*). Angry, he doused the brothel's porch with gasoline and lit it, himself and Nellie on fire.

Reuben even saves the story of Reuben as one of its newspaper *minkisi*. The authorities arrest Reuben for impersonating a lawyer and jail him overnight. He returns home the next day to read his story in the *Pittsburgh Post-Gazette*. He knows what it will say. As part of his morning ritual, he reads the daily, codified stories about Black people every day. Now, he is one of them. He begins to read the story with the headline: "HOMEWOOD MAN ACCUSED AS IMPOSTER" (188). He skims the paper and lands on "two short columns of print about himself. Too much for a tombstone, too little for a page in a book" (189). He then hesitates.

> He wasn't ready for his story to be real again—the cops, the cell, the long night listening to dying animals prowling their cages. When he read his story, it would be real again, happen again. . . . A Reuben chained by words, Reuben locked up forever. (191)

The newspaper voice uses all of the easily recognizable codes. It subjects *Reuben* to the type of treatment that the narrator of *Writing to Save a Life* observes in the court martial file of Louis Till, whom the U.S. military hanged for the crimes of rape and murder. "The Till file works the way any good, old-fashioned novel works. It may sprawl all over the known world, but by the final scene, the plot's resolved, accounts settled, order restored, characters receive their just deserts" (Till 99). He later calls the Till story a running "serial" (Till 180). The newspaper continually runs this serial, with a cast of stock characters in a repeating, racial melodrama. It defines Reuben and the people of Homewood through familiar language such as "impostor" "poor persons," "lawyerlike representations," "phony," and "misguided advice." *Reuben* thus presents a fictional character, reading about a fictional character in a fictional daily newspaper. It's a scene of infinite regress. Nevertheless, the light in the endlessly reflecting mirrors bounces off of some original being they did not create or produce. Both accounts capture aspects of a living spirit, of a perhaps lost and irredeemable soul who nevertheless experiences hurt, was loved, and can be saved.

When Reuben finishes reading the story, he concludes: "It's all there in the newspaper. Unbelievably plain and simple. His life story in three hundred words or less staring back at him. The unvarnished truth" (195). Reuben's reading conjures the arresting power of the final paragraph of Chinua Achebe's novel, *Things Fall Apart*. After reading 191 pages about a Nigerian named Okonkwo, the reader finally confronts the thoughts of a colonial administrator who reflects on the story of a "man who had killed a messenger and hanged himself. . . . One could almost write a whole chapter on him" the administrator thinks. "Perhaps not a whole chapter but a reasonable paragraph at any rate" (191). Reuben equally tackles this rhythm of the dominant narrative. After reading 195 pages of *Reuben*, the reader knows it is not Ruben's story, and it is not true; or that it can only be true if they apply a version of the Igbo proverb that Wideman repeats throughout his later novels and locates in Achebe's work: "All stories are true." Reuben thus uses the spirits arrested by daily journalism to perform a counter spell unveiling newspaper stories and the "deeply flawed national narrative" (Torres and Gonzalez 87) as fictions inexorably used for a threatening purpose; the base materials of a fetish.

A Secular *Nzo a Nkisi*

As a magical bundle, Reuben works as a tool that brings it beyond the mere crossing of ontological and epistemological boundaries for the fun of it and beyond the pessimism of the irredeemable. Wideman crafted the work during a time of immense suffering and emotional agony that found him powerless before the fictions of threatening legal processes. Although Wideman's son, as Byerman notes, rarely makes an overt or fundamentally "literal" appearance in his work, *Reuben* nevertheless works almost plastically to capture or save his spirit while salving the agony of the author. It keeps something alive the way Wideman's work kept alive a brother who was suffering "death by incarceration" (Robert Wideman). Indeed, this product of Black Atlantic craft functions like the efforts of an African American artist named Henry Dorsey that Thompson describes in *Flash of the Spirit*. Thompson offers the elaborate decorations that Dorsey made to his home in Brownsboro, Kentucky as a syncretic example of African American cultural retention of elements from Kongo cosmology. According to Thompson, Dorsey's craft enabled him to go beyond the violence and pain imposed by the racism of the dominant society. "Dorsey taught us to master things rather than to complain about them, to subdue them with artistic weapons of humor and generosity," Thompson observes (151).

> The house of Henry Dorsey remains a secular *nzo a nkisi*, a charm for the denial of hurt, for the redirecting of spirit, to greet provocateurs with laughter and generosity, teaching us how to endure, how to bestow honor, even as the ancient Greeks taught the progeny to honor the gods, parents and strangers. (158)

In a similar way, *Reuben* uses its collection of *minkisi* to redirect spirits captured within the fetishes of a dominant culture that has then deployed them to pillage a community and place its people beyond redemption.

Reuben, like Picasso's *Les Demoiselles d'Avignon*, thus functions as Wideman's first major attempt at a *"toile d'exorcisme"*; a work of or that perform the rite of exorcism (Malraux, *Tête* 19). Yet, Picasso, like African sculptors, worked in the visual arts where a brush stroke of pigment on a canvas, a pinched and formed piece of clay, or even the gathered objects of a bundle or collage, could stand under their own power without reference to an original object or concept. The written word does not have this freedom. It comes inexorably attached as a representation to something spoken. It arrives as a dead, spiritless thing, always representing and seemingly incapable of escaping its original purpose. Yet, *Reuben* asks if words—if a written text—can actually do other work and successfully achieve what other media seem to do so effortlessly. As part of its struggle with its own limitations as representation, the text launches a thirty-year conversation in Wideman's oeuvre with the shaman, priests, necromancers, alchemists, and sorcerers producing "works of exorcism" and charms in other media including jazz musicians, painters, illustrators, sculptors, filmmakers, and photographers, who in the words of a character from the 2008 work, *Two Cities*, blast "holes in the world [and] Free others to free themselves" (117–118).

This conversation begins as Reuben lifts from a library shelf a book of pictures by nineteenth-century photographer Eadweard Muybridge. Although he plies his magic through words, Reuben also disparages their inadequacy. "Words are bred in books and newspapers . . . words didn't matter, didn't care . . . words faltered on their last legs . . . desperate to keep their power, to be seen as well as heard, seen as real by weak creatures like himself" (60). He becomes mesmerized after opening a folio called *Animal Motion* (15), which in the text doubles Muybridge's, 1879 collection of photographic studies in movement, *Attitudes of Animals in Motion*. Reuben sees ancient African wizardry at work declaring, "the album of dead faces and dead bodies no plaything [. . .] This Muybridge joker right at home among the pharaohs" (20–21). Through photographs that used a bank of cameras like a more modern strobe light, Muybridge's work reveals to Reuben that all "motion a series of stills, succeeding one another fast enough to create the illusion of motion" (16). In other words, the album exposes the fact that life itself—"And motion was life, wasn't it" Reuben asks (47)—is an illusion, a narrative, a story, a "suspension of disbelief" (16) and the effect of "black magic tricks" (17). The pictures unmask a "million *heres* and each one separate, discrete, enduring" (126). Reuben thus reflects that the frozen pictures are "accomplishing what the Egyptians attempted when they embalmed dead bodies" (21), even lightly suggesting to himself that film works like the "bandages" that wrapped mummies.

Reuben thus begins ruminations imagined twenty years later for Frantz Fanon in *Fanon*. Fanon labels pioneering French filmmakers Aguste and

Louis Lumière "wizards and necrophiles" (195) who "discovered how to catch, cook, fast-freeze the dead images [. . .] preserving this stuff on strips of celluloid they shined light through" (196). Historically, Muybridge first conceptualized the brothers' work in his freeze-frame photographs and his later invention of the zoopraxiscope, a hand-cranked machine that predated the film projector and reanimated individual, frozen etchings of motion on a moveable glass disk by projecting light through it. Reuben performs a similar feat, creating his own porn video, and bringing to life a deck of Muybridge photographs of a naked woman:

> Extraction was the problem. Releasing the genie from the jar, cutting the strips of photos into separate frames, multiplying them infinitely, stacking them and flipping through them fast enough so they ripple into motion, life. Illusion of course, but one that's slick enough to grab you're your attention, your belief for as long as it takes to fly through the stack. (47)

So, somehow, through the visual medium of photography and as a progenitor of motion pictures, Muybridge had found a way toward the captured life of a spirit. Indeed, at one point, "the ruffle-bearded, breathless white man" thrusts himself into Ruben's trailer for a conversation about the medium and a lesson about its mystical capabilities. He tells Reuben that everything "ever spoken, ever learned, loved, and lost" remains "available for an instant on the end of a pin" (61). It arrives to wash "away the dust of the past" leaving behind "a single bit of [. . .] stuff [. . .] a concentration of vital force, incandescence, a final focused energy [. . .] a final, life sustaining flash of the spirit" (61).

Reuben thus struggles to work in the manner of this cleansing medium, or like the sweeping broom of Clement, the mentally disabled, preternaturally silent, white-haired, 20-something-year-old errand boy and janitor, claimed by nobody, who "swept out the barbershop, the Velvet Slipper, anywhere they let him" (142). This includes the streets of Homewood extending from *Reuben* all the way forward by nearly thirty years to *Writing to Save a Life*. In *Reuben,* Clement sweeps the "pavement on two sides of the Homewood AME Zion church [. . .] What are you trying to do boy? [. . .] Nobody knew [. . .] Clement regular as rain whipping his broom back and forth" (141). In *Writing to Save a Life,* the narrator says the broom-sweeping and "the silence of the name *Clement* [echoes] in the legend of a colored boy/man in Peru who swept day after day a barbershop floor, a monastery's stone paths" (191). Clement thus conjures the "trademark broom" (Writing 190) and spirit of Saint Martin de Porres, a powerful and protective *mystery* or arrested spirit of Santeria, a Black Atlantic religion. His broom performs *barradas* (sweepings), a ritual of spiritual cleansing (Padilioni 102). Similarly, *Reuben*, like the efforts of Muybridge and Picasso, performs such exorcisms.

It struggles to transubstantiate written words into a different medium that would not only battle against "unknown threatening spirits" but sweep away other encumbrances, extracting, and releasing "the genie from the jar" and reanimating or saving life that had been deemed by the dominant culture as beyond redemption.

The work thus struggles to accomplish a similar feat performed by Isis of ancient Egypt; a deed that Ishmael Reed saves in his 1971 work *Mumbo Jumbo* in which a ruler murders, dismembers, and scatters the body parts of Osiris, who threaten his law-and-order regime. Beloved and not forgotten, the magical spirt-embodying body parts of the dismembered man get reclaimed, pieced together (literally re-membered), and then brought to life by his grieving widow, Isis. Wideman imbeds a revision of this story in an essay about slain Civil Rights leader, Malcolm X (Wideman, Malcolm X). It is similar to a story that Reuben tells Wally. Yet in Reuben's story, a parent replaces Isis and Osiris is replaced by a son.

> Reuben once upon a time told the story of a woman whose son was torn into thousands of pieces and the fleshy fragments tossed into the wind and the winds scattered the body to the earth's four corners. . . . After she had mourned . . . she . . . set out gathering the remnants of her lost son. Up and down the land. One by one she searches out every quivering morsel. Molded them together like you'd shape your fingers wet clay from a riverbank . . . one day the son was reassembled and she breathed the smoke of life down his lungs and they danced off together. (107)

Such is the functional destiny of the bundle in the form of a work named *Rueben*: "Behold, a son!"

Chapter 2

Philadelphia Fire and the Art of Bundling the Inchoate

It may have once been possible to layer the novels of John Edgar Wideman onto the *Norton Anthology of African American Literature*'s rubric of contemporary, less-functional art concerned with intimate relationships, family history, and broad, non-confining (non-narrowly Black nationalist) ideas of aesthetic experimentalism. Yet, the work of Wideman's in the 1980s and 1990s brazenly undermines this characterization as the writer uses his voice and art not only to address major, topical controversies such as mass incarceration and the use of police force against African Americans; he also takes a stand on how society of the emergent neoliberal era violently suppressed the counter culture of the 1960s and 1970s and the threats posed to hegemony and official power by the idea of Black liberation. Moreover, Wideman's work had begun to shape the public discourse about such issues as mass incarceration and was cited, for instance by Civil Rights lawyer Michelle Alexander in her 2010 book, *The New Jim Crow* which helped change the way many in the United States came to think about prisons for the next decade. Meanwhile, *Philadelphia Fire* (1990) challenged major lapses in America's memory of the 1980s. It actively saved the memory of a public, extrajudicial mass execution, influencing and framing how academics and writers approached its legacy. For instance, it performs in the background of Robin Wagner-Pacifici, 1994 study of the atrocity, *Discourse and Destruction: The City of Philadelphia versus MOVE,* which analyzes the crisis of language that led to the fatal decision by the mayor of a major American city to bomb a row house in an African American community, kill its eleven inhabitants and lay waste to a city block in 1985. *Philadelphia Fire* captures this moment, which was not long after President Ronald Reagan told the country that it was "morning in American" in his 1984 reelection campaign. The text remembers and pits itself against a somnambulistic society, blindly in the process of erecting the prison industrial complex as it violently struggled to contain the remaining vestiges of the Black liberation and counter cultural movements of the previous decades.

Philadelphia Fire begins with the story of a character named Cudjoe, a somewhat frustrated African American writer living in self-imposed exile on a Greek island much as Wideman had once retreated from the problems of Pittsburgh and Philadelphia to Laramie, Wyoming. In his exile, Cudjoe becomes haunted by accounts of a young child (Simba Muntu) who survives a fiery police raid on his Philadelphia home. The boy had inhabited a house with ten other people living vestiges of a life once projected by the utopian visions that drove the countercultural and Black liberation movements of the 1960s and early 1970s. They reject many of the life-devouring trappings of consumerism and advanced capitalism. Their neighbors, however, complain about the strange, dreadlock-wearing people who: "Didn't want no kind of city, no kind of government" (86). The mayor reacts to the complaints, and the police attempt to evict the group from its home by bombing it. Everyone is killed except a woman and the little boy whose fleeing profile haunts Cudjoe. Cudjoe returns to America,—to Philadelphia—to find the lost child and the lost utopian dreams the child embodies.

Despite its functional, urgent, and topical theme, *Philadelphia Fire* is not a documentary work. Instead, like *Reuben* it is a timeless product of the Black Arts. Yet, as with *Rueben,* its functional, eclectic form evokes for many late-twentieth-century critics the writing of its literary contemporaries and the structures of the postmodern novel. Its first reviewers, such as writer Darryl Pinckney, disparagingly describe it as "a self-conscious combination of European modernism, the black oral tradition, and, most recently, the atmosphere of deconstruction and canon-bashing closing in on black academic judgments." He characterizes it as "[d]isorganized, fractured, inchoate" (Pinckney 19–20). Such critics read the novel as merely representative of a fragmented, postmodern reality—as about something rather than *being* something in and of itself. Yet, like *Reuben*, it is also a functional work of Black Atlantic magic that works against the hostile fetishes of the dominant culture. It captures, "saves," and magically bundles together the voices and stories of an African American community under siege, untying the imaginative knots of malevolent spirits and threatening official processes. It performs as an antidote to the type of categorical or epistemological panic that seems constantly to arise when ordering official power comes into contact with the unofficial, discredited, and unknown forces that liberated Blackness has come to embody in the Western imagination. As a Black Atlantic charm, it confronts and contaminates its readers with this contagion of disorder as it becomes the very "[d]isorganized, fractured, [and] inchoate" thing that critics expect it to merely describe. It thus performs as an instrument of healing, prophetically teaching and enabling readers to accept and come to terms with the unknown, the fragmented, the unstable, the open-ended, and the dislocated—the type of threatening inchoate that the establishment endeavored to bring under control with a police bomb in 1985 and still struggles against in the second decade of the twenty-first century through brazen displays of force against people who dare to script their own lives or imagine a better society.

DOCUMENTS, REPRESENTATION AND THE BLACK ATLANTIC BUNDLE

Like the powerful bundles of Black Atlantic religions such as Vodun and Santeria, *Philadelphia Fire* appears as a miniature of the cosmos reminiscent of the crystal ball that sets the tone of the work from the onset. Cudjoe describes holding the object in his hands and toying with it.

> Cudjoe is remembering the toy from his grandmother's cupboard. A winter scene under glass. Lift it by its black plastic base, turn it upside-down, shake it a little, shake it, don't break it, and set the globe down again watch the street fill up with snow the little horse laugh to see such a sight and the dish run away with the spoon. He wonders what happened to his grandmother's souvenir from Niagara Falls. When did she buy it? Why did he always want to pry it open and find the music and snow wherever they were hiding when the glass ball sat still and silent? (7)

Similarly, *Philadelphia Fire* shakes up the world and turns things upside down, bringing the dead and inanimate to life and redeploying their spirit. It exposes what was disremembered or hidden in plain sight through the clear, glass-like container of language. This is the work of a particular type of Black Atlantic charm: a *minkisi* container. To peer at the contents of such a charm, says Robert Farris Thompson in *Flash of the Spirit*, is like "looking through the clear water at the pebble-strewn bottom of a river" (118).

Like this container, the novel overflows with wildly divergent elements, which led many of its early critics to treat it as an example of late-twentieth-century postmodernist writing. Such writing, says novelist and literary critic, David Lodge, in his 1990 essay, "Mimesis and diegesis in modern fiction," resounds with chaos and the indeterminate and, in some ways, realistically mirrors the unhinged quality of the postmodern world. The postmodern text, says Lodge, actually revives and perpetuates "the mode of classic realism" (24).

> The confusions, distortions and disruptions of the post-modernist text, in contrast [to classic realism], reflect a view of the world as not merely subjectively

constructed (as modernist fiction implied) but as absurd, meaningless, radically resistant to totalizing interpretation. (26)

A polyphony of worldviews and voices in a Romare Bearden-like collage, or motley crazy quilt of incompatible cloths, jagged seams and rough stitching characterize these texts which mock ideology, journalistic reading, and a simplistic search for conventionally rendered historic fact. Many critics of the late twentieth century, who in the words of Aldon Nielson, "are far more likely to assume what was said during the Black Aesthetic period and reargue the issues from there" (17), would view such postmodernist play as diametrically opposed to the over-serious and constraining aesthetic of the Black Arts Movement. Yet, *Philadelphia Fire* as a functional work tied to African and Black Atlantic cosmology, links itself to that aesthetic although its form seems anchored in the conventions of postmodernism.

In fact, the actual form of the Black Atlantic charm, at first, seems to present all of the superficial characteristics of postmodern fiction as it struggles to "save" or capture—not represent—the force that drains from modern life the way sweat drains from the body of Cudjoe's dying grandmother. "Sweat is what gives you life. He figured that out as life drained from her. Her dry bones never rose from her bed. . . . He'd wiped it from her brow, her neck. Dried the shiny rivers in her scalp" (7). As Cudjoe soaks up this life sustaining sweat, the novel soaks up, captures, and saves a spirit than can be described as *àshe*; a force that shakes things up the way Cudjoe shakes up the little globe. According to Thompson in *Flash of the Spirit*, this is "the power to make things happen" (5). As it deploys àshe, such an object may seem to resist "totalizing interpretation" because it unravels all critical, aesthetic, and generic attempts to fix it down. Says Thompson: "A thing or work of art that has *àshe* transcends ordinary questions about its makeup and confinements: it is divine force incarnate" (7). As a container of àshe, *Philadelphia Fire* thus challenges the imaginative field and its ordering of reality rather than comfortably and perhaps playfully settling with representing it.

Works of what Nielson calls the "Black Aesthetic period" embraced "functional art" as an enduring quality of African art. They openly valorized African and Black Atlantic cosmology. As stated in the previous chapter, so does Wideman's *Reuben*. And so does *Philadelphia Fire*. Both texts evince the structuring influence of Haitian Vodun and Kongo cosmology as elaborated by Thomas and work as "secular *nzo a nkisi,* a charm for the denial of hurt" (158). Like the charm, *Philadelphia Fire* also consists of numerous disparate forms of *minkisi,* or powerful, spirit-arresting objects, that lend it an eclectic, incongruous, and fragmented aesthetic quality. Yet, the craftsperson working under the guidance of this system does not chose each *nkisi* for its aesthetic or representational quality. Instead, the practitioner choses it for its power and effect on the world. Rather than represent a certain notion of reality, *minkisi* capture or arrest the essence of a life. "Minkisi containers are various: leaves, shells, packets, sachets, bags, ceramic vessels, wooden images, statuettes, cloth bundles, among other objects," says Thompson (117–8). Bundles of these objects divert the power of the spirits and use it for binding, locating, divining, protecting, and healing. *Philadelphia Fire* crafts its *minkisi* through written stories that save. In English, "to save" means:

> "1. To rescue from harm, danger, or loss. 2. To keep in a safe state: safeguard. 3. To prevent the waste or loss of: conserve. 4. To keep for future use: store." (Webster's 617)

As charms, *Reuben* and *Philadelphia Fire* perform such saving. *Reuben* serves to save rather than redeem the writer, a ravaged community, and an imprisoned brother and son. *Philadelphia Fire* develops and expands upon this work. It pits itself against the capturing magic of discourse and hostile narratives as it performs works of extraction and abstraction of a captured life spirit redeploying it for healing and protection. It both liberates these spirts and saves them in a charm that undermines and transcends not only the limiting discourses of history and journalism but of all closed or dead-end systems of signification.

This might even suggest a somewhat formative influence of the work on what has come to be known in the second decade of the twenty-first century as Afropessimism, which also seems anchored in the anti-essentialism of postmodern and poststructuralist theory. In his book, Afropessimism, Frank Wilderson reflects on and rejects dead-end systems of signification and the "narrative mode" of European epistemology with its parasitic relationship to the "aporia" of the Black person as a "Human subject," which it could never allow it to be.

> I had looked to theory (first as a creative writer, and only much later as a critical theorist) to help me find/create the story of Black liberation—Black political redemption. What I found instead was that redemption, as a narrative mode, was a parasite that fed upon me for its coherence. (16)

Philadelphia Fire similarly embraces if not lays the foundation for such pessimism as it turns away from this "narrative mode" of dogmatically embracing the totalizing structure of language as constituting reality. It thus channels the imagined words of photographer Eadweard Muybridge from *Reuben* who proclaims: "The word's dead. Long live the deed" (61). Like *Reuben,* it also rejects the narrative of redemption for Black people as it dabbles in the type of Black art discredited by forms of Western knowledge and performs acts of saving.

Thus, the difference between *Philadelphia Fire* and the documents describing the tragedy is the difference between action and description. As the best of documents describe the disease, *Philadelphia Fire* functions as an antidote to a sickness of the dominant imagination that responds to the aporias of liberated Blackness—the inchoate—with a sense of terror that then guides the hands of real-world power that inexorably asserts law and order through life-destroying acts of acts of horrific violence.

Minkisi and the Fire of Philadelphia

Philadelphia Fire deploys words, polysemy, disparate voices, literary figures, techniques of intertextuality, and iconic stories culled from the African American experience to reclaim the essence and spirit of life that animates the normally more plastic media of the Black Atlantic fetish. Even its title, through the proper name *Philadelphia,* functions as a divination device that not only enables readings of Wideman's other work but allows for what African American novelist Ishmael Read more mystically calls "readings about the future" (O'Brien 16). Significantly, the "fire" of the novel's title conjures the fire that smolders in *Reuben* and the title character's memory. In a conversation with Wally, Reuben tells of falling in love with a prostitute named Flora. In the act of consummating this love, he recounts, a group of White fraternity brothers crash into Flora's bedroom as one of their number douses the house with gasoline and lights it afire. Meanwhile, the brothers chain Flora to her bed while they bind and beat Reuben. Eventually, Reuben and the brothers escape through the window, leaving Flora to perish in the flames. The proper name "Philadelphia" thus conjures this atrocity story, or the repeating, scripted American rhythm of what Reuben calls: "Fires and whores. White boys up to their usual shit" (90). It immemorially repeats a timeless, iconic story of African American racial memory as it tragically divines the future.

Three years after Wideman wrote *Reuben*, an actual, angry, drunken White boy, "up to" the "usual shit," torched an infamous bordello, burning to death its owner and himself in Natchez, Mississippi. Thus, as Reuben's story conjures Flora, it also saves as a *nkisi* the spirit of an iconic story of the future and of a Natchez bordello's madam, a woman named, Nellie Jackson, who even seems to physically resembled Flora in addition to maintaining an establishment that serviced an all-White clientele. A 2017 documentary, *Mississippi Madam: The Life of Nellie Jackson* and two newspaper articles in *The Times Picayune* of the early 1990s, tell her story. The *Picayune* articles, "Two Badly burned in Former Brothel" (*The Times*

Picayune) and "Death of Madam Ends Era in Natchez" (Rose), document how Nellie was burned to death in the brothel after she refused to admit a drunken, 20-year-old customer. Angry, he doused the brothel's porch with gasoline and lit it, himself and Nellie on fire. These newspaper stories, capture what Ishmael Reed calls a "rhythm" of American society, the basic substance of the Black art of "necromancy." Newspapers provide the "guts of the dead" for the literary necromancer. Indeed, print newspapermen traditionally filed away, and entombed "dead stories" in a place they referred to as "the morgue." In the eyes of the necromancer, these stories throb with a life rhythm that awaits reclamation. Reed describes how this works in a 1971 interview. "Necromancers" he says, "used to lie in the guts of the dead or in tombs to receive visions of the future" (Reed, O'Brien 16). The literary practitioner of necromancy prowls the morgue, reclaiming the life contained in the undead stories of American journalism. The necromancer, says Reed, thus lies "in the guts of old America and makes readings about the future" (Reed, O'brien 16).

Wideman also performs such work. Most notably, a short story, "Newborn Thrown in Trash and Dies," written two years after *Philadelphia Fire,* takes the undead pulse of an actual August 14, 1991, *New York Times* story by George James with the headline: "Newborn is Thrown in trash and Dies." While perishable old news expires with the date emblazoned on the front page, gets discarded, and sometimes serves to line bird cages or wrap fish or is finally laid to rest in the "morgue"; within Wideman's story the life within gets reclaimed, saved, and redeployed through the speech of a voiceless baby now resounding beyond the clutches of conventionalized, and journalistic time and space. It throbs with life. The story acts as a charm that saves a ghastly American rhythm which launched a new decade. "Last year," James reports, "nine newborns were abandoned by mothers in trash bins or similar places, and so far this year, at least seven" (James). The Wideman story captures this American rhythm: "In 1990, nine discarded babies were discovered in New York City's garbage. As of August this year, seven have been found" (123).

One can uncover this return to the "morgue," in other Wideman stories that predate this one. The earlier stories of Homewood and *Reuben* also abound with facsimiles and renderings of newspaper articles that save the spirit of the undead. In *Reuben,* one story tells of the "band of strip-and-run wreckers who have plundered seven city homes since January" (191). The headline for this story reads: "Strip-and-run Home Wreckers At It Again in the City" (191). Even Reuben's own story makes it into the newspapers: "Homewood Man Accused As Imposter" (188), reclaiming the spirit and story of the type of Homewood denizen, inexorably marginalized, denigrated, criminalized, and used against the community by the popular media in the 1980s.

The proper noun, *Philadelphia* thus functions as a divination and decoding tool to make "readings" and record the rhythms of racial injustice, gendered violence, love, hate, brutality, tragedy, and even haunting responsibility. "We all have our Philadelphias," Reuben tells Wally.

> Mine's as much about love as it is about hate. . . . All black men have a Philadelphia. Even if you escape it, you leave something behind. Part of you. A brother trapped there forever. Do you know what I mean, Wally? My Philadelphia's strange because for all the horror, more of it's about love. Have you had yours? (91–93)

Reuben, and the word Philadelphia thus function much like the song described at the end of Toni Morrison's novel *Beloved,* where a group of women get together and sing in an effort to exorcise the unearthly figure that has haunted 124 Bluestone road. The "voices of the women searched for the right combination, the key, the code, the sound that broke the back of words" (Morrison, *Beloved* 261). The word, Philadelphia, similarly functions as a word-breaking "key" and "code." Indeed, in his book *Blackness and Modernism: The Literary Career of John Edgar Wideman*, scholar James Coleman observes that Reuben's Philadelphia story has "a timeless quality and contributes to the myth [. . .] They've slipped from time" (124). The word thus saves life rhythms that reach out to the past and future of Wideman's other work including *The Homewood Trilogy, The Lynchers, Philadelphia Fire, The Cattle Killing, Two Cities, Fanon* and *Writing to Save a Life.*

As an actual place, occupying a central role in Wideman's biography, "Philadelphia" also evokes promise and the aspirations of the burgeoning Black middle class. Through a basketball scholarship to the University of Pennsylvania, an Ivy League school, Philadelphia lifted the future writer away from the Black underclass in Pittsburgh and granted him access to the once-impelling American dream of integration and upward mobility at the beginning of the 1960s; the dawning of the age of Aquarius. He graduated with honors from the University in 1963, the same year as Martin Luther King, Jr. delivered his "I Have a Dream" speech at the March on Washington. He left for England as a Rhodes Scholar, returned to the United States in 1966, and found himself again in Philadelphia, teaching at the University of Pennsylvania in 1967, during the high-water mark of the counter cultural and Black liberation movements. Within *Philadelphia Fire,* the word "Philadelphia" saves this moment, where utopian dreams attempt an escape into the actual world through the insubordinate speech, postures and performance of groups that radically sought to transform a society through the force of their imaginations.

Dreams have a unique rhythmic force and tension in African American speculative thought. There is the dream of the integration of the despised other into American society, and there is the dream that celebrates the radical otherness of Blackness and the possibilities of a fundamental transformation of the American imagination. *Reuben* integrates this tension through a gloss on the prophetic rhythms of one of the most well-known and endlessly quoted passages form a Langston's Hughes: the "Harlem" section of *Lenox Avenue Mural*. "What happens to a dream deferred? /Does it dry up/ like a raisin in the sun? [. . .] Or does it explode?" (Hughes, Harlem 1319). Questions structure this powerful excerpt from the poem. Yet the questions posed by Hughes are not really questions at all; they are divinations, warnings, and prophecies about the risks of deferring a dream. In *Reuben*, the rhythms of these questions structure Wally's musings about Philadelphia, triggering associations with Hughes' poem. Wally's thoughts have the same questioning structure as he improvises around Reuben's conception of Philadelphias: "Or did he mean pain [. . .] Was it like a jail sentence? Hard time. A state of mind" (112–14).

"Philadelphia" thus captures the bitterness of vapid success in a parasitic society organized around and dependent on the oppression of Black people. It preserves the possibility of a middle-class conscience troubled by American caste boundaries and the internal distress resulting from a historic flight to mostly White communities that left behind "a disproportionate concentration of the most disadvantage segments of the black urban population" as describe by sociologist William Julius Wilson in his 1987 book *The Truly Disadvantaged* (58). "Philadelphia" thus pulses with the guilt of this flight, in addition to that of the dreams of the Civil Rights and Black Power struggles and even of those of the Harlem Renaissance, as once also described in the 1920s by Langston Hughes. In his 1926 manifesto declaring literary liberation from the constrictions of racial uplift, "The Negro Artist and the Racial Mountain," Hughes explores the deeply structured tensions of the "dream deferred" describing the aporia of the "desire to pour racial individuality into the mold of American standardization" (Hughes, Negro 1321) and the more rewarding effort to embrace the irreverent, destabilizing, uncontrollable, and inchoate Blackness of the "low-down folks, the so-called common element" (1321).

In the 1960s, the emergence of the Black Arts and Black Power movements forced this deadly rhythmic tension of the artists' imagination into actual life. Groups like the Black Panther Party for Self-Defense relentlessly upset the way America imagined itself and the way it imagined Black Americans. They rejected what Kwame Ture and Richard Hamilton in their book *Black Power* called "cultural terrorism" (35). Their revolutionary agenda aesthetically defied "the mold of American standardization," described by Hughes. The "Panthers stood the commodity fetishism of capitalism's 'society of the spectacle' on its head," says Kimberly Benston, using thoughts from French Marxist theorist Guy Debord in her introduction to the Black Arts and Black Power movement in the *Norton Anthology of African American literature*. They performed "revolutionary effects from an assemblage of signifying objects and poses" (Benston 548).

Such performances played with fire. Indeed, they perhaps had a more devastating effect than the Panthers' actual gun battles with police on the American streets, which were like the "real" hold ups, described by Jean Baudrillard in his essay, "Simulacra and Simulations." From this perspective, such an actual confrontation "only upsets the order of things," whereas the "revolutionary effects"—the simulation—"interferes with the very principle of reality" (180). They thus attacked the whole dominant, post-Enlightenment machinery, which through the sorcery of the word "light" in its very name, ruled over the inexorably looming chaos of darkness or the Blackness the revolutionaries now brazenly embraced. Through its categorizations, rational processes, scientific understanding, technocratic conversions of unknowns into knowns, and "narrative modes," the fetishes of this machinery alchemized the un-expendable, inherently White human subject from the base matter of the expendable other—the Black person—and imposed law and order. The performances exposed the inner workings of this charm, pulling open the curtain hiding the wizard. His captured genie threatened to escape its "real" bottle, which was nothing more than a fragile enchantment, a confinement of language, fictional tropes, and figures; a charm woven by Western "word magic" and fictional stories that masqueraded as fact and history.

In the increasingly conservative America of the 1980s, groups like MOVE, arrived as holdovers from the 1960s and 1970s, and continued to threaten the dominant society's hold over the reins of reality. On the most basic level, as a life-loving group with no clear political ideology, MOVE resisted the vagaries of imaginative classification and categorization that validate the power of civil authority. Indeed, everything went downhill for MOVE the day the group decided to pantomime the postures of armed revolt. In May 1977, group members staged a spectacle in response to endless police harassment. They "dressed in jumpsuits and green berets" and posed with (or with what looked like) rifles, putting on what they called a "'guns on the porch' display" (Puckett and DeSilvis). So, with the very "principle of reality" under attack, the Philadelphia authorities responded with the ages-old rhythm of escalation that violently ended with them containing the threat and setting fire to the performing Black bodies that "posed" it in 1985.

Capture and the Fetish of Narratological Re-Enslavement

The fire ignites in Part Two of *Philadelphia Fire*, as an author figure watches as a "city burns on the screen" of a television set. At first, he decides it "must be happening in another country" (100). Then he realizes that he once lived on the burning block. This triggers a familiar response in readers of 1990, who, on the surface, expect the novel to imaginatively explore an actual historic event (the bombing of a Philadelphia row house by police in 1985), perhaps just as Toni Morrison's 1989 work, *Beloved*, returns to the historical decision of an enslaved woman, Margaret Garner, to murder her child rather than allow her to be taken back into slavery in 1856. As with Garner's story, newspapers had lavishly documented the Philadelphia tragedy, and the readers of the time perhaps hazily remembered the basic facts. On May 13, 1985, at 6221 Osage Avenue in the city of Philadelphia, policeman in a helicopter dropped a bomb (an incendiary device) on bunkered rowhouse, killing eleven members of an organization called MOVE. In *Philadelphia Fire*, a first-person narrator named John Wideman (who was born in 1941) observes a similar event. He had also written a novel called *Reuben* and is "a middle-aged, middlingly successful writer, teacher, father husband and all the rest" (106). He has a wife named Judy and a son who is in prison. So, *Philadelphia Fire* presents a parallel event to the bombing of MOVE. It also occurs at 6221 Osage Avenue in Philadelphia. Yet, beyond that, there is little more information about the specific time of this event. A character named Cudjoe (who arrives through the text's use of the third-person voice) researches the event. Cudjoe has a wife named Catherine and two sons. He is not a successful writer, father, or husband. Cudjoe's life has a timeline within *Philadelphia Fire*, but its chronology does not conform to any registered dates. The reader does not know when he was born, or how his acts tick through the time of the text. The reader does know, that he lived, taught, and experienced the dreams of the 1960s, and even had some of his own.

In *Philadelphia Fire*, "John Wideman" and the annihilation of MOVE correspond to "real" people and events living in a "real" time recognizable by the reader. Meanwhile, the character Cudjoe, a group called the Family, and its members—Margaret Jones, Simmie, and King (aka James Brown)—live in a world that is tenuously connected to actual time. They live in the time that literary scholar, Karla F. Holloway, in an essay on Morrison's *Beloved*, calls that of the "mythic voice of the community" (521). Such an immemorial voice possesses, what Jean Francois Lyotard calls in *The Postmodern Condition* an "ephemeral temporality" (22). It is a part of community property. Everyone possesses it. It speaks itself, and for this reason, it is always spoken. It thus hovers outside of what theorist Walter Benjamin calls the linear "homogenous empty time" of clocks and calendars that structures the Western imagination and gives rise to its notion of progressing history (Benjamin 110). Instead, the lives and stories of people in *Philadelphia Fire* have a timeless flavor which rhythmically links them to other ritualized stories about atrocities committed against the descendants of enslaved Africans in America. The particular details of such stories—names and dates—wither away in importance. Everybody within the community knows the rhythm of these stories. They don't have to be remembered or recited, like the prayers Kwansa utters as she puts her son to sleep: "the words came and said themselves . . she wasn't sure who was speaking the words first, realized that she was following as much as leading" (58). *Philadelphia Fire* imbues the MOVE tragedy, with this "ephemeral temporality" (Lyotard 22). It extracts its spirit from capture and use by the hostile fictions of the dominant narrative (anchored in "homogenous empty time" and the fictional renderings of time, space, and history) of daily journalism and a relentless American narrative—a capturing fetish that in the words of Reuben sows "chaos, fear and trembling" (186).

The American fetish works by first capturing the spirit of resistant Blackness and then deploying it in an aesthetically bundled object that functions to preserves the myth of American exceptionalism or what media analysts Joseph Torres and Juan Gonzalez describe as the "deeply flawed national narrative of heroic European settlers battling an array of backward and violent non-white peoples to forge the world's greatest democratic republic" (87). The endlessly running scripts of television, films and the popular news media perform this work as they activate and inexorably apply a theory of progress and societal evolution through unremitting race war. This theory, according to social historian Thomas Gossett, immemorially asserts that "nonwhite races are oppressed, poverty-stricken, and of an inferior social status for no other reason than their innate lack of capacity" (173). Indeed, asserts Afropessimist Frank Wilderson, such a theory is merely a manifestation of the "narrative mode" of Western thought that inexorably depends on the subjugation of Black people for its "coherence" (15).

As a moving, vague, often performative, and relentlessly inchoate entity, MOVE panicked the fictions producing American identity and validating its hold on power. In short, MOVE emerged as a living embodiment of the "inchoate" or as an actualization of the linguistic meta-aporias elaborated by Afropessimism. "MOVE itself comes to represent the intolerable inchoate" argues Robin Wagner-Pacifici in her 1994 study, *Discourse and Destruction: The City of Philadelphia versus Move*. "All civilizations have a form of terror at the inchoate, the unknowable" (148). Anthropologist James W. Fernandez elaborates this term in his book, *Persuasions and Performances: The Play of Tropes in Culture*. The inchoate, he says, is "all the dark at the bottom of the stairs [. . .] it is all the other images and contexts that are swung into association with that central and organizing image to cast light upon it—and which are part of its polysemy and overdetermined quality" (215). In short, the MOVE tragedy resulted from the authorities' response to this terror of a darkness that defied regulation and categorization in language, argues Pacifici.

> In fact, I believe the whole endeavor to label the group was a dead end and actually a bar to a resolution. But the social minds of human beings press forward the process of identification and categorizing, and when a group like MOVE falls through the categorical cracks, a certain panic arises. (26)

For Philadelphia authorities, the inchoate nature of the group induced an epistemological breakdown, or an implosion of the narrative fictions that model time and space, confer identity, give rise to a sense of community, and enable people to imagine who, what, when, and where they are.

As a response, Philadelphia officials struggled to regain their footing by ceding their agency to the steadfast racialized script of American minstrel shows, Westerns, and the endlessly repeating structures of original blockbuster films such as *Birth of a Nation*. These narratives alchemize actual genocidal murderers and homicidal maniacs into heroic characters who save the race and civilization from the chaos, disruption, and disorder of savage dark forces. When the police stood in front of the MOVE house in 1985, one of them took a blowhorn and uttered an incantation, speaking more as a heroic character—imposing the order of a melodramatic script—than as natural man directed by human agency. "Attention MOVE" he squawked, "this is America. You have to abide by the laws of the United States" (quoted in Wagner-Pacifici 42). Government officials functioned as characters moving through a fixed plot with a beginning, middle, and cathartic end. Wagner-Pacifici, for instance, presents the image of an official who steps out of a meeting planning the siege of the MOVE house who seems struck by a paralyzing fatalism. He describes a room where there "was almost a dread [. . .] so thick you could have cut it with a knife" (quoted in Pacifici 113). Meanwhile, Wagner-Pacifici describes sentimentalist, melodramatic, and television fictions contaminating the minds of law enforcement officials and city bureaucrats. Children die because the image of a clothed child sporting a haircut "like that kid on *The Cosby Show*" (62), playing with plastic toys, watching television, eating a hamburger, and using a flushing toilet is preferable to that of a dreadlocked, unclothed child, eating raw fruits and vegetables, and burying his feces in the yard like a cat. MOVE thus induces an epistemological crisis that inevitably leads to its destruction through an exercise of brutal power.

Yet, before and after the tragedy, dominant, journalistic narratives worked to contain such disruptive force and that of the counterculture of the 1960s and 1970s by imposing coherence through spells of narrative capture that validated the running script of parasitic White supremacy and Black subordination. Indeed, as a response to the type of epistemological crises induced by MOVE, the American media during the last quarter of the twentieth century performed a cultural ritual of containment dating back, at least, to the original Black-faced minstrel show, America's first distinct form of popular entertainment. According to minstrel-show scholar Stanley Lemon, in his article "Black Stereotypes as Reflected in Popular Culture, 1880-1920," these shows emerged when "race relations were extremely bad [. . .] The general public tried to render one of its most fearsome problems into a funny one" (104). Indeed, an 1867 *Atlantic Monthly* magazine story about the first minstrel show performs this containment ritual. According to minstrel show scholar Eric Lott, in his article "Love and Theft: The Racial Unconscious of Blackface Minstrelsy," the story depicts a White man borrowing the tattered clothes of a Black beggar to perform the first Black-faced minstrel show on stage in the 1830s. Toward the end of the performance, the naked Black man steps out onto stage and demands his clothes back, asking for his "nigga's t'ings." Lott summarizes the effect of this article which, he says, captures the "return of the repressed," "miscegenation and homoerotic desire," "the economics of slavery," "racial expropriation," and "the plundering of black culture" (41). Although the Black beggar was not enslaved, Lott argues that the *Atlantic Monthly* article through "successive subordination of Cuff in Rice's minstrel performance and in [the reporter's] use of dialect [. . .] narratologically re-enslaves a black man who evidently turned out to be more competitive and enterprising than he should be" (43).

The American popular media engaged in similar rituals of narratological re-enslavement in response to the 1960s counterculture and the emergence of groups such as the Black Panthers. The Panthers as an inchoate force and by the specter of their violent annihilation by American law enforcement induced "a 'moral panic' [. . .] in the media response to" them (57), says media scholar Michael Staub in his article, "Black Panthers, New Journalism, and the Rewriting of the Sixties" (57). Soon, however, the media adapted to this breakdown by conjuring the original containment spells deployed by the *Atlantic Monthly* article about the first minstrel show.

> as the decade wound to a close, from December 1969 onward [. . .] the panic over the Black Panthers set in, and quite dramatically, escalating steadily through the first half of 1970. And yet this particular panic followed an unusual course, one that would ultimately shift away from demonizing rhetoric to trivializations and that would finally present the Black Panther member more as oversexed media sweetheart than violence-prone social menace. And it was that trivialization that has left the most lasting legacy. (Staub 57)

Indeed, during this period, journalism—often described by American reporters as the "first rough draft of history" (Shafer)—openly turned to the techniques of fiction to restore coherence to the American narrative in a time of epistemological or "moral panic" as described by Staub. Using these techniques and the alchemy of the minstrel show writers crafted fetishes to contain the Black threat, transforming one of its "most fearsome problems into a funny one" (Lemon 104) while also deploying it to validate the narrative of irradicable Black inferiority. One of the most influential journalistic works of the period performs this function: Tom Wolfe's 1970, *New York* magazine article, "Radical Chic: That Party at Lenny's." Within this article, writing itself performs as a Black-faced minstrel show, embracing tropes that depend on stylized Black masks, ventriloquizations, and White men prancing around, rolling their eyes, stuttering, and exuding what Lott characterizes as "functional unruliness" and "supreme disorderly conduct" (Lott 28). Wolfe's work harvests and translates the original, threatening Black spirit of the actual Black men and women participating in a toney fund raiser in the New York apartment of the outspoken liberal orchestra director and composer Leonard Bernstein. Wolfe's literary delineations give the article a comforting aura of verisimilitude that tells readers that Blackness is neither more nor less than a harmless, subordinated mask concocted and donned for their entertainment.

Wolfe's essay and similar pieces of New Journalism effectively squeezed the genie back in the bottle and transformed the media coverage of African Americans and the counterculture. It influentially helped frame and interpret an entire decade before it had ended, argues Staub. "The memory of the sixties (both as historical event and metaphysical reference point) was being fought over almost immediately; history, in short was getting written as it was happening" (54). It had a powerful effect. In her article, "Fanning the Flames of Racial Discord: The National Press and the Black Panther Party." Jane Rhodes describes elements of these media fetishes, which propagated the idea of "black degeneracy" (115) through "grossly stereotyped misrepresentation" (102). Indeed, her presentation of press coverage of the Panthers tracks much of the "coded antiblack rhetoric" that Michel Alexander locates in ensuing coverage of the African American community in the 1980s (56). It's a repeating script. According to Rhodes, the "racial discourse of the 1960s' press was not far removed from that of the turn-of-the-century writers who described black Americans as 'lazy, thriftless, intemperate, insolent, dishonest, and without the most rudimentary elements of morality'" (Rhodes 114–15).

Extracting the *Minkisi* of Black Power

Philadelphia Fire extracts and abstracts the genie. The text works like the imagination of Reuben, cutting, duplicating, and rifling through a stack of

Muybridge photographs, reclaiming the vestiges of an actual, lived life. For him, "Extraction was the problem. Releasing the genie from the jar cutting the strips of photos into separate frames, multiplying them infinitely, stacking them and flipping through them fast enough so they ripple into motion, life" (47). Similarly, *Philadelphia Fire* extracts, abstracts, saves, and redeploys the rippling motion or rhythms of spirits, bundling them together. As such a bundle, the work actually takes on the inchoate form, once recognized and disparage by its early critics. Yet, as such an inchoate work, *Philadelphia Fire* works against the "moral" and "categorical" panic induced by the aporias of liberated Black power.

Philadelphia Fire thus functions as a Black Atlantic charm, a container of *àshe* and a bundle of *minkisi* or "spirit-embodying materials." Indeed, the figures of the work function more like the spirits of Haitian Vodun than like literary characters. They abstract and distill the power of actual, once-living, still-living, and historical people whose spirits had been commandeered in service of the American national myth of race war and justified violence against Black people. Thus, the figures of the text function as the reclaimed spirits or the *lwas* (loas) of Haitian Vodun. According to, Maya Deren in her influential 1953 work, *Divine Horsemen: The Living Gods of Haiti,* these spirits are extracted from once actual, historic beings. "There is no loa who can be remembered by a human being," Deren asserts (32). The text reclaims these living spirts as its bundled *minkisi*. These include those of actual living and dead historical figures, the more general ones of children and their promise, the animating force behind sport and African American expressive culture, and those imprisoned by Western narrative concoctions of identity and human subjectivity.

EXTRACTED HISTORY

Philadelphia Fire relentlessly performs such acts of historical extraction. Simmie at first closely resembles the actual Birdie Africa, who survived the MOVE bombing. In the novel, Simmie is never found. Policeman, however, rescued Birdie (later renamed Michael Moses Ward), and journalistic documents about the tragedy follow-up and track the movement of his actual life. Vincent Leaphart (who also took the name John Africa), the founder of MOVE, dies in the bombing. In *Philadelphia Fire*, however, a figure named James Brown lives on. The spirit of King, the founder of the Family in *Philadelphia Fire*, becomes James Brown, whose name conjures a particular, rebellious and funky, Black American spirit. A graduate of the University of Pennsylvania, Brown also extracts a particular tempo of Wideman's actual life, so he resonates with vestiges of Black middle-class guilt, utopian dreams differed, and the Philadelphias of "Fires and whores. White boys up to their usual shit" (Reuben 90). He even invokes the spirit of the ubiquitous homeless bum of the streets, who lives on delicacies taken from "the best Dumpster for half a mile in any direction. Full of boxes and packets that seal flavor in. Almost like buying your own meal" (176). Through James Brown, sporting the dreadlocks and army fatigues of MOVE members, the abstracted, reclaimed spirit of MOVE emerges from the fire.

> Him and no other turning his J.B. back on the famous flaming city and walking away like *shit*, it ain't nothing to me. . . . Don't mean a thing. Don't' mean a thing. (156)

Indeed, James Brown might even escape the pranks played on him by an unchecked gang of children who light him afire one day as he sleeps on a park bench.

EXTRACTED CHILDREN

Philadelphia Fire also abstracts and saves the spirits of lost, abandoned, neglected, and orphaned children, or ones that die or are removed from life too soon. These children resound with the spirit of the hopeful future immolated in 1985 when the police of a major American city dropped a bomb on a home where children lived. At one point, a first-person narrator named, John Wideman, intrudes on the text and asks:

> Why would we allow anyone, adult or child, to suffer untended, alone, an agony enacted not deep in the forest but in a so called civilized city, in a building with a number, on a street with a name, in a cell with a tiny window we pay people to watch? (116)

Meanwhile, this figure's textual double, Cudjoe, works like Reuben, and perhaps like the actual craftsman of the inchoate text. A sorcerer, he also slips in and out of time weaving together a bundle of stories and words to save or reclaim the life of a friend's daughter, who predeceases her father in a car crash. The friend is a book editor named Sam, who in some ways corresponds to Wideman's original, beloved editor, Hiram Haydn. Haydn worked for Harcourt Bruce Jovanovich, died in 1973, and like Sam, once lived on an island, Cape Cod. When Cudjoe arrives in Philadelphia to investigate the fire, he wakes up in a hotel room and looks through a bathroom window. He searches for a naked woman that he earlier spied in an apartment across the alleyway. Suddenly, he remembers his former wife, Caroline, and the first trip they took to Sam's island home. On that trip, Cudjoe hands Sam the manuscript of a novel (a novel that Sam ultimately rejects). Unable to sleep while Sam may be reading it, Cudjoe walks about the house, looks through a small window, and accidentally catches a glimpse of Sam's daughter, Cassandra, swimming in the ocean before taking a nude shower in the moonlight. Sam's daughter (Haydn had an actual daughter, Miranda, who outlived him) captures the living anguish felt by a parent upon losing a child and the dreams of future vindication children embody. In Cudjoe's ruminations, Cassie, promised a "better Sam, reborn penitent, wiser for having sinned grievously. Capable of unconditional love" (65).

Then, through his "word magic" Cudjoe grants Sam a reprieve. Via his narration of events, Cudjoe imposes an alternative timeline, reversing the chronological order of events that mercifully allow Sam to predecease his daughter, and grant Cassy a womanhood denied by death. He relates events out of order and admits to weaving together the story of Cassy with bric-a-brac and found objects taken from his environment: a panoramic landscape picture, cinematic descriptions, and a hippie caravan he encounters on the road while driving to Sam's house on the island. In the seemingly infinite regress of a fictional work about an actual event with a fictional narrator telling and then reversing the events of a fictional story about a fictional child, *Philadelphia Fire* extracts and saves the truth of a spirit. His telling embodies the Black or African magic of a version of the Igbo proverb that Wideman repeats throughout his later work: "All stories are true."

Philadelphia Fire abstracts the life of another child of the late 1960s, who rests her head on the kitchen table as she reads a box of cereal because no one has made her breakfast. "Cereal is her company this morning" (136). Home alone because her mother is out, the child struggles to remain awake because she stayed up too late watching the "Johnny Carson Show" on television. This *minkisi* saves with her spirit that of her idealistic teacher, a 1960s figure. The teacher, Cudjoe, choses the girl to play Miranda in a funky, quixotic staging of Shakespeare's *The Tempest*, where a man with "heavy, heavy dreadlocks" (120), who resembles Leaphart, King, and James Brown tries to "unteach" his precious students and enable them to "separate the good from the bad from the ugly." In this unrealized yet captured performance, the children come alive, cast off "flimsy bits of homemade costumes, fling masks, superfluous ornaments into the threshing crowd our children's, your children's, my life, your lives are vindicated" (132). Again, all stories are true.

Throughout all of this floats the spirit of abandoned children. Cudjoe, for instance, cinematically captures a tableau vivant of the family he abandoned: his wife and two sons standing in a train platform, wrapped in the steam of an anachronistic locomotive. Someone else's discarded, endlessly swooping gang of dangerous children paint the world with graffiti, join the

Kids Krusade or Kaliban's Kiddie Korps, worship "Money Power Things," costume themselves like Klansmen, obey imagined commands from "Vator, king of the universe" (162), and play in vacant lots, jumping on a mattress that is "the nastiest thing melting down like a dead body with ugly shit inside when the skin rots. . . . Jump on it and bounce till one them rusty springs pop through tear up Lester's leg" (163).

EXTRACTED EXPRESSION

The throbbing of a basketball resounds throughout the text, 10 years before Wideman actually published his book, *Hoop Roots* (2001). Basketball also arrests a spirit. In a 1983 interview, Wideman describes the game as "a means of self-expression" and an "Afro-American cultural inheritance" (Wideman, Samuels 23). Basketball players have magical abilities that capture something timeless. According to Wally in *Reuben,* a good basketball player, "can skate on the thin ice of the air, maneuver on that invisible plane three feet above the floor where the best ones played the game" (Reuben 99). Indeed, basketball, he says, "has an essence." In one of its most lyrical passages, *Philadelphia Fire* saves this essence or spirit of the game through a description of a group of men playing in a park past dusk. "If you keep playing, the failing light is no problem [. . .] You could be blind and play if the game's being played right so you stay out the point people really seeing" (39). Wideman returns to the game in *Two Cities* and in *Fanon*, where the text imagines Frantz Fanon exercising the same skill of being able to play in the dark, an idea that also captures the spirt of his writing. This power renders Fanon into an extracted spirit, or in the words of the text, it make him "uninventable [. . .] He's no more or less a fiction than any person writing about him. Fanon's been here and gone. Played the game till it was too dark to see the ball. You can't touch that" (163–64).

The text also saves another powerful spirit of African American expressivity through its capture of Black orality. At the height of the Black Aesthetic movement, observes Aldon Nielson, in his 1997 book, *Black Chant,* many writers stylized (9), privileged (18), and "idealized" (19) Black speech as a shaky indicator of a text's authenticity. *Philadelphia Fire* captures this spirit as one of its *minkisi*. Indeed, insubordinate Black speech characterized MOVE, particularly in its harangues of the neighbors who called for the group's eviction. Before the bombing, journalists and judges easily used language to frame and devalue a group, which almost singularly defied the incipient new neoliberal era, the increasing militarization of American society, and the burgeoning, thinly disguised war against African Americans (masquerading as the war on drugs). By the 1980s, many saw them the same way people came to see such groups in the twenty-first century, whose anachronistic ideas about legal conspiracies against African Americans, says Michelle Wallace in *The New Jim Crow,* were "initially dismissed as far-fetched, if not downright loony" (7). Out of step with the times, they denounced police harassment as they conveyed their grievances in profanity-laced African American Vernacular English that blasted the return to normalcy of the increasingly conservative era. According to a University of Pennsylvania history of the group, MOVE would "stage non-violent but disruptive protests that featured what they called "strategized profanity" (Puckett and DeSilvis). *Philadelphia Fire* captures their orality through the tape-recorded speech of Margaret Jones, the lone adult survivor of the bombing. For instance, when speaking about King, she says: "He's right even if he did things wrong sometimes, he's still right cause ain't nothing, nowhere any better" (15). An actual survivor of the bombing, Ramona Africa, uses her words in a similar way. At her court trial, she rejects legitimacy and refuses to acquiesce to her capture by the inherently hostile narratives of the American legal system. She argued her own case saying, "See MOVE people been telling people since MOVE that it ain't no justice in these courtrooms" (Anderson 345).

Margaret Jones thus functions as the extracted essence of Roman Africa, and the spirit of MOVE orality. Perhaps she also channels the spirit of Gayl Jones, and her 1975 novel, *Corregidora,* which once helped Wideman in the 1970s to explore the poetics of saving Black speech within a written text. In his 1977 article titled "Defining the Black Voice in Fiction," Wideman asserts that Jones' novel allows "Black speech to do . . . everything any other variety of literary language can do. . . . A black woman's voice creates the only valid terms for *Corregidora*'s world; the authority of her language is not subordinated to other codes" (81). Though Jones is only captured within the first part of the work, her unsubordinated speech seems to validate the "terms" for *Philadelphia Fire's* world for some readers. This is acknowledged by writer Jan Clausen in her feminist reading of the work, "Native Fathers." At one point, Clausen asks of a latter, worrisome section of the work: "What in the world would Margaret Jones have to say?" (53).

The text also saves another aspect of Black orality as it positions the hip voice, of Cudjoe's middle class, African American friend, Timbo, against that of people such as Jones. Indeed, historical accounts present the MOVE conflict as one between the insubordinate members of the group and "their largely middle-class African American neighbors" (Puckett) and people such as Timbo. Timbo serves as an assistant to the African American mayor who makes the decision to bomb the Family. Paradoxically, like Jones, Timbo also imports African American orality into the work. Indeed, he is, in some ways, an inchoate figure who unsettles Cudjoe (newly returned from his Greek island exile), through the constant code-switching of contemporary discourse which displays a brazen lack of taboo subjects, naked plays of power, and an indeterminate attitude toward the conventional racial roles that Cudjoe thought he placed behind him when he left America. "Who's zooming who?" Cudjoe wonders. "A new language. New license. Niggers and dagos. Cityspeak. No secrets, no history, what you see is what you say. Things have changed since he's been away" (76). Through this language Timbo cavalierly sounds out, summarizes, and puts a 1980s spin and end to the once actualized dreams of 1960s.

> We had them on their knees, man. Begging and pulling out their hair. Tried everything to put us down but we were strong. We were righteous. Couldn't nothing stop us. . . . We was superbad. On the tube. In the movies. . . . They snatched back the car keys, the house keys. We got slogans and T-shirts and funny haircuts. And AIDS. Make love not war. Grateful Dead. Woodstock. Black Power. Sheeit. (82–83)

Finally, despite all of the displays of insubordinate code switching, Timbo, "elegant, skinny" and wearing "gray, double breasted, laser stripped suit" (74), drops the pretense of underclass solidarity and unexpectedly underscores his allegiance to the unimaginative forces of racial uplift now tied to reactionary official power. He manifests the "politics of respectability" of Black leaders which validated the law-and-order policies of the late twentieth and early twenty-first centuries, as analyzed by Michelle Alexander in *The New Jim Crow* (263). She observes "that today some black mayors, politicians, and lobbyists—as well as preachers, teachers, barbers, and ordinary folk—endorse 'get tough' tactics" and spend most of their time "chastising the urban poor for their behavior" (266). Timbo captures this attitude. He first chides Cudjoe about his absence from the country, as they eat a lunch of "crab cobbler" and "a sampling of pâtés" (76). Then, Timbo finally confides to his friend the real reason why the mayor had to drop the bomb. "They were embarrassing, man. Embarrassing. Trying to turn back the clock. Didn't want no kind of city, no kind of government. Wanted to live like people live in the woods. Now how's that sound? A Garden of Eden up in West Philly?" (81)

EXTRACTED IDENTITY

Within *Philadelphia Fire,* Wideman even deftly abstracts his own life essence for use in the minkisi container. Although, Clausen says Wideman "appears to identify intensely" with Cudjoe, there is nebulous autobiographical similarity between the author and this character. Then, in Part Two, a new, first-person, author character emerges (like J.B. emerging from the fire) and the novel cavalierly blends the seemingly factual recollections of this Wideman-like character with those of Cudjoe. The text asks: "Why this Cudjoe, then? This airy other floating into the shape of my story. Why am I him when I tell certain parts? Why am I hiding from myself? Is he mirror or black hole?" (122). The term "black hole" mobilizes the inchoate "readings" that attach to the loose, ahistorical rhythms of the writer's unconventional notions of the self. In a 1989 interview with James Coleman, Wideman describes his problems with the narrative capture of conventional, stable notions of identity.

> And my own sense of identity, or the sense of identity which I am evolving as I write books, has a lot to do with [. . .] what is fragmentary, what is discontinuous, more and more so. . . . So that my whole way of looking at human beings and lives is changing all the time. I probably believe that more than most people that the notion of a stable, underpinning personality is itself a fiction. That people have different stages and go through different personas and they are really drastically, drastically different in the sense that you could talk about one person's life as many lives. (Wideman interview, Coleman 159)

Whatever lies outside or beneath, or resonates within the conventional narrative of the self, exposes itself to extraction and redeployment. It is, in the language of one of the narrators of *Fanon,* "uninventable" (Wideman, *Fanon* 164). Within *Philadelphia Fire*, this spirit also lies within conventional representations of the unstable, inchoate Black community that the text extracts, saves and redeploys.

Perhaps avoiding conventional narrative capture is the reason why the historical Jake so rarely appears openly in Wideman's work as noted by Byerman. A later, 1992 story responds to such capture by conventional narrative of an abject tragedy involving a child. This story abstracts the essence of a *New York Times Headline,* "New Born Thrown in Trash Dies" and uses the thoughts of a dead baby to underscore the inherent violence of forcing life into the dead chronotope of journalistic representation: "As grateful as I am to have my story made public you should be able to understand why I feel cheated, why the newspaper account is not enough, why I want my voice to be part of the record [. . .] I believe facts sometimes speak for themselves but never speak for us" (Wideman, "Newborn" 124). The baby, who is thrown down a garbage chute, all but compares the conventional renderings of voice, time and space to the trash compactor toward which it heads: "My time is different from this time. You can't understand my time. Or name it. Or share it" (128).

Meanwhile, *Philadelphia* Fire abstracts the rhythm of an iconic story, and the immemorial anguish of an impotent parent before a child being thrashed by internal and external fictions. In one of the most unsettling passages of the work, the authorial spirit of *Philadelphia Fire* addresses the powerful necessity of learning somehow to embrace the inchoate as he ruminates over his son's mental illness (which resulted in an unspeakable crime) and the lurking dangers of stability, integration, and desire for conventional closure. Indeed, for his son, thriving, holding on, means resisting capture by the hostile fiction of a unified identity—an identity that leads to acts of violence and destruction when whole.

> How does it feel to be inhabited by more than one self? Clearer and clearer, in my son's case, that he is more and less than one. Perhaps his worst times are those when he's aware, in whatever horrifying form that awareness takes, that he must live many lives at once, yet have no life except the chaos produced by divided, warring selves. The utter frustration, loneliness and fear accompanying such an awareness are incomprehensible. If there ever is an I, a me beyond the separate roles he must play, its burden would be to register the damage, the confusion wrought by his condition. To take stock, to make sense, to attempt to control or to write a narrative of self—how hopeless any of these tasks must seem when the self attempting this harrowing business is no more reliable than a shadow, a chimera coming and going with a will or will-lessness of its own, perverse, delusive as the other shadow selves that vie for ascendancy. Is he doomed to fail? Doomed to come apart no matter how hard he struggles at constructing an identity, an ego, a life, an intimacy with who and what he is? Is madness the inevitable result? A part of himself, a self exploding with pent-up rage, another part numb and bewildered, approaching catatonia as it beholds its predicament. Helpless, appalled, avoiding any motion, any act that might aid and abet the furies. Waiting. Playing mindless, repetitive games, locked in but also grateful for the cage of inactivity, the stasis that for a while can pass for peace, control, coherence. Sanctuary. A blessed oblivion consciously sought, an oasis between wrenching, explosive takeovers.

As a response, the text extracts and frees this spirit, incorporating it into the type of powerful bundle that Robert Farris Thompson calls a "secular *nzo a nkisi,* a charm for the denial of hurt" (158).

The *Govi*

All of these elements compromise a Black Atlantic bundle destined to extract and save the promise of the "dream deferred." *Philadelphia Fire* resists the limitations of prefabricated discourses and narratives. Indeed, its historical abstractions and acts of reclamation lead in the direction of another form of prophetic Black Atlantic vessel that extracts spirits from captured history—the Haitian *govi.* According to Deren, this crafted object not only contains the life of a spirit but resounds with a prophetic voice.

> Where there was once a person, there is now a personage. Transposed to this dimension the summoned voice in the *govi* is no longer intimate, advisory; it is an objective oracular authority that booms as if from the bowls of the earth. (Deren 29)

Philadelphia Fire pours the spirits of the dead; of utopian dreams both deferred and blown up with a bomb; of wailing parents; of orphaned, neglected, and languishing children; of complicit forgetfulness; of law, order, indifference and violent containment; of the last quarter of the "American century" into its eclectically crafted *govi*. It extracts the spirit of inexorably timely stories, that should have perished with the expiration date of their printing in the daily news. Yet this functional, Black-American style *govi* speaks with an "oracular authority that booms as if from the bowls of the earth" in the time of the present, capturing the timelessness of an endlessly repeating American script.

Chapter 3

The Cattle Killing and the Art of the Slavery Narrative Conjure

Like *Reuben* and *Philadelphia Fire*, John Edgar Wideman's *The Cattle Killing* (1996) overflows with stories that capture a particular rhythm of American life. Yet, unlike these other works it seems to exit the hardscrabble time and space of the urban street and move into the densely layered time of speculative fiction. It begins as an incarnation of the author steps "out the hotel door and into another skin," and takes off down a Philadelphia or Pittsburgh Street. He morphs into a younger self of the early 1950s, of today, or possibly of the eighteenth century, and of other times. For that moment, he bears the name "Isaiah" or "Eye" for short. "Eye, any kid, your kid, you, me, mine, one or both of the boys blown away at the party last night" (11). Hustling away, he morphs again, moving through space, time and identity, undercutting any attempt to read *The Cattle Killing*, as a familiar, journalistic account of right now as he seems to mobilize all of the powers of speculative fiction to leave behind newspapers, sociology, radical groups, protest, prisons, and the contemporary streets under his moving feet. He pulses with the archaic rhythms of another soul, echoing a strange, florid, self-consciously literary voice that lacks any trace of the Black American orality that Wideman studied and used so abundantly in his earlier fiction. Indeed, according to Jacqueline Berben, one of the earliest scholars of Wideman's work, the writer worked hard to successfully become "relaxed," and "confident" in his ability to authentically render the Black voice in fiction. She writes in 1987 that he had learned to adapt this voice to the "literary genre, rendering [it] altogether understandable, competent, and convincing for [. . .] black and white readers [my translation]" (282). *The Cattle Killing* seems to undercut these efforts. Indeed, most of the work flows from the experiences and florid voice of a young, anonymous preacher who traverses the city of

Philadelphia and its environs during the yellow fever epidemic that ravaged the area at the end of the eighteenth century.

The reveries, memories, and visions of this preacher largely give rise to other stories that make up the text. This voice, layered with other voices, echoes with prophetic warning as if from the Haitian *govi*. An ancestral voice of the immemorial present, unravels and denounces the myths, dreams, fake news, and false prophecies that relentlessly drive individuals, a people, and a whole society toward repeated acts of self-destruction: A young prophetess, moved by a vision, prompts the Xhosa people to participate in their own genocide through the slaughtering of their cattle; African American boys gun each other down as they meld into images of cattle moving blindly through slaughterhouse killing chutes; and a small, abused, orphaned boy satisfies his rage by setting fire to an orphanage of children.

The Cattle Killing stuns the reader with its departure from the conventionalized voices of contemporary urban America and its decision to capture the archaic, yet deliberately tactical and fraught voice of the eighteenth- and nineteenth-century slavery narrative. Other works of the late twentieth century had done similar work, comprising a new genre that African Americanists call neo-slave narratives. From the mid-1960s onward, these texts engaged in acts of historical revision, rewriting and updating the slavery narrative for the moment while mostly distancing its archaic voice and form. And for Wideman, resurrecting the antebellum voice of the ex-slave narrator seems a step backward. The voice of the slavery narrative is fraught with the primordial violence of European capture and its unending crusade against Black bodies and Black thought. Early critics disparaged the narratives as artless; parroting or largely imitative of or actually being produced by writers of the sentimentalist genre of American fiction. In the 1990s, scholars of the neoliberal or long Reagan era rescued (perhaps from the fingers of what they saw as orally obsessed Black Power activists) that voice in critical anthologies. For instance, in the late 1980s, Henry Louis Gates edited and coedited two important slavery narrative anthologies, *The Classic Slave Narratives* and *The Slave's Narrative: Texts and Contexts*. For Gates, the written voice itself reacted to the actual life and death struggle of slaves for recognition as humans. "The slave narrative represents," says Gates "the attempts of blacks to write themselves into being" (Gates, Classic xxiii). Yet, African Americans no longer seemed to need this particular strategy in the incipient "post-racial" America at the turn of the twenty-first century. And Gates mostly had use for the narratives as an aesthetic starting point, divorced from their context and their urgent politics. For him, they establish a tradition for a distinct academic field of studies that his tireless work helped to reconstruct away from the exigencies of Black Cultural Nationalism. So why channel this voice of a creature still trying to prove its worth through the self-consciously literary language and a florid style that bore no traces of the funky Black English that writers had learned to represent by 1996?

THE CATTLE KILLING

The Cattle Killing, like slavery narratives and the turn of the twenty-first century novels of Wideman (*Reuben, Philadelphia Fire*, and *Two Cities*) has an eclectic, motley style consisting of fragmented swatches of different narratives and samples of various texts. It begins as an author leaves a conference of writers to find and read his latest book to an ailing father. As he exits the conference, his dreams and memories of a youth spent in the city (or one like it) engender what follows. The writer reads his new book aloud to his father about a young, anonymous, itinerant preacher, who crisscrosses the Pennsylvania countryside and the city of Philadelphia at the end of the eighteenth century. Meanwhile, this preacher equally speaks aloud, or tells his tale to an unnamed woman (perhaps a river goddess, a once-enslaved woman, or a contemporary lover), who desperately needs the story to cure a fatal illness. The spoken dreams, memories and visions of the preacher engender other stories which then cross all boundaries of place, time, race, and gender. Loosely woven together, no single story dominates. Sometimes, the stories seize the preacher and tell themselves. Altogether, they capture various recurrent patterns of American life, which include the plague that ravaged Philadelphia in 1793. They save the rhythms of a prominent American patriot, his blind wife, and their enslaved servant, a young woman who suffers repeated sexual assaults from her master as she takes dictation for a diary and sentimentalist book the wife wishes to write. The preacher tells of his encounters with an aging artist, who is taken as a slave from Africa, serves as an apprentice to an English anatomical illustrator, gains his freedom, and retreats to the isolated, Pennsylvania wilderness with his White English wife, masquerading as her servant. Driven by hate and terror, the White villagers burn the couple to death in their isolated home. The preacher also has a vision that sweeps over time and space, relocating to 1850s South African where a 16-year-old Xhosa prophetess dooms her people to famine with a false prophecy, commanding them to kill their cattle in order to free the land of European oppressors. Against this backdrop, the tales conjure a love story between the preacher and an anonymous woman whom he seeks out and heals with his words. Throughout, the rhythms of false prophecy resonate through time and space, pulsing through Philadelphia as an immemorial city of the past, present and future. The preacher incants: "I found in that city of brotherly love the country of sickness and dying the African woman's dream foretold. And Philadelphia was a prophecy of other cities to come" (149).

Dystopian tales of mass indifference to the oppressed, the murdered, and the dead structure the work which describes: "Apocalyptic machines hovering in the air . . . with the power to swoop down spattering death" (206) and which are driven by incantations of "prophecies deadlier than the machines" (207). "Black boys shoot each other" (7); the Xhosa destroy themselves" (7); men lose "faith in their gods, their maps, reneging on the promise they'd pledged to themselves to endure, hold on no matter what" (14); and children in "savaged row houses" bleed (14). Yet, *The Cattle Killing* throbs with less anguish and more optimism than *Reuben* or *Philadelphia Fire*. Both *Reuben* and *Philadelphia Fire* foreground the absence of a missing child. *The Cattle Killing*, however, begins as a child seeks out his missing father. Indeed, as the man moves toward his father, his rhythmic double searches for, reunifies with, and cares for an ailing woman with whom he imagines a more hopeful future. While the novel captures the agony of a sad, murderous child, other children escape the diseased thinking of the plague and enjoy a life filled with possibilities. For instance, the novel contains a dedication to Wideman's actual child, Jamila, who barely survived a premature birth, but who also lives out her father's dreams of becoming a professional basketball player. It ends with an Epilogue that begins with the name of another of Wideman's actual sons, Dan, who is a writer. Father and son exchange letters, reading each other's work.

These eclectic, bundled tales comprise the *minkisi* of a functional Black Atlantic bundle calculated to capture, save, resurrect, and mobilize the spirits of the living and the dead. They deploy the spirit of the slavery narratives, which activated the empathy of their readers and transformed imaginations once deadened by a society structured by non-caring for *les misérables* or the most wretched of the earth. While these narratives may have established the cornerstone of a movement that resulted in the abolition of slavery, *The Cattle Killing* rekindles their urgency as a response to the new form of slavery and violence against Black people that had taken hold at the turn of the twenty-first century in the form of mass incarceration and extrajudicial murders by police. This analysis will, therefore, explore the form of the slavery narrative as consisting of magical and functional texts that are deeply structured by the cultural retention of African cosmology found in practices such as quilting, and which exhibit the same eclectic structure as *The Cattle Killing*. It will then present this channeling of the slavery narrative as the appropriately urgent response to the recurrent rhythms of American society which had once again imposed the logic of slavery on Black Americans of the late twentieth century; the incipient age of mass incarceration. It will then explore *The Cattle Killing* as a quilted narrative, or a Black Atlantic *minkisi* container, that uses for its swatches of cloth the stories of Liam, the African; the spirit of "Philadelphia"; the Xhosa Cattle Killing; and Kate, the enslaved amanuensis.

It will explore how these stories work to save spirits that give the work the power of the Haitian *govi*, a vessel of prophecy.

The Slavery Narrative

The slavery narratives were functional art. They first emerged as polemical, tactical, and powerful weapons against slavery—both as an institution and as a looming threat to their fugitive writers who often feared capture and re-enslavement. Critics thus relentlessly anchored them within their timely moment of production, treating them as nineteenth-century agitprop. According to early critics, says Gates, the narratives functioned because they went "right to the heart of their readers" (Gates, *Classic* xii) strategically conveying "all the original Romance of Americans" (xxi). They did this through openly emulating the popular codes of the nineteenth- century "sentimental novel" with its "florid asides, strident polemics" and "melodramatic imagination," Gates observes (xv). Meanwhile, the often fugitive writers fought against and undermined looming legal processes that could lead to their recapture. They crafted works that would both assure their safety and generate a desperately needed income. Furthermore, as patchworks of misdirection, the narratives resisted efforts at generic categorization, exploiting the tension between the categories of historic document, autobiography, and novel. The writers crafted these works for a tactical purpose, not to conform to the rigors of genre. They, therefore, dexterously manipulated an "authenticating machinery" that assured a popular readership in nineteenth-century America, says Robert Burns Stepto in his 1979 essay "I Rose and Found My Voice: Narration, Authentication, and Authorial Control in Four Slave Narratives" (229). Many of the narratives blur the distinction between fiction and nonfiction in an effort to divert their masters from their path (228). Often, these works undermine the role of authorship subordinating the writer's voice and control over the narrative to that of others, imbedding into the work letters and documents authored by White publishers (228), abolitionists (228), law makers (236), politicians (236), and even themselves (239–40). The writers often appear powerless or seem to cede control as they vacillate between the roles of editor and author, at once accepting and denying power over the texts and their contents. Because of this, says Stepto, many of the texts appear to lack the "integration" of truly "aesthetic" works (241). Stepto uses the label "eclectic narrative" (227) for the most loosely structured form of slavery narrative. In this form, "authenticating documents" are appended to—rather than integrated into—the tale. Historically, the patchwork craft, tactical purpose, misdirections, and play with historically authenticating documents worked against serious critical consideration of the slavery narrative for much of the twentieth century.

These narratives also presented a hidden danger. For the enslaved, and particularly for enslaved women, harnessing the abstracting and primordial power of what the African captive, Olaudah Equiano in his early 1789 narrative calls "talking books" (an idea Gates treats as an emergent trope of the slavery narrative and African American literature) works as a dangerous two-edged sword. It takes as it gives, submerging, controlling, and invalidating other types of knowledge not beholden to Western writing; other ways of knowing and acting upon the world. Still, the patchwork form of the eclectic narrative resists such capture as it also seems indebted to what Toni Morrison calls "discredited knowledge" and the ordering aesthetic of another eclectic and powerful Black Atlantic practice: quilting. The Black American quilt (though it also has an evident European lineage) manifests qualities of powerful and functional Black Atlantic art. Like the *minkisi* bundle, it also pieces together various material objects of spiritual power, binding, protecting, disorienting, and creating possibilities. Yet, early critics of Black American quilts evoked the original critical reception of the "eclectic" slavery narrative by denigrating the shabby objects made from "fabric remnants, scraps of cloth, pieces of old clothes" says folklorist Michael Prokopow in his 2009 article "Material Truths: The Quilts of Gee's Bend at the Whitney Museum of Art" (62) "Notable for their unusual colors and the obvious ways in which they did not follow a known or familiar pattern, they were considered as imitative, generally poorly made, and certainly not tangible examples of cultural retention and aesthetic innovation" (62). Nevertheless, says Robert Farris Thompson in *Flash of the Spirit*, such craft deploys a "resistance to the closure of the Western technocratic way" (222).

In the 1980s, scholars began to observe that African American quilts indeed manifested and modeled alternative aesthetic possibilities that went beyond representation and possessed the functional power to protect and to save that indeed models the aesthetic structure of *The Cattle Killing*. In fact, in her 1986 article, "African Symbolism in Afro-American Quilts," Maude Southwell Wahlman, a student of Thompson, argues that the eclectic form of quilts bore a transformative relationship to writing and underscored an aesthetic approach to words that gave them a use as things that went beyond their acting as mere representations. In her discussion of quilting, Wahlman references the Black folkloric practice of using artifacts of print culture in the form of discarded newspapers to confuse and divert unwanted visitors the same way some Black Americans scattered grain at entrance ways for protection. "Newsprint placed on the walls of Southern homes, and into shoes as well, protected against the elements or evil enslaving spirits, who, it was believed, 'would have to stop and read the words of each chopped up column' before they could do any harm" (72). Wahlman then argues that quilts "have the same function as newspapered walls" (72).

In her 1984 book, *In Search of Our Mothers' Gardens*, novelist Alice Walker explores how a novel can work in the same way as quilting. In the title essay, she recovers the concrete, generative power of a Black Atlantic craft that men had relentlessly disparaged as "women's work" as a model for her aesthetic approach to her 1982 novel, *The Color Purple*. In the essay, she presents herself in a museum standing before a famous quilt crafted by an "anonymous," enslaved African American woman. The quilt, she observes, "though it is made of bits and pieces of worthless rags [. . .] is obviously the work of a person of powerful imagination and deep spiritual feeling" (239). Walker then struggles to infuse her own work with the power of such craft, linking writing itself to the concrete act of quilting. She quilts, she says, as she writes *The Color Purple*, an epistolary work that stitches together letters from two sisters. Such craft underscores the nature of the Black arts and a powerful practice conjured by the *Cattle Killing*. This work also embraces the eclectic structure of the slavery narrative and the crazy quilt as it deploys the powerful force of *àshe*, which, when captured, Thompson says, enables a work to transcend "ordinary questions about its makeup and confinements" (7).

The New Slavery

Yet, capturing the urgent force of *àshe* or crafting the archaic and functional equivalent of a patchwork slavery narrative at the turn of the twenty-first century seems patently unnecessary if the work isn't designed to engage in acts of remembering or historical revision. By the end of the twentieth century, politicians, public policy, and the larger American public in their dismissal and unraveling of affirmative action held that it was time for African Americans to place slavery behind them. It was long over. Yet, the late 1990s cried out for functional narratives that would respond to a particular rhythm of American society in which a form of American slavery had become the new normal. Indeed, asserts Cornell West, quoting the words of a Civil Rights activist in his Forward to Michele Alexander's *The New Jim Crow*. Slavery "didn't end; it evolved" (West, Forward xxxviii).

In the 1980s, the administration of President Ronald Reagan launched its war on crime. Then, in the 1990s, the self-styled "progressive" President Bill Clinton accelerated this war, which had a devastating impact on Black life in American. According to Michelle Alexander in *The New Jim Crow*, "Clinton escalated the drug war beyond what conservatives had imagined possible a decade earlier" (71). He lorded over the growth of "a penal system unprecedented in world history" (53). Alexander then cites the statistics: "More than 2 million people found themselves behind bars at the turn of the twenty-first century, and millions more were relegated to the margins of mainstream society, banished to a political and social space not unlike Jim Crow" (73), which itself was just a mere evolution of slavery.

Yet, Clinton merely performed as a recurrent figure, acting as a character within an old, American script. Such acts of re-enslavement form a particular, American "pattern, dating back to slavery" says Wallace (20). "Since the nation's founding, African Americans repeatedly have been controlled through institutions such as slavery and Jim Crow, which appear to die but then are reborn in new form, tailored to the needs and constraints of the time" (27). Meanwhile, youth-driven, popular entertainment toxically structured the American imagination the same way the nineteenth-century minstrel show rendered the dehumanization of African Americans both necessary and normal if not pleasurable and amusing. Wallace excoriates the entertainment of "an era in which black people are criminalized and portrayed as out-of-control, shameless, violent, oversexed, and generally undeserving" (216). Even combating the conspicuous evils of slavery seems more straight-forward than fighting against the re-enslavement of the neoliberal era, she argues.

> In many respects, the reality of mass incarceration is easier to avoid knowing than the injustices and sufferings associated with slavery or Jim Crow. Those confined to prisons are out of sight and out of mind; once released, they are typically confined to ghettos. Most Americans only come to "know" about the people cycling in and out of prisons through fictional police dramas, music videos, gangsta rap, and "true" accounts of ghetto experience on the evening news. These racialized narratives tend to confirm and reinforce the prevailing public consensus that we need not care about "those people"; they deserve what they get. (227)

In other words, the conditions of slavery still loomed over American society in 1996 and called out for a tactical slavery narrative which could perform the old work of healing the imagination, working against the pattern of re-enslavement, and producing a sense of caring where there is none. *The Cattle Killing* performs this work.

The Quilted Narrative

Wideman's *The Cattle Killing* has many of the characteristics of a quilted, eclectic slavery narrative. Nothing reveals this more than the reactions to this novel by its early reviewers. For example, Sven Birkerts almost laments this aspect of the work in his 1996 review for the *New York Times Book Review*.

> Plot is not the point. Stories, memories and visions bleed together in the narrator's stricken soul [. . .] Filaments of story, of precious sense, are woven like

bits of rag into a rug of colorful, but also perplexing and complex suggestiveness. (20)

In other words, *The Cattle Killing*, thorough what Birkerts calls its "textual strata," emulates the quilt-like form of the eclectic, antebellum slavery narrative. In many ways it has the same effect as that described by Stepto in his discussion of William Wells Brown's narrative, *The American Fugitive in Europe* (1855), which rejects the lofty and conventional structures of genre and literary form for more tactical goals.

> Brown's personal narrative is hardly an aesthetic work, but that is because Brown had other goals in mind. [. . .] He is willing to abandon the goals of true authorship and to assume instead the duties of an editor in order to gain some measure of control over the present, as opposed to illuminating the past. Brown's narrative is present and future oriented. (241)

So is *The Cattle Killing*. It's cavalier skirting of ontological and temporal boundaries enables the work to roughly stitch its "filaments of story" through and around readers—their here and now—while enveloping them in a mist of there and then. It functions as a magical slavery narrative, a product of craft in the Black Atlantic tradition.

Other early critics responded to the tactical function of a work destined to perform its magic on the American imagination at the turn of the twenty-first century. Gene Seymour, for instance, underscores this aspect of the work in a 1996 review for *The Nation,* titled: "Dream Surgeon."

> Through style and content, Wideman has made it his calling—really his burden—to chart deficiencies in imagination, both collective and individual. Because Wideman is an engaged, highly visible, black writer in twentieth-century America, readers assume that racism, not imagination sickness drives his work. But what is racism, after all, but a breakdown of the imagination?
>
> But, as is the case with fellow modernist dream masters like Faulkner, Toni Morrison, Ornette Coleman, and any Abstract Expressionist you can name, Wideman demands that his readers work with him in making connections, drawing conclusions, following the map of his characters souls. . . . *The Cattle Killing* is the latest and, quite possibly, the greatest testament to his heroic struggle against imagination sickness. (Seymour)

The Cattle Killing engages this "heroic struggle" through a text that fights against its own medium as a printed document consisting of written representations of the spoken word. As it layers voice upon voice in acts of speaking or telling, it struggles to transform writing into more concrete, plastic work, much as original African praise singers—the *griot*s of Sahelian Africa—forged voice and sound with the same knowledge blacksmiths used to pound metal, carve masks, and fabricate charms. *The Cattle Killing* foregrounds the effort of the writer who works like the once-enslaved author/editor, or the quilting African American woman "[o]rdering the universe" (Walker 241) and using ancient and discredited knowledge to produce tools that would not just represent, but render a service. Indeed, it augments and deploys the magic of the quilted narrative. Each colorful patch extracts the essence of a spirt, the spark of lived life, or the tenor of an ancestral voice booming with magical substance in a bundled fabric of *minkisi;* a prophetic, Haitian *govi* of voices; or even the unsettling song of a griot, which one scholar says, tells a history of the past with tactical, concretized words that *"may as quickly malign as praise"* (Jablow 522).

LIAM

Through its speculative turn, fantastic movement through time and space, conjuring of an archaic eighteenth-century voice, and capture of the antebellum slavery narrative, *The Cattle Killing* represents a departure, or perhaps an intensification of the form and type of Black Atlantic craft deployed in *Reuben* and *Philadelphia Fire*. Indeed, it engages in a primordial struggle with words as concrete tools and continues the preoccupations with more concrete media (sculpture, music, film) that animates *Reuben* and ensuing works. These works place the writer in the company of other artist working through different forms to protect, safeguard, capture, and save in a fight against threatening processes and evil spirits. Again, this gives the work its crafted, eclectic, patchwork quality, resembling the "newspapered walls" of Southern homes that press the representations of print into the service of a charm against what Seymour calls "imagination sickness" (Seymour).

As the itinerant preacher of *The Cattle Killing* enchants his listeners, casting his "spells," he conjures the power of the slavery narrative, relinquishing control over his "authorship" and ceding it to one of its captured spirits. At one point, Liam, an eighteenth-century African takes over and then recounts his own slavery narrative. He arrives in the work after he rescues the anonymous preacher from freezing to death in a snowstorm. Liam then channels the voice of the slavery narrative as an artist—a painter—struggling to transform the confining representations of art into pliable, tactical tools. Through Liam, *The Cattle Killing* meets the extracted essence of Wideman, an artist at the turn of the twenty-first century using his craft to battle against the absence of memory, "forgetfulness," "silence," and "utter lack of concern" (13) producing the "devastated landscape" of contemporary American life (7).

The ability to craft work that can move beyond representation and actually restore or save depends on discredited Black Atlantic knowledge. *The Cattle Killing* indirectly links such knowledge of converting representative words into things by conjuring the eclectic quilting of the slavery narratives, including *The Interesting Narrative of the Life of Olaudah Equiano or Gustavus Vassa, the African. Written by Himself*. Gates calls this 1789 work "the prototype of the nineteenth-century slave narrative" (Gates, Classic xiv). Like Equiano, Liam is born in Africa; he too is an "Ebo" (Igbo). Liam's wife speaks of his originally telling tales, tactically wooing her with sound. His story is, in many ways, Equiano's. "The gift of his words painted worlds for me," she recounts. "He'd voyaged round the globe, fought in great naval battles, escaped the chains and torture of a dungeon, lived among savages in faraway lands" (102). Yet, for many years, Liam had remained silent and blocked, unable to free "the colors inside me," particularly after his arrival in America where madness subdued the imagination. "I call the whites' attitude toward us madness" (113), he tells the preacher. "We were brought here to serve and die. Serve or die" (127). Yet, with the arrival of the preacher, Liam begins to paint with words again. These words connect him to his past as a direct heir to a magical legacy. Liam tells the preacher: "had I not been stolen from Africa, I would have become a holy man, a healer of soul and body in my homeland. My father was a renowned wizard" (104). Liam casts spells over the anonymous preacher and *The Cattle Killing* that function like the reordering magic of the rain that the older man once observed moving downward on a window before a panoramic of trees; uprooting the world behind it:

> Trees floating, the solid earth left behind. . . . Reversed the natural order. Downward was upward. . . . A different world hidden in this one. A world that couldn't be, yet there it was in all its simple glory, being what it couldn't . . . I look out now at these trees and remember they have the power to fly. (133)

The preacher also has knowledge of this black art and describes it as he hears enslaved Africans telling conflicting stories about the plague ravaging Philadelphia. "I believed each story," he says. "My way of reckoning learned from the old African people, who said all stories are true" (53). Liam is also one of those "old African people." Yet, he needs the arrival of the preacher to reconnect with the powers of an African craft that treats words as substance. He tells the preacher, "I couldn't begin to talk, son, till I learned you were willing to listen" (181).

Liam tells the preacher that he first informally apprenticed as painter in the guise of a servant to George Stubbs, an anatomical illustrator whose work bears the traces of necromancy. An actual, historical figure, Stubbs risked his health and reputation by dissecting dead animals and eventually dead humans, which linked him to the infamous eighteenth-century "resurrectionists," or physicians who unearthed dead bodies for dissection. Liam calls them "a ruthless depraved crew" (115). Yet, Liam admires Stubbs' capacity to copy "nature directly" (114), "his decision to seize life, do with it as he saw fit" (125), and his obsession with a craft dependent on dissected dead bodies and fed by "an empire built corpse by corpse" (128). Yet, everything changes for Liam when he witnesses Stubbs' enthusiasm at an auction for the dead body of a pregnant African woman. "His imagination teeming already, daydreaming possibilities the African woman and child present for his art" (135). Liam's horror resonates to a basic problem of representation and of writing realist African American literature. It touches on Wideman's previous work, such as *The Homewood Trilogy,* which, through techniques and conventions of verisimilitude, took the dissected ruins of African American life to produce art. Intersubjectively, Liam projects a response to such works: "Wonderful drawings. . . . Nature revealed. . . . To what end? . . . Could they restore what's been torn apart?" (129). He then ponders: "What art could I invent to expose the lie of the madness? How many layers peel from a white body to free the black, how many from a black body to free the white" (127). In the wake of these questions, Liam remains blocked as an artist until the preacher arrives and Liam begins "to talk again. Talk, talk, talking [. . .] Master again of talk," his wife says (101). This talk reconnects him to the powerful, discredited magic of African storytellers, or *griots*—the blacksmiths of the word.

In Sahelian Africa, griots often belong to the same caste of artists—*nyamakala*—as blacksmiths, who forge farming tools and weapons as they carve masks and fetishes. Griots perform this same work as they forge words from a primordial substance—*nyama*—the way smiths pound metal taken from the earth. Indeed, the notion of functional art embraced by Black Arts movement writers comes from their understanding of griots and functional African art through the writing of such major Sahelian thinkers as statesman and poet Leopold Senghor. *Griots* possess the awesome power to produce functional words that are not just representations but actual tools or things in and of themselves. According to Christopher Wise, a scholar of African literature and philosophy, "the *nyamakala* include griots [*djelu*], blacksmiths [*numu*], tanners [*garanke*], hunters [*donzo*], basket-weavers [*fina*] as well as Islamic praise-singers [*funé*]" (21). In "Nyama and Heka: African Concepts of the Word," Wise cites research that asserts that the "griot is someone who 'know[s] how to handle *nyama*, as one would handle a tool'" (27). *Nyama* deploys the primordial force of sound, says Wise. To underscore this, he cites a translation from an interview with an African philosopher who says: "there are certain sounds that exist, pure sounds that have been passed down through the centuries. [. . .] If such a person utters these sounds, he can gain access to the archive wherein the totality of human history resides" (quoted in Wise

33). *Nyama*, says Wise, is thus "'power' or 'means'" (26). In channeling the voice of Equiano—whose first master was an African goldsmith—and telling his story to the unnamed preacher, Liam taps into *nyama* or the force that makes tools of words and governs the crafters of fetishes and charms.

Still, the "mad" villagers seek out Liam and his wife, burning them to death in their home. Although *The Cattle Killing* apparently presents this horrific scene chronologically, it moves against the rain, later saving Liam, bringing him back to life as a master of *nyama*, quilting liberating force into a nude painting of his wife that defies conventional representation as it acts on and changes life. Seemingly out of order, the text last shows Liam alive many pagers after his death. The preacher describes sneaking up on a barn and overhearing lovemaking and "conjuring" sounds coming from the building which also serves as a blacksmith's shed. He unexpectedly spies Liam, alive again, painting a nude portrait of his wife.

> If there is a woman on Liam's canvas, she is beset by a storm of paint. A forest of paint. Flapping pennants of paint. Triangles and rectangles. Colors he'd never seen before, mashed, streaked, spattered, running like yolk from broken eggs. Feathers of paint. Ladders. Ropes. Dark fists inside the paint pounding to get out. Somewhere in the holler of it, the woman's figure surely was forming, surely as patches of familiar melody formed the quilt of Liam's tune.
>
> When he looks at her again, beyond the canvas, through it, she's changed. Transformed as air and water and fire had turned her into different women, many women crowding the room that first morning when he had watched her bathe in the split cask beside the fireplace.
>
> Not the woman stretched on this burning straw, not the woman twisting free of rainbowed serpents of paint. Not what Liam imagined or he imagined or she imagined, but what could come next. After this time. Next and next. Always unknown. Always free. (181–82)

This portrait melds with *The Cattle Killing* and its eclectic, non-integrated, fragmented, non-linear structure—commenting on itself. It rejects the false prophecies of conventional, chronologically organized, plot-driven narrative techniques as it strives to capture and save a devastated world. Invoking the non-developing time of the quilt, its swatches of cloth capture and liberate the "flash of the spirit" of the dead, the disremembered, the devastated, and those toward whom contemporary society has shown an "utter lack of concern" (13).

PHILADELPHIA

The name "Philadelphia" works as another rough stitch linking the pulsing, eclectic colors of *The Cattle Killing*. A borrowed stitch, it draws from the previous two novels. In *Reuben*, the word Philadelphia conveys the rhythms of: "Fires and whores. White boys up to their usual shit" (90). In *Philadelphia Fire*, the word captures a moment when utopian dreams structured the imagination and attempted a transformation of society. It then becomes the apocalyptic incineration of the American dream and dreams of a better self and future as represented by children. *The Cattle Killing* rhythmically takes up this word as the pattern of slavery and American oppression that Michelle Wallace says, "appear to die but then are reborn in new form." Philadelphia booms with "a prophecy of other cities to come," telling tales of false prophesies, racial hatred, mutual suspicion, madness, and despair. Yet, as the nameless preachers observes about the word, Philadelphia: "Love is buried in its name [. . .] The city would not have survived without it" (49). So, this swatch of cloth also has colors of redemption, healing and discovery. The nameless preacher tells the sick woman: "So I went to Philadelphia to fight the plague, to purge myself of hate, to find you" (149).

The Cattle Killing explores the recurrent patterns resonating in the word Philadelphia: the historical yellow fever epidemic that decimated the city in 1793; the suppression of the Black liberation movement; the terror of drugs and crime; the excuses that led to mass incarceration; and the devastating effect of always fake news when it comes to chronicling the lives of enslaved Africans and their descendants. The preacher deftly explores the textures of the pattern in his description of the plague.

> I learned in rapid, whispered exchanges with coach drivers and footmen the plight of the city's Africans.
>
> We are being blamed in the newspapers. They say we are immune to fever and require no assistance. They say black slaves, refugees from the troubles in Haiti, brought the fever to these shores. Mark my word, it is the contagion of freedom they fear. The lie of our immunity, the blame foisted upon us, are preposterous cowardly excuses for beating us, denying us employment, avoiding our stalls and goods, revoking our hard-won rights.
>
> All of us, black and white, equally marooned by poverty, but the stark necessities of our lives. No spare time for the frivolity of race hate. Then the fear, anger, arrogance and cold distance of city-dwellers fleeing the plague soured our simple truce.
>
> If rumors held any truth, we had been declared guilty, sentenced to die for the crime of plague. Though we too were its victims. (34–35)

He describes Philadelphia of the 1790s, but like Liam's painting, the colors of the city are "mashed, streaked, spattered" and run "like yolk from broken eggs." Philadelphia is South Africa, contemporary Pittsburgh, the 1960s, 1970s, 1980s, 1990s, the 1850s, and the "prophecy of other cities to come."

THE XHOSA CATTLE KILLING

Like a quilted fabric, *The Cattle Killing* refuses to linearly separate space and time: the now from the then or the here from the there. It often rejects the historic past tense, presenting fragments of thought that hover in present impressions. The writer walks up a hill that can be in Pittsburgh, or Philadelphia, or any American city and ponders over the wanton murder of African American people. The unnamed preacher lies in a field and has a vision of a 16-year-old girl in 1850s South African, who becomes a prophetess and leads the Xhosa people to slaughter their cattle resulting in a famine that kills more than 40,000 people. They occupy the same rhythmic patch.

The story of Nongqawuse and the Xhosa cattle killing saves the deadly rhythms of the consumerist culture of the 1980s and 1990s and its capture by children. Nongqawuse lives in the time of encroaching European domination and the elders of her ethnic group and their traditions seem weak, impotent and incapable of battling intensifying oppression. "Our chiefs could not lead, our warriors could not fight, our women deserted their children, our young men began to worship alien gods" (145). In response, Nongqawuse goes against the elders and proclaims a prophecy directing the Xhosa to slaughter their cattle, the most important source of their livelihood, for protection. The child instructs that to save themselves the people must "kill their cattle." The elders scoff. "The people are the cattle, the elders said. To kill our cattle, they said, would be to kill ourselves. What devil has taught this child a terrible lie" (147). Yet, the people eventually submit to the prophecy, kill their cattle, and begin dying en masse of starvation. "Too many dead to bury [. . .] The Xhosa homeless, destitute, sick, begging food from settlers, skulking in the shadows, ghosts roaming the bush at the edges of European towns, a proud people become like the worthless dogs they always had been in the whites' eyes" (7).

The Cattle Killing stitches this texture of the 1850s prophecy next to the 1980s and 1990s and the rise of gangsta rap and thug culture, even perhaps prophetically linking it to the death of the young, immensely popular, twenty-five-year-old rapper Tupac Shakur, whose murder coincided with the 1996 publishing of work. As noted earlier, Michelle Alexander views "gangsta rap" as one of the "racialized narratives [that] tend to confirm and reinforce the prevailing public consensus that we need not care about 'those people'; they deserve what they get" (227). Such attitudes, she argues helped lead to the mass incarceration epidemic—a new plague—returning many African American men to the state of near slavery. With its prophetic warnings about children exposed "to the madness," *The Cattle Killing* rails against glorifying tales of self-destruction. It laments Liam and his "African brethren ripped with him from the land of their fathers to preach false prophecies" (148). As the writer climbs the Hill, he imagines a violent battle between the children who attend parties on the Hill. In these fights, the knives and fists of his youth transform into the guns of the turn of the twenty-first century. A child gets killed—shot. The word "shoot" conjures the word "chute," cattle chutes, the Xhosa Cattle, and false prophecies. "Black boys shoot each other. Murder themselves. Shoot. Chute. Panicked cattle funneled down the killing chute" (7). *The Cattle Killing* abstracts, captures, and saves the spirits of that contemporaneous carnage, working against the violence of an "utter lack of concern" for Black life of a "distant and abiding and memoryless" society (13). As the writer walks "he unleashes himself from this time, this moment beginning the climb to his father. What is the name of the space they occupy now. All of them. The black boy always fifteen, the two boys freshly dying, the long gone African, his father" (131). *The Cattle Killing* abstracts the story Nongqawuse and of children like Tupac Shakur as warning prophetic voices, exploring the raw contents of a crazy quilt, or a *govi*-like container.

KATE

Finally, *The Cattle Killing* returns to the slavery narrative, the transformation of the conventions of genre, writing and authorship into tactical tools that halt enemies and safeguard freedom, and the spirit of women such as Harriet Jacobs. Jacobs self-published her slavery narrative, *Incidents in the Life of a Slave Girl*, under a pseudonym in 1861. According editors of the *Norton Anthology of African American Literature,* Jacobs' narrative now "occupies a crucial place in the history of both African American and American women's literature" (222). Indeed, her work openly and daringly surpasses the descriptions of the exploitation of women under slavery of other narratives written by men. Furthermore, her work overflows with descriptions of what Black Americans call motherwit, or the knowledge guiding womanly, Black Atlantic craft. In one of the most gripping episodes in all of American literature, Jacobs describes escaping from her master who had relentlessly used his power (eventually threatening to sell her children) in attempts to sexually dominate her. She hides from him in a tiny attic crawl space of her grandmother's house. In what she calls her "attic retreat," Jacobs, an accomplished seamstress, describes sewing, reading, and writing. Similar to Walker who writes and quilts; Jacobs reads, writes, and sews. Jacobs then melds the three together in an extraordinary display of Black Atlantic craft. She takes half a sheet of newsprint that a friend says "was round a cap I bought off a peddler" (Jacobs 582); picks apart the cabalistic seams of a newspaper that she says "systematically abuses the colored people" (582); and expertly quilts the garnered "snippets" into a new patchwork that, she then says, "was made to render them a service" (582). She had read the paper for its representation of New York locales. She takes this information and re-bundles the newspapers original aesthetic work, impressing it into letters that that she asks a friend to take to the North and then post to her master. Like an expertly crafted charm, the letters entrance her master, mislead him, and compel him to think that Jacobs is hundreds of miles away while she lies hiding in an attic for seven years, sometimes just above his head.

Jacobs' craft of misdirection worked so well that her narrative received scant critical attention after its original publication and many twentieth-century critics found little use for the few existing copies of the work. In fact, it remained out of print until 1987 when a scholar hounded the ephemeral tracks of the historical Jacobs, wading through the swamp of misdirections, scattered grains and "chopped up" print of her patchwork craft and authenticated the narrative. Before then, the works deliberate, enemy-confusing misdirections, and a pseudonym (Linda Brent) led scholars to question the narrative's written authenticity. It openly seemed to be a case of the type of "amanuensis" problem where critics suspected it was a novel written by a White abolitionist woman similar to Harriet Beecher Stowe, who accelerated the Abolitionist Movement, with a novel, *Uncle Tom's Cabin* (1852), and a key that openly cribbed from the oral and written testimonies of enslaved Africans. The *Cattle Killing* captures and reverses this notion through the story of Kate, who takes down the story of her blind mistress.

Kate's story has much in common with Jacobs' narrative. As noted earlier, Jacobs' narrative kept enemies off her tracks for more than a hundred years because critics thought abolitionists had written it. Meanwhile, unlike most of the other slavery narratives, it possesses an expressly gendered component as she addresses her narrative to northern White women, struggles against the overwhelming power and sexual advances of her master, and tackles the "fake news" and myths surrounding the practices of the vaunted, "patriarchal institution" of slavery.

It is nearly impossible for contemporary readers of Jacobs' narrative to believe that the man who had absolute, life-or-death power over Jacobs did not take what literally belonged to him and sexually assault her. "You are my slave," he tells her, "and shall always be my slave" (Jacobs 507) Yet, in many ways, Jacobs narrative reveals that her master was as enslaved as she was by the laws and narratives of propriety and property and by the way they produced identity, power, and status within their antebellum community. Jacobs master was fixated—fixed—by his identity and public image. She calls him "conscientious," "scrupulous," "politic," and obsessively protective of how others saw him. "Bad as are the laws and customs in a slaveholding community, the doctor, as a professional man, deemed it prudent to keep up some outward show of decency" (472). He thus dreaded rebuke and being "exposed . . . in the eyes of his children and grandchildren" (478) and religiously avoided the appearance of "violating" what historian Edward Crapol calls the "three antebellum societal taboos—illicit sex with a slave, miscegenation, and selling his bastard offspring" (Crapol 65). Yet, at one point in the narrative, in a twisted declaration of love, the master tells her: "You have been the plague of my life" (483). Jacobs thus plagues her master, manipulating him while sending him into fits of rage and shame. Eventually, she runs away, sends him off her track through her quilted letters, and finally crafts her own narrative, exploiting the "authenticating machinery" (Stepto 229) of the eclectic slave narrative, which masks her identity and pantomimes the undermining of authorial control as she seems to all but turn over her story to the controlling idea of a White woman amanuensis.

The Cattle Killing conjures the rhythms of this gendered narrative of impotence and power through Kate; her master, Dr. Thrush; and his wife, the blind woman. Mrs. Thrush wants to write a novel or confessional diary, but her blindness hinders her. She, therefore, turns to her enslaved assistant, Kate, for help. She proclaims, "I depend on you, dear Kate, in this writing business as in so much else—your arm to guide—your ear to listen—your eyes to see—depend on you to write my words and then read them back to me" (162). Thus, the voice of Mrs. Thrush, the blind woman, is captured by Kate, who transcribes her mistress' words onto paper. This voice tells the valiant story of Dr. Thrush and his efforts to cure those affected by the plague and advocate for the Africans who, despite their efforts to redeem themselves, had been made into scapegoats by the White people of Philadelphia. It also tells the story of Mrs. Thrush, who teaches at an orphanage erected for children whose parents had died of the plague. The voice does not, however, explicitly tell the story of its writer, Kate, who has been repeatedly raped by Dr. Thrush and bears his child. Still, Mrs. Thrush eventually finds out about Kate's pregnancy, but keeps it a secret from the history she writes—from *her*-story.

> We share a secret now—a secret neither of us has said the words of—we are not ready to say them, though we both know we must—words shaming us, so unsaid—words locking us into an unholy silent pact—we say only what we need to say to preserve the silence—words stillborn—no words for the roundness of belly she grasped my hand and forced me to feel—no name for the touchable shape, nor name for the untouchable shape inside it—no name we can say now—wounded doubly by silence—the pain of it stretched between us—the pain of not having attempted to break the silence—until now—until the pen is unmoving on the page and there is only waiting, no words for telling more. (198)

The whole story—of the publicly respectable, privately lascivious husband; of the noble, betrayed, blind, and somewhat sensitive wife; of the invisible, wronged, and ultimately triumphant servant; and of the unborn, unnamed, and unknown child blend and form another distinct capturing color of the quilt. Again, this open secret of vicious racial exploitation, not violating social taboos, and protecting the relentless assaults of racism saves a particular American pattern that had also reemerged in the bourgeoning post-racial, neoliberal climate at the turn of the twentieth century. In her 1990 book, *Playing in the Dark,* Toni Morrison blames similar "moeurs" for suppressing consideration of the structuring role of slavery and racial oppression in White American literature. According to Morrison "ignoring races is understood to be a graceful, even generous, liberal gesture" (9–10). It is the same type of "unholy silent pact" that has led to mass incarceration, rendering the imprisoned, in the words of Alexander "out of sight and out of mind" (227).

This swatch also captures the implicit, enemy distracting tension of the slavery narrative and its play with authorship through the relationship between Kate and Mrs. Thrush. *The Cattle Killing* inverts the expected relationship of the abolitionist amanuensis who uses formal writing to capture the oral speech of an enslaved or once-enslaved source. This presents a particular racial rhythm involving written representation. In his academic writing, Wideman has compared the Depression era, transcribed and written interviews of the formerly enslaved by White government functionaries to a type of ritualistic dance. In "Charles Chesnutt and the WPA Narratives," he observes:

> The whites, who have the advantage of establishing the outward forms of the dance, design the ritual to display their superiority, their dominance; the dance is a metaphor of their power. For the blacks who, like the whites, must perform for two audiences at once, the objective is to find room for maneuver within the rigid forms dictated by the whites, maneuver which allows space for private communication with the other black participants. (Wideman, Chesnutt 65)

The Cattle Killing conjures this struggle as the enslaved servant transcribes, struggles against power, and ultimately frames as "fake news" the delusions of the blind White woman's story.

The voice of Mrs. Thrush speaks in the florid, written style of a sentimental novel. Yet, the passages lack the conventional markers of quoted speech. Dashes instead of periods and commas separate sentences. The fragmentary, free nature of the dictated diary structurally evoke "representations" of speech, though the reader also knows that the passages are supposed to be transmissions of Kate's actual writing. Meanwhile, the blind woman recounts her-story, her version of official American history through Kate. She presents her husband, Dr. Thrush (modeled after Benjamin Rush, a signer of the Declaration of Independence) as the archetypal, scrappy American Yankee. A devoted husband, he befriends the Negro, champions the underdog, and fights against adversity. He helps found the African Methodist Episcopal Church and enlists the aid of Negro nurses in fighting the plague. Like the historical Benjamin Rush, he advocates what became known as "heroic" intervening medicine through a controversial (indeed deadly) cure for the plague—"mercury purges and extensive bleeding" (175). The actual Benjamin Rush thought the human body held much more blood than it did, and he thus weakened the body's natural defenses against yellow fever, weakening, and often killing his patients.

Meanwhile, throughout the text's transcription, an italicized voice interrupts the written diary, framing the lies of the official record, this time another her-story, with unofficial, maneuvering utterances. It works much like the "Afro-American oral performance" that tactically slips through and re-frames narrative capture that Wideman describes in his analysis of the WPA testimonies. Ultimately, he observes, the "dialect comes full circle" and is "turned against the oppressor" (64). In *The Cattle Killing* such a voice intervenes throughout the blind woman's diary. For example, the third paragraph of the first entry begins

> I love Kate—*she owns*—I take her free hand in mine—tell her not to stop writing with the other—dear Kate, you must learn to speak my heart—a task fitting and proper because you, Kate, truly reside inside my breast—a second tender tremor there. (162)

Like the rain observed by Liam, the italicized words *"she owns,"* reverse the intended flow of the passage. Suddenly every word written has double meanings which compel readers to acknowledge the rhythms of two separate version of truth. When Mrs. Thrush utters: "I taker her free hand," "tell her not to stop," and "you must learn," such pleadings are not directed at a free White man. To the contrary, they are directed at an enslaved Black woman. In this context, Mrs. Thrush's over-emotionalized language is a flagrant exercise of power. The blind woman forces the slave to write her story.

Still, the enslaved woman tells her own story through these invocations of speech, which frame the narrative, disclose secrets, and capture the colors of Jacobs' narrative, American history, and oral testimony. Jacobs' master, the historical Dr. James Norcom, religiously avoided the appearance of transgressing the "three antebellum societal taboos" (Crapol 65), while endlessly pursuing, sexually harassing, and wielding his power over her. Thomas Jefferson slept with and had children by Sally Hemmings while extolling the virtues of liberty. And the enslaved Kate of *The Cattle Killing* tells the open secrets of American history, demystifying its mythologies. Kate's unrecorded, parenthesized voice, therefore, violates the "moeurs," taboos, and secrets of "an unholy silent pact" that structured a Democratic republic founded on slavery, and continued to re-enslave Black people in 1996, sounding rhythms which, as Michelle Alexander observes "die but then are reborn in new form, tailored to the needs and constraints of the time." It thus pulls down the Confederate Monuments of American narrative and prophetically lays the foundation for the nearly seventy monuments physically removed from the American landscape twenty years later, following the 2017 murder of a protestor at a rally defending such memorials and the 2020 murder of George Floyd at the hands of a Minneapolis policeman.

PROPHECY

Within *The Cattle Killing*, the spirt of enslaved women get extracted from history and saved as a "she" who haunts the text. Throughout the work, the unnamed preacher searches for an indeterminate "she" who "appears" (37) in its first pages. Like the preacher, she either has no name or many names. The narrator hears and believes many different stories about her. At first, like Kate, "she" is "a female servant, a slave," a "young African woman" (50), a "Cassandra-like" woman who "threatens her masters with prophecy," and a "*bozal*, fresh from the West Indies" (51). "She" is a woman on her sickbed, whothat must be cured by the preacher's stories—and who also melds with the writer figure's ailing father to whom he reads his work. Then, she is a woman on the road, who carries a dead baby and disappears, naked, into a lake. At one point, this woman of the lake reappears, then transforms into the dying woman in the bed. Meanwhile, a woman's voice often intrudes on the preacher's consciousness. She morphs from the African river woman into an aging, equally nameless, English woman—the wife of Liam. The preacher finds himself, lying on his back "in the Africa of Liam's stories" (143), dreaming before an "Old woman, girl, black, white. Bald, fiery-haired. The dream of the African girl who'd told the people they must kill their cattle" (144). Toward the conclusion, a nameless woman, who has the same history as Kate, enters the narrative. She also needs the preacher's stories to "save" her (203). She, too, cradled a dead baby by a lake. The text reads: "The language coming apart in my hands. The way the blue gown shredded when you knelt in the sand beside the lake and pulled the tired cloth over the child's golden crown of curls" (206). Then, in this passage, the pronoun "she" becomes a genderless "you." The narrator continues to address this same "you" at the close of the narrative when he brings up names, places, and other references which evoke the 1996 present, Ramona Africa, Nelson Mandela, Alfred Hitchcock, Cape Town, Pittsburgh, and Philadelphia. Capturing these spirits, *The Cattle Killing* resounds with the prophecy of the Haitian *govi*, predicting, and issuing dire warnings about the racialized "madness" infecting the America mind during the yellow fever epidemic of 1793 and continuing unabated in the COVID-19 epidemic at the dawn of the second decade of the twenty-first century.

Chapter 4

Two Cities and the Art of Breaking Writing's "Spell"

In her 1953 book, *The Divine Horsemen: The Living Gods of Haiti*, artist Maya Deren describes the crossroads of Voudoun cosmology and the powerful entities that safeguard its boundaries.

> Legba, then is the guardian of the sacred gateway. Of the Grand Chemin, the great road leading from the mortal to the divine world . . . he was once the newborn infant sun . . . and is now the old sun, walking with a cane—the "third leg"—in the afternoon of life . . . an old tattered man, shuffling down the road, with his crude twisted cane or crutch. . . . Already he is linked to Carrefour, whose other hand holds firmly that of Ghede, Lord of the Underworld, God of the Dead. . . . For it is Carrefour who may loose upon the world the daemons of ill chance, misfortune and deliberate, unjust destruction. . . . If Legba commands the divinities of the day, Carrefour commands the daemons of the night. (Deren 98–101)

Two Cities (1998) is a bridge novel; a mystical work of the crossroads. It seems to begin in Philadelphia on the "Spring Garden Street Bridge at taint time" (3)—a vague, gray time which is neither day nor night—as a shuffling old man, walking with a cane—"a taint man sure enough" (7)—communes with the spirit of the dead. Hobbling along, like Papa Legba of Haitian cosmology, he traverses the bridge with "John Africa his partner" (2), yet laments: "Poor John Africa dead. They say the cops never found his head . . . body parts mixed up in the ashes to say it was a dead man. Say it was John Africa" (7). John Africa, a figure from *Philadelphia Fire,* and the chosen name of Vincent Leaphart (the actual leader of MOVE, who died in the 1985 bombing), thus infiltrates *Two Cities* from the other, pervious works as a denizen of the dead; a talking, dismembered head, "whose features refuse to detach themselves and become his face again" (4). He emerges in *Two Cities* like "Ghede, Lord of the Underworld, God of the Dead," as he lets "loose upon the world the daemons of ill chance, misfortune and deliberate, unjust destruction,"—a cycle of the blues, captured by African American music. On the bridge, he proclaims, "We getting ready for the struggle. Ready for whatever it takes" (10). He intends to stage a "Confrontation" (218) with law and order. His group is arming itself, building a bunker on top of a row house, and reminding the city and the police of the plot-driven, narrative "duty" (218) that inexorably leads to the "Homes bombed. Women and children roasted alive," (7) that once released its spirit to the earlier work.

Before this bridge takes shape, *Two Cities* begins with another level of communing with the dead as the reader first confronts the "spell" of the lifeless, atomized, and fixed words of a dictionary as the essential elements that comprise the text. Base material for an art that struggles against its very form, they manifest an aspect of an artist's continuing effort to transform his medium from an act of representation and delve into the Black Atlantic space of the crossroads that ties the written word to the concrete matter of functional art. So, the work begins with the words, "He read the definition again," as an ambiguous someone reads the definition of the word "zoo" from a dictionary (1). Thus, an unanchored pronoun lacking an antecedent sets off a chain of densely packed associations, of connotations and denotations, of historical fact and fictional rumination, and of indeterminate relationships between space and time. The words commune with the dead as the text takes a vague shape. They conjure the relentless gaze of dead Swiss sculptor, Alberto Giacometti, who once analyzed the nose of a face until, he said, the "form dissolved [and] it was little more than granules moving over a deep black void, the distance between one wing of the nose and the other is like the Sahara, without end, nothing to fix one's gaze upon, everything escapes" (Giacometti 18). The "He" of the text wages a similar struggle with the granular words of the dictionary—"Words to make sense of no sense" (8). Then, in *Two Cities*, the fixed and elusive words of the dictionary begin to give form to "taint time"; the limping old man, Martin Mallory; his ghostly friend, John Africa; and the bridge itself.

> Everything connects; nothing connects [. . .] Once upon a time he stood on the Spring Garden Street Bridge with John Africa. Today he's in another city, alone in a room on Cassina Way. Then and now. *Two Cities* . . . Now. No words for what separates and connects these moments. He couldn't understand, could only witness (7).

In its first chapter, "Missing John Africa," *Two Cities* thus continues the project of *Reuben, Philadelphia Fire, and The Cattle Killing* of sculpting words like matter and fashioning a functional Black Atlantic charm for healing and protection.

These figures on the bridge—a disembodied head and a shuffling spirit—wield the power of the crossroads. Given form by words from the dictionary (conjuring the spirit of Malcolm X, who similarly recalls "spelling" out and reading through the words of a dictionary in his transformative autobiography), they bridge the text to the spirit of the Black liberation movement, once again pitting it against the intensifying emergent destruction of Black life in the America of the twenty-first century. *Two Cities* therefore continues the project of Black Arts writers to make their work matter and of transforming writing into a usable, physical force. It resounds with the performative incantation of Amiri Baraka in his 1965 poem, "Black Art," which avows: "We want live words of the hip world live flesh &/coursing blood" (Baraka 219). It performs as a work of linkages; a bridge work. Like much of Wideman's work, it ties together the fictional and the autobiographical, taking up more visual and perhaps European preoccupations with art and aesthetics. Along with the writer, it negotiates connections and the vast abyss between writer and character; between middle and old age; between different marriages, families, and lovers; between Europe and America (and America and Africa); between Pittsburgh and Philadelphia; between other works of art, other works in the writer's oeuvre, and other media; between the sacred and the profane; between the spirituals and the blues; between witness and activism; between then and now; between being and nothingness.

Through the emergent and developing eye of Mallory, an itinerant photographer who is influenced by the speech of his African American elders and their art forms as well as by the gaze, sculptures and thoughts of Giacometti, *Two Cities* explores the bridges and linkages between words and the other media of photography, sculpture, painting, and music. The text thus enters into a conversation with those crafting powerful objects to protect, safeguard, capture, and save life in a relentless struggle against the inexorable "duty" of oppressive processes. It functions as a work of Black Atlantic craft that ultimately mobilizes what Robert Farris Thompson calls in his book *Flash of the Spirit*, "the lessons of the crossroads" (19). According to Thompson, "one must cultivate the art of recognizing significant communications, know what is truth and what is falsehood, or else the lessons of the crossroads—the point where doors open or close, where persons have to make decisions that may forever after affect their lives—will be lost" (Thompson 19). The text mobilizes these lessons through the two spirits on the bridge who wield the force of Eshu-Elegbara a compound figure of Black Atlantic cosmology, whose figure is often crafted of stone and clay. According to Thompson:

> Eshu-Elegbara eludes the course nets of characterization. Even his names compound his mystery. Some call him Eshu, "the childless wanderer, alone, moving only as a spirit." Others call him Elegbara (or Elegba), "owner of the power".... He is, of course, all of these beings and more—the ultimate master of potentiality.... Cubans blacks associate Eshu with change: "favorable he modifies the worst of fates; hostile he darkens the most brilliant happenings." (Thompson 19)

Like the limping Mallory coupled with his companion John Africa, Eshu-Elegbara deploys the force of the spirituals and the blues, the sacred and the profane, possibility and destruction. Such a spirit has the power to freeze enemies in "their tracks" (Thompson 131) or unleash the "potentiality" or the "duty" of "wanton destruction" arrested and then deployed by the hostile fictions of the dominant culture. In the words of Mallory, this power can also blast "holes in the world" and free "others to free themselves" (117–118), bringing them beyond the precipice of despair. As a character who sings the blues without vocalizing a note, Mallory, a photographer who plies a literally undeveloped art, mixes up facts, times, and places, pursues a one-sided correspondence, and dares to ask a haunting question: is "art a lost cause"? (119). Can writing break the spell?

Two Cities thus takes up the work of the author figure that links his efforts to transcend literary representation to the magical work of European and Black artists in other media such as photography, sculpture, and music. The work presents a photographer, Martin Mallory, who similarly tries to transform his camera into a powerful saving tool of the Black arts as he links "fixing his camera" and taking pictures to the sculptures of the Swiss surrealist Alberto Giacometti, the collages of African American artist Romare Bearden, and the music of jazz pianist Thelonious Monk. Like *Reuben, Philadelphia Fire, The Cattle Killing,* and Wideman's other turn-of-the century works, *Two Cities* functions as a Black Atlantic bundle consisting of spirit embodying material carefully culled from the Black community and quilted into place. The text itself mirrors the aesthetic and magical intentions of Mallory, a World War II veteran and confidant of John Africa who haunts the streets of Philadelphia and Pittsburgh as he tries to save his dying community through film and the lens of a camera.

Eight sections or chapters ("Missing John Africa," "Dancing at Edgar's," "Lamentations," "Playing Ball," "Mr. Mallory," "Philadelphia," "Pittsburgh," and "Zugunruhe: A Postscript") comprise *Two Cities*. As it overflows with the energy of the crossroads, *Two Cities* is a text that subverts itself as a novel, conjuring instead the aesthetic form of what jazz musicians call a "fake book" (a collection of jazz "heads" or the standard melodies jazz musicians use for improvisation). On one level, it seems to center itself around a plot—a love story between a man and a woman—that it destabilizes through the flagrant layering onto the text of equally important secondary stories that threaten to overwhelm the narrative. These include ones that capture the disruptive tales of Mr. Mallory and John Africa; a repetition of borrowed, Homewood and Philadelphia stories as "jazz heads"; another work upsetting the text through its epistolary form; and a final bundling of the work into a Black Atlantic charm destined to give hope, save life, heal, and subdue the wanton destruction of a place where the blues of the crossroads "rule," as it actively modifies "the worst of fates" (Thompson 19) and in the words of Mr. Mallory, frees "people to be themselves."

A PLOT: ROBERT JONES AND KASSIMA

If the work is a novel that has a plot, and if that plot has main characters, *Two Cities* offers a love story between a mostly anonymous young woman in mourning, and a man whose life, persona, and physical description extracts those of John Edgar Wideman. As a character, Robert Jones, bears much of the background history of the fleshed-out works of what critics refer to as *The Homewood Trilogy*. Jones grew up in the Homewood community of Pittsburgh at 7215 Cassina Way, a street that immemorially threads its way through Wideman's life and much of his writing. Many of the recurrent common places established by the earlier works lend both form and substance in the reader's memory to the scant sketch of Jones in *Two Cities*. Readers of Wideman's fiction recognize Jones' life. Jones says he has a sister and brothers. He doesn't give the number and he doesn't name them. He does indirectly name his grandmother (Elizabeth Alfreda Jones) in a story told (remembered for him) by another character. This story furthers his likeness to Wideman and his Homewood characters, conjuring the "Begat Chart" and "Family Tree," of his Homewood Works and allowing some readers to fill out the form. They imaginatively lend Robert three brothers, a sister, and a grandmother who bears the same scar on her finger as Freeda Holinger, who tells the same story about that scar to her daughter (Lizabeth), which becomes part of the family memory enlivening the other works. Robert also has Homewood memories of his grandfather carrying him on his shoulders throughout the streets of the community, an act that wends its way throughout Wideman's work. Like the John of the "Family Tree" and like the writer, Robert is tall, balding, and passionately plays basketball well into middle age. Despite such resemblances, the few intimations of Robert's history divert from the "John" figure of Wideman's other works and of his biography. Jones attends Howard University, not the University of Pennsylvania. And the novel provides no information about his previous marriage and family. A misty character, overly dependent on other characters from other works for a form, Robert at, one point, questions his own formal integrity. At one point, he cryptically refers to himself as "another dead man" (110).

In the second chapter, "Dancing at Edgar's," Jones meets the women, who remains unnamed until the last few pages of the work. She is more of a composite figure than a character, given form by mourning and tragic loss. Indeed, in broader cultural memory, she evokes the Isis figure of Ishmael Reed's 1971 novel *Mumbo Jumbo,* or the story that Reuben told, "once upon a time" about "a woman whose son was torn into thousands of pieces and the fleshy fragments tossed into the wind and the winds scattered the body to the earth's four corners" (Reuben 107), and a similar "she" once described in an essay by Wideman on Malcolm X. In this essay, Wideman elaborates this spirit of a woman who suffers the betrayal, death, and dismemberment of a loved one.

> Then she comes, always she, inconsolable, her tears a frozen rain drenching the land that has not cycled past winter since her lost one disappeared. She will scour the whole wide world until she finds every fragment of her beloved. And when she has gathered them and united them and breathed life again into the body, the earth too, as if it has been kissed, will begin softly to stir again, bud, bloom, warm as she does, her outstretched arms and smile open wide as a horizon in welcome. (103)

Such mourning—the blues— give immemorial form to her character. In fact, she admits to Jones that she discovers a record of her life—"Found my story. My song" (54)—in the lyrical passages of the Biblical *Book of Lamentations.* "Scared me" she affirms, "to find my story in a book" (51).

Along with autobiographical details from his Wideman's actual life, the tragic dimensions of the woman's spirit leach into the novel from the author's other work. On some levels, the she of *Two Cities* appears nearly interchangeable with Kwansa from *Reuben*, whose loss and mourning also give her form. Kwansa is a recovering drug addict, former prostitute, and teenage mother. She is also an orphan, who was raised by a grandmother (Big Mama), who drags her to a sanctified church and cares for the child with copious amounts of shame and tough love. Big Mama dies shortly after she ejects Kwansa from the house because she is pregnant. Kwansa seeks legal advice from the title character as she wanders the streets looking for her lost son, whom her unstable boyfriend has kidnapped.

The "She" of *Two Cities* has much in common with Kwansa and figures from other works, yet, unlike Jones, she also has a rich, detailed history that is largely native to the work. She is thirty-five years old, boney, and very pretty. She has two younger, named sisters: Chantal and Yolanda, whom she helps raise. She doesn't know her father, and her mother dies in childbirth.

Orphaned (a major motif of Wideman's later work), she and her sisters are shuttled about and raised by a variety of elders, who scrub them and drag them to a church that she associates with shame and judgment. Meanwhile, she mourns an unfaithful husband, who dies in prison of AIDS. Within a year, her youngest son, Marcus, kills himself while supposedly playing Russian roulette, and her oldest son, Kwame, gets hunted down by gang members and murdered in the doorway of his home in a way reminiscent of the actual murder of Wideman's nephew, Omar, to whom *Two Cities* is dedicated. She and Jones meet at Edgars bar in Pittsburgh, fall in love, break up because she can't bear the notion of his dying like the other men in her life, and then reconcile over the death of a mysterious tenant (Mr. Mallory) in her house.

Despite such detail, "she" still has spirit-like odors and a face which lose their integrity and inexorably conjure other women. At one point, Mr. Mallory, as he regards her, has to "stop to ask himself which woman. Which face, which ears and eyes" (101). Indeed, she remains nameless until the last few pages of the work when she begins to imagine a new life, perhaps becoming pregnant by Jones, and giving her own name, Kassima, to a baby girl. Yet rather than fixing her down as "handle," this name resonates toward the crossroads and passageways that energize the work, phonically evoking the street—Cassina Way—that meanders its way through Wideman's work and art.

The Second Line: Martin Mallory and John Africa

The conjuring of passageways leads to the two other figures, who are secondary to that plot—the figures on the bridge and at the crossroads that begin *Two Cities*: Martin Mallory and John Africa. Recalling the irregular gait of Esu-Elegbara or Papa Legba, Mallory shuffles into the text on a cane, the result of a wound he receives in World War II at the hands of American soldiers, who hunt down him and a friend as the two innocently party one night with two White, Italian women on the beach and in an isolated cabin in the literally picturesque Italian countryside. The soldiers spray the cabin with the machine gun fire of tracer bullets, lighting it afire, killing the women and Mallory's friend before wounding Mallory who, like Reuben in the earlier novel, escapes from the fire. His wound and shuffling gait inherently conjure Wideman's own memory and his long struggle with research about the lynching of Emmett Till and the military court martial file of his father, whom the U.S. army hanged for the crimes of rape and murder.

Nearly twenty years later, Wideman saves the spirit of this immemorial story in *Writing to Save a Life* (2016). This work recalls the usual pattern of race hatred and an American atrocity story. During World War II, eighty-three of the "ninety-six American servicemen executed by the US military" for war crimes were African American (Smith 13). These executions often stemmed from the U.S. military's imposition of American Jim Crow law in Europe. Black "soldiers were executed for even the hint of fraternizing with white women," asserts Valerie Smith in her 2008 article, "Emmett Till's Ring." She further observes that "African American soldiers in the segregated armed forces were executed at a much higher rate than were their white counterparts for the same or lesser offenses" (157). Mallory's wound thus resonates with the spirit of this casual American atrocity committed during World War II by what journalist Tom Brokaw calls in a 1998 book, America's "Greatest Generation." The story thus resounds as an iconic, African American atrocity story of the type described by Rueben and packed into the word Philadelphia. It is a spirit of "Fires and whores. White boys up to their usual shit" (*Reuben* 90). It is Mallory's Philadelphia over which he layers the bombing of MOVE as one of the repeating, traumatic events of his memory. He asks: "Did he hear flames crackling. Screams" (195). Speaking to John Africa, he links the stories together through a summary of the official written record or the "enemy activity report" which leads to a lifetime pension for his wounds from the military. He melds together the Italian cabin with Osage Avenue, the site of the bombed MOVE house. "In separate incidents one U.S. soldier KIA, one wounded, two civilians dead from enemy fire blah, blah, blah. . . . All dead in It-a-ly. All dead on O-sage-Ave. Same dying. Same lies to cover it up" (197). Mallory thus arrives in the text bearing traces of Reuben's Philadelphia. And like Reuben, he, too, is an ambiguous Homewood fixture that no one knew by name, but who "appeared one day and soon stopped being a stranger because you would see him everywhere" (205).

Yet, Mallory has a vague, dispersed and fragmented history in the work. It has to be pieced together or re-membered by a reader who takes on the role of the "she" described by Wideman in his remembrance of Malcolm X. They, too must scour the text, collect the scattered pieces, breathe life into them, and participate in an act of re-membering by actively assembling the life of Mr. Mallory. Mallory grew up in Philadelphia, had some university schooling, traveled extensively, and once lived in Washington, DC where he had a wife and children, though he never says how many. He abandons them—"Stole myself. Like a runaway slave" (107)—when he joins the army during World War II where he gets wounded. He then, returns to Philadelphia before moving to Pittsburgh in the wake of the trauma induced by the MOVE bombing. In Pittsburgh, he boards with Kassima, where he is identified as much by a smell or sound in her house on Cassina way where the toilet has been known to flush by itself. He is as much a rhythm or song structuring the interstices of the text as he is a character—a blues that he carries within himself but could never be heard singing. When his thoughts dictate the narrative, he cryptically refers to himself as "dead too" (85). He describes himself as peeping through windows, voyeuristically and guiltily taking on the character of a written text saving and capturing the lives of others "because he couldn't imagine such a life for himself, a body and feeling anchored, touching, being touched" (85). He thus exists more as a consciousness of the text, channeling the thoughts of an aging writer cavalierly making art of life, mixing up time, space, facts, and dates that openly defy and subvert the "blah, blah, blah" and lies of any factual, historical record. "How crowded his mind is . . . no space to be his own dying, dreamy self and also hold on to the dates and times and places and names . . . *Two Cities*, old man. You've got everything mixed up, friend" (173). Mallory thus looms over the text, as an extracted spirit of the writer and of an artist struggling to perform the work of a text that seeks to transcend its own medium of letters, words and writing; images that move linearly across the printed page that have trouble maintaining their integrity.

Mallory originally works as a professional photographer who, says Kassima, "took pictures of dead bodies in a hospital. When they autopsy people, his job photographing the body parts. Hearts, livers, lungs" (219). This original job evokes the spirit of Liam of *The Cattle Killing* and his work with George Stubbs, the anatomical illustrator. Liam witnesses Stubbs' ability to "copy nature directly," down to its smallest, atomized detail (Cattle 114). Liam also becomes an artist, yet he disparages such realistic representation and seeks to invent an art that could "peel" back the layers, "expose" what's beneath (Cattle) (127), and produce a new and different way of understanding the world and unsettle what he calls the "lie of race." Mallory struggles to do the same thing with photography, channeling the lessons of another text, and the lessons of Stubbs and anatomy. He wanders Philadelphia and Pittsburgh with a camera that he fixes to take layer upon layer of pictures that one day someone might figure out a way to develop. "I want to enter the wound, cut through layer by layer like a surgeon, expose what lies beneath the skin. . . . Free others to free themselves" (119).

The other figure on the bridge is John Africa, who has almost no history native to *Two Cities*. He literally appears as a disembodied talking head that accompanies Mallory throughout the text, dominating and structuring the work from the margins of its bridging latticework. He embodies, the twin spirit of Papa Legba compounded by the name Eshu-Elegbara, who, says Thompson, can darken "the most brilliant of happenings" (19). He wields the power of the blues and the crossroads, which inexorably cuts things loose as, according to Thompson, it equally beckons "misfortune and deliberate, unjust destruction" (19). As more of a spirit—a loa of Haitian cosmology—or a blues than a character, John Africa imports the discredited spirit of the holdover, countercultural movement of the 1960s; the mother wit and knowledge of African American vernacular culture and speech; and the soul of an agonistic, uncontrolled, and uncontrollable Blackness that poet Amiri

Baraka posited as motivating the Black Arts movement of the 1960s when he said: "But we Bad, in fact we was trying to get Badder dan Nat" (Baraka, Movement 499).

John Africa has thus accompanied both Wideman and Martin Mallory since the 1985 bombing of MOVE. *In Philadelphia Fire*, he enters the text as King, who also bears the name James Brown. A bum, mystic, and the former leader of the "Family," he abstracts the spirit of the MOVE group and that of Vincent Leaphart, the actual founder of MOVE, who went by the name of John Africa. Leaphart's severed head, was unearthed among the rubble of the bombed MOVE house in Philadelphia (Anderson and Hyenor 185).

When MOVE emerged, Philadelphia city officials seemed unready for the group started by a charismatic, semi-literate, handyman and dog walker. Members of the movement wore dreadlocks and took Africa as their last name, but they weren't clearly Black nationalists and they weren't the Black Panthers. They weren't Maoists or Marxist revolutionaries. They didn't advocate the armed overthrow of the United States and world capitalism. Instead, neighbors, the police, and city officials observed them living healthy lives, getting up at five in the morning to jog, and abstaining from processed foods. At first, it seemed that their worst crime was a refusal to kill the roaches infesting their home (and moving into adjoining row houses). They based their lives on a book that advocated respect for all life. "Animal rights are equal to human rights as a part of MOVE philosophy, and so the vermin were not removed" assert John Puckett and Devin DeSilvis in their history of MOVE (Puckett and DeSilvis). The name, John Africa thus abstracts the contagion of insubordinate Blackness, idealism, and disorder that destabilizes identity, tearing things loose, and threatening the confining lies, and "blah, blah, blah" of the official record, or the cover up of an "understanding" that John Africa tells Mallory is "in our souls if we just go on and use it" (149). He is the spirit of the type of art that Liam and Mallory pursue. He tells Mr. Mallory that "Our job's about making people see what they don't want to see. What's right in front of their eyes. . . . Just got to let people know a war's on [. . .] system want invisible war. System don't want you to know who your real enemies are" (218).

At the Crossroads: A Fake Book of Heads

The two figures on the bridge embody the spirt of New Orleans second-line jazz parades, named after the reveling stragglers of the periphery and not the instrumental concerts of the center. As figures of the crossroads, they instigate a "jam session," or the type of in-between performance in which employed big band musicians would originally "squeeze in" or "jam" in playing time for themselves and for pleasure at the smaller clubs around town after the paying gig. For instance, in his autobiography, *To Be or Not to Bop* (1979) the transformative jazz trumpeter Dizzy Gillespie says he was never employed at the club where he, Charlie Parker, and Thelonious Monk explored the radical, new sounds of Be-Bop: "I went there to jam. . . . That's where we all used to go after hours, until daylight to play" (Gillespie 140). Another formative figure of jazz, bassist Charles Mingus, affirms this idea in his autobiography, *Beneath the Underdog* (1971). He says "jazz musicians play for love. . . . That's what jazz originally was, getting away from the usual tiddy, the hime, the gig" (Mingus 191). So, jazz, like other Black music, dwells in what Houston Baker calls in his book *Blues, Ideology, and Afro-American Literature* (1984) places of "juncture," "crossroads," and "crossings." Baker juxtaposes these notions against the idea of "fixity."

> Fixity is a function of power. Those who maintain place, who decide what takes place and dictate what has taken place, are power brokers of the traditional. The "placeless," by contrast are translators of the nontraditional . . . their lineage is fluid, nomadic, transitional. Their appropriate mark is the crossing sign at the junction. (202)

In their writing and interviews, jazz musicians reveal that this notion is also expressed through their preoccupation with musical structures such as "bridges," "channels," and "breaks." Within the music, these places of juncture become the inviting space for solos and improvisation where musicians feel free to identify themselves, their individuality and their style. "The inside of the tune (the bridge)," Monk once told saxophonist Steve Lacy "is the part that makes the outside sound good" (Lacy).

This suggests another, generic or engendering "genre" for *Two Cities* that goes beyond that of the written, novel. It extracts elements of what jazz musicians call, a "fake book." This is the name for the often ramshackle, illicit, mimeographed, Photostatted, Xeroxed, or once hand-copied collection of what the musicians also call "jazz heads." This notion is invoked in the introductory chapter, "Missing John Africa," by the head of John Africa which performs as a "jazz head," or the eventually memorized, standard melodies around which jazz musicians improvise. For instance, at one point, Mr. Mallory takes John Africa and performs a jazz-like ritual with him as he works on a melody resounding from another text in Wideman's oeuvre. He tosses him in a river. Mallory "snatches Dogman, who's light as a feather now, from the walkway of the bridge. Tosses him over the bloody rail and Dogman hits without a splash, laid out gentle in the water on his back with almost a smile on his face the way they would have fixed him in a funeral parlor if they'd found his head" (10–11).

Like much of *Two Cities*, aspects of a similar musical ritual occur within Wideman's other work. For instance, in the later work, *Fanon*, the character of Thomas unexpectedly receives a severed head in the mail and eventually tosses it in a river. Late in *Fanon*, the speaker of the text admits that this ritual had entered the work through the short story, "Damballah" (an actual work by Wideman) saying: "At the end of the story a slave boy on a plantation in the American South rescues the severed head of a murdered fellow slave, carries the head to a river, and tosses it in. A kind of burial. A kind of grim wish for more life" (184). In *Fanon*, the speaker laments such a conventional, craftsman-like tying up of loose ends that evoked praise from literary critics. Yet, within the work, such a neat end also leads to a beginning—a head—and another way of thinking about the millennial work of Wideman. The severed head suggests a way out as much as it presents a return.

Such repetition evokes the hope implicit in African American expressive culture. In jazz, "the heads" collected together in the "fakebook" are the copied-out melodies of a familiar jazz tune. They establish the harmonic structure and rhythmic parameters of the piece that help structure solos and improvisation. They stage and invoke memory while suggesting alternative futures and possibilities. Rather than look backward; they project forward. The head imposes the familiar, demanding its recognition. "Pat your foot & sing the melody in your head, when you play," Monk tells Lacy (Lacy). Yet, unlike classical, scripted music, such a performance also foregrounds detour and departure from the "seen" written script (improvise, from the Latin word *improvisus*, which quite literally means "unforeseen," hinges upon a form of the verb "video" which means "to see"). The jazz head thus invokes transgression, violating and defying the property of copyright laws; the musicians taking and fooling around with what doesn't belong to them while bending, breaking, and even sometimes destroying the rules—revolting against the "fixity" of seen writing and thereby its "function of power," as described by Baker in his exploration of the crossroads. "These pieces were written so as to have something to play, & to get cats interested enough to come to rehearsal," Monk tells Lacy. "Don't play everything (or every time); let some things go by. Some music just imagined" (Lacy).

Therefore, musically, the head of John Africa performs as a "jazz head," as do many of the Homewood stories of the text. Another of them begins as a woman—who could be anyone's mother, daughter, wife, or sister—witnesses a scene through her window in a Black American community. As she sits helpless and glued to her chair, an armed figure emerges from the shadows of a Pittsburgh back alley, stalking the lover and husband she awaits in her spot behind a glass boundary. A spectator looking through glass, she is inside in a well-lighted domestic space; they are outside in the liminal world of the streets—the crossroads—where anything can happen—and does. Meanwhile, an actual, concrete barrier of brick and glass separates them, locking them into the endlessly repeating roles of the cliché, tragic, inner-city script of perpetrator, helpless victim, and witness. Outside, an interchangeable perpetrator stalks his endless stream of prey. Inside, the exchangeable witness sits in her chair by the window; viewers of the TV news sit fatalistically on their sofas; and readers know what to expect, their eyes scanning from left to right and the words inexorably moving in a foreseen, determined direction—from beginning to tragic end. All await the expected outcome—the "duty"—structured by the rhythm of the American imagination that relentlessly menaces and consumes Black life. But then, something unexpected happens. The woman rejects the scripted outcome—performing an act of black magic—and pierces the boundary separating her world form theirs. She rejects the predetermined role of passive observer, victim, and witness; jabs her fist through the window—"blasting" a hole in the world (118)—; and screams, breaking the spell. Freed, her husband dodges around a corner and away to safety. The would-be assailant also flees as his weapon clatters to the ground. This head, this one, saving, magical, and likely autobiographical moment involving Wideman's grandmother and grandfather, had such an impact that it is saved, and repeated as a "head" in at least three different works: the 1983 novel *Sent for You Yesterday*, the short story, "Lizabeth: The Caterpillar Story," and again in *Two Cities*.

These are themes to be taken up again at later dates and improved upon with re-imagined possibilities. And *Two Cities* doesn't just return to these heads, it daringly corrects them, rendering a pat ending—all pat endings—suspect. By retelling the "Caterpillar Story" or the story of Damballah as a head, it reopens something that had seemed finished and closed in a previous text. This, perhaps, is the optimism of *Two Cities*, a book of fragments, orphaned stories, misguided plans, "false starts," and misdirecting heads. Nothing is closed. Like the best experimental Black American music—alto saxophonist Anthony Braxton, for instance, has written music to be performed on several planets—*Two Cities* is a transformational work, laying down paths and creating possibilities, structures, styles, images, and language for another time; a yet to be imagined future. It moves through barriers that once opened, cannot be closed again.

An Epistolary Form: The Letters of Mr. Mallory to Alberto Giacometti

The "Caterpillar Story," thus also formally functions as a "head." It is a family story told in the text and throughout Wideman's oeuvre by several generations of women. As such a story, it captures or saves something about the story telling of Wideman's mother that he describes in his later work *Fanon* and cuts and pastes as part of a literary collage into a 2019 essay on the visual collages of Black American artist of Romare Bearden, "Between the Shadow and the Act." In these collages and in his mother's storytelling, Wideman locates a particular functioning of Black Atlantic craft.

> Romare Bearden's collages remind me of how my mother talked, still talks to me today, years after she's been gone. Her stories flatten and fatten perspective. She crams everything, everyone, everywhere into the present, into words intimate and immediate as the images of a Bearden painting. (209)

Indeed, such cramming—or jamming—extracts the aesthetic qualities of the collage, the minkisi container, or the patchwork quilt that Wideman sees through the eyes of Bearden. Bearden's eyes, Wideman imagines might "linger over a swatch of antique, patchwork Alabama quilt alive under his gaze as he rotates and rubs it, discovering new, mellow harmonies among its once brightly colored threads. Sweet funk of it as he brings it closer to his eyes."

In an aesthetically formal way, this practice connects *Two Cities* to a work such as *The Color Purple,* and African American writer Alice Walker, whose actual quilting modeled the epistolary form of that work. Indeed, within the interstices of *Two Cities,* the patchwork of an another, imbedded text takes shape through an unread, "one-sided" correspondence (an idea rendered oxymoronic by the eyes of the reader) consisting of 6 letters between Mallory and Swiss sculptor Alberto Giacometti (178). This correspondence and the shadow, epistolary form enables the text to embrace an alternative, Black Atlantic structure as it delves deeply into the journey of an artist at the crossroads, who is in search of a form for his work that would function like the storytelling of Wideman's mother and, says Mallory, like the "old voices taught" him by elders speaking in the discredited tongue of African American Vernacular English. "I speak this despised, motherless, fatherless tongue" he asserts. He then describes it as a language that "I want my pictures to speak" (128). Such a language in art would work like the sculptures of Giacometti, the music of Monk; and the collages of Bearden. Through this correspondence Mallory constantly asks in different way: "How can I make [. . .]" (91).

Still, as he struggles with form, Mallory also expresses a relentless sense guilt at the failures of his art and of conventional forms of representation. He feels like a traitor, whose medium and skills fail him, rendering him a thief, voyeur and impotent witness "eavesdropping on someone else's life, a scavenger [. . .] surviving on what he steals through the yellow squares" emblazoned on the film in his camera (102). In one letter to Giacometti, Mallory implicitly compares this freezing of life through conventional representation to the awesome power of Medusa and "the stare that freezes and kills." He explores this problem as he ruminates over her tale.

Medusa's story made me uneasy from the beginning. Nasty as she was, for some reason I felt sorry for her. Turns out the hero didn't go after her because he was trying to rid the world of evil, he just wanted to steal her evil power for himself. Chopped off her head and carried it around to freeze his enemies. (118)

This image not only haunts *Two Cities* but seems to be a major preoccupation of Wideman's work since *Reuben*. Is it possible that the "stare that freezes and kills" also betrays an anxiety of the writer who captures and represents his world through the written word, which itself seems lifeless, frozen and dead? So says Paul in his second letter to the Corinthians: "The letter kills" (II Cor. 3:6).

Despite such anxiety, the story of Medusa is also the story of a trickster figure, who knows how to channel the power saved within something dead or deadly and turn it against enemies, and in the words of Robert Farris Thompson in his description of the power of Black Atlantic charms, "arrest" them "in their tracks" (131). Wideman's work overflows with such trickster figures who know how to undermine and disarm those who threaten them through a power over words. He explores how the once enslaved took control over their written form in his analysis of Charles Chesnutt and the slave narratives and his study of the novel *Corregidora* by Gayle Jones. He lends what he calls the power of "word magic" to the character of Reuben in *Reuben*, to Margaret Jones in *Philadelphia Fire*, and to the enslaved Kate in *The Cattle Killing*. Such figures, says Mallory in a letter to Giacometti, have the power "turn things loose," and "blast holes in the world." Mallory struggles to deploy this power through the pictures he takes.

> You probably know the story. Why I am recalling it now. A stare that freezes and kills just the opposite of what you do, and Mr. Bearden and Mr. Monk. You turn things loose.
>
> And I keep pulling the trigger, snapshot after snapshot blasting holes in the world, pretending nothing changes, the ducks still sit on the water untouched, calm, waiting until I'm ready to shoot again. My pictures are pretty postcards with the world arranged nice and neat. But I don't want to hide the damage. I want to enter the wound, cut through layer by layer like a surgeon, expose what lies beneath the skin. Go where there is no skin, no outside or inside, no body. Only traffic always moving in many directions at once. Snapshots one inside the other, notes played so they can dance away, make room for others. Free others to free themselves (118–19).

This shadow, epistolary novel exposes a work and an artist in the search of a medium that will deploy the world-changing, functional power of the crossroads.

Mallory pens his letters to Giacometti, a Swiss painter and sculptor obsessed with the problem of imbuing his work with life and movement; moving beyond the conventions of representation that "freezes and kills." So says art scholar Richard Stamelman in "The Art of the Void: Alberto Giacometti and the Poets of 'L'Ephémère.'" "The problem Giacometti faced from the start of his career, [Jean-Paul] Sartre observes, was 'comment faire un homme avec de la pierre sans le pétrifier [how to use stone to make a man without petrifying him]'" (23). According to Stamelman, Giacometti developed a visual language for rendering absence present, inspiring a group of mid-twentieth-century French poets—poets of the Ephemeral—through his exploration of the crossroads, guiding them to

> that point of intersection where existence and language dialectically interpenetrate, where world and book unfold in a co-presence that transforms the poem into an object that, like a Giacometti statue, is fragmented, scarred, torn, hollowed, fissured, pulverized, and brought as close to a state of nothingness and silence as possible. (17)

Giacometti was equally obsessed with heads, or a head, which dominated his work since 1936. He writes about this himself in a 1947 letter to art collector Pierre Matisse: "A head (I quickly abandoned figures, that would have been too much) became for me an object completely unknown and without dimensions." In the development of his technique, Giacometti's journey tracks that of Liam of *Two Cities* and of Mallory, who writes: "I'm not an artist, but I'm learning from your art to use my camera in new ways" (81). Giacometti's work performs the type of jamming Wideman observes in Bearden's art as well as in his mother's speech, as she "crams everything, everyone, everywhere into the present." Deploying such jamming in writing leads to a density that challenges conventional techniques of realism, verisimilitude, and mimesis that Giacometti explored with a visual language of absence. Stamelman describes this quality of "Giacometti's eye."

> But part of Giacometti's problem in capturing the real was his belief that merely representing figures alone, without copying the density and materiality of their circumambient space or without representing the distance between himself and the object of his perception, offered an incomplete and inauthentic picture of reality. Giacometti's eye was profoundly sensitive to different kinds of empty, so-called "negative," space: to the vacant, airy space surrounding or passing through his statues; to the white, sometimes gray, space which like a halo encircled the heads of his painted portraits; to the corrosive space of paper eating into the unbounded network of lines that precariously shaped a head in his drawings.

Ultimately, Stamelman observes, the "void is a constant presence in Giacometti's work" (20). And the complete effect is "to transform emptiness into a palpable, almost measurable substance" (15–16).

In his letter, Mallory connects the effects of Giacometti's technique to the Black Atlantic aesthetic, as he also inherently conjures Ralph Ellison's description in his novel *Invisible Man* of

> three boys on a subway platform. . . . These fellows whose bodies seemed—what had one of my teachers said of me? "You're like one of these African sculptures, distorted in the interest of a design. . . . For they were men outside of historical time, they were . . . men of transition whose faces were immobile. . . . Do the others see them, think about them, even those standing close enough to speak?" (440–442)

In his letter, Mallory queries this "real" aspect of African American life. "Did you know you were sculpting Africans, Mr. Giacometti" he asks. "High-butt Watusi warriors rippling down a city street, crossing an intersection in the corner of someone's gaze, our flying people with their steel cable legs and chunks of lead for feet, yet lighter than air, invisible when a passerby halts midstride and turns to check out what she thinks she just might have glimpsed over her shoulder" (92).

Mallory further asks Giacometti if he knows the work of Romare Bearden, asserting that the art of the Swiss sculptor has much in common with that of two, "homegrown," African American Artists: Bearden and Thelonious Monk.

> And though I lack words to say how, our homegrown African music, like your sculpture and Mr. B's paintings, helps me with my picture-taking. In the piano solos of Mr. Thelonious Monk I hear familiar tunes drifting in and out, hiding and uncovering each other, and songs playing something new, music no one's ever heard before. (117)

This suggests the existence of an African American tradition—a tradition of the Black Arts—that embraces the transgressions that inspire Mr. Mallory (who tries to fix his camera so that he too can copy "the density and materiality of . . . circumambient space" by shooting a plethora of different images on one frame of film) as well as Wideman.

In his essay on Bearden's art, Wideman invokes the spirit of Monk and his music, describing it as a force that both inspires (is inspirited) and possess. "Working on collage is too hard, impossible really, unless he [Bearden] hears something resembling music whose rhythms guide his eyes, hands. His feet shuffle beneath the work table's edge like Monk's feet under a piano" (209). Within the history of African American expressivity, Monk is a preeminent figure of the crossroads, whose music pulses with the spirit of "Carrefour who," according to Maya Deren, "may loose upon the world the daemons of ill chance, misfortune and deliberate, unjust destruction" (Deren 101). Indeed, jazz scholar Brent Edwards names his 2017 collection of essays that are "experimentation in pseudomorphosis—new possibilities found by hearing across media" (253), *Epistrophies*, after a 1941 Monk jazz head, "Epistrophy," a corner stone of any quality "fake book." In his essay, "*Zoning* Mary Lou Williams *Zoning*," Edwards explores the fraught musical and written relationship between Williams as a jazz traditionalist and the contagion of post-1930s, new music led by the original work of Monk, her former student. In Williams eyes (and ears), Monk's music embodies the spirit of the Haitian zombie, inexorably animated by Carrefour as it lets lose demons or what she calls "A Fungus Amongus" (her whimsical title to a Monk-like musical pastiche that names one of her own "heads"). Like an invasive fungus, Monk's music inspired the jazz "avant-garde, foreign composers, black magic, commercial rock" Williams laments. All of "this began to enter in and destroy the true feeling of Jazz" (quoted in Edwards 164). The continuing effects of Monk on "avant-garde" jazz pianist Cecil Taylor, with whom she recorded a live record, led Williams to exclaim to Taylor (in her own one-sided correspondence of a letter that may never have been sent): "You are actually destroying yourself" (169). A seminal teacher, mentor, and jazz scholar who either taught or befriended the major architects of jazz after the 1930s, Williams, Edwards says, seemed to figure "'avant-garde or free' music as a sort of invasive organicism [that] sows mistrust and dissension into the structure of the ensemble" (158). Edwards presents Williams betraying both a wariness of Haitian religious practice and a cavalier attitude toward interstitial jamming. She simultaneously praises and disparages Monk as a figure whom she tacitly derides with terms like "zombie" and "after hours" (jamming): "He was one of the original modernists all right, playing pretty much the same harmonies then that he's playing now. Only in those days we called it 'Zombie music' and reserved it mostly for musicians after hours" (quoted in Edwards 157).

Through exploring Williams' invocation of "the living dead" in her characterization of Monk's music and the influence of its spirit on avant-garde pianist Cecil Taylor, Edwards develops what he terms, an "aesthetics of disposal." He links this aesthetic to the Black Arts and the work of poet Amiri Baraka. *Two Cities* extracts this spirit, which Edwards addresses through an analysis of Baraka's *The System of Dante's Hell*, and its provocation of "wars of consciousness" (161). This notion easily names Mallory's pursuit of a new art and John Africa's instigation of acts of violence that would make "people see what they don't want to see" (218). According to Edwards, Williams, through a technique she calls "zoning," attempts to contain this contagion within Taylor's musical approach in her writing and in their live concert. Her work "girdles Taylor's approach as a species of the living dead. This is not just moralizing; it also serves as something like an exorcism" (167). This is the opposite of Mallory's approach. For him, Monk's music "blasts holes in the world" and performs the type of "saving" of the "flash of the spirit" native to Haitian cosmology, invoked by the term "zombie music," and deployed by the work of Wideman since the novel *Reuben*.

For Edwards, this spirit is also named by "an aesthetics of disposal, where innovation is predicated on putting in place or putting away . . . a 'place of naming' in the mind: it serves not as a 'receptacle' but as a kind of methodology" (161). In the work of Baraka, it has the force described by Thompson, of freezing the enemy in his tracks. Says Edwards: "So dis-posal here means something like 'putting in hell', freezing an object in the bottom-most ring, an allegorical 'process' that is necessary for the intuition of an angle of ascent" (161). In Taylor, he says, it produces "a sound that coagulates in space, and in it coming together is able to take up 'scatter'd deposits'" (172).

> Taylor's historiographic sensibility approaches the past as a *deposit,* as a sedimentation of poesis that allows certain organic approaches to construction [. . .] Any such deposit of prior stylistic practice contains elements of "deposition," and the player must be primed to take the testimony—one might even call it the haunting—of a "spirit" or "passion" that "informs" the methodological approaches of the black aesthetic tradition. And by implication, an aesthetic "evolution" must involve another factor, as well, a certain violence that characterizes that unearthing or haunting, a force that not only founds but simultaneously "deposes"—overthrows or sublates. (168)

Taylor's music thus works like a *minkisi* container, gathering and deploying "spirit-embodying" material.

Such deposits are conjured throughout *Two Cities*, by the notion of caring, of remembering, of "saving a space" that in the work of Giacometti, says Mallory, keeps "the sting of absence present" (82). In one letter, Mallory thanks Giacometti "for piecing something together out of nothing, for remembering what's lost" (83). Even as Mallory dies, he ascends to Kassima's room, and lays his head on a pillow which later leads Robert Jones to think: "It should have been my head on her pillow, me guarding her not some dying old man saving a place for me. What kind of goddam place is that, anyway" (116). But Kassima has many such saved places in her home, stirring her to reflect on the "kind of" space she once saved for an often absent, now dead son thinking: "no matter what else went down he had a mother who loved him and saved a space for him, protected it, keeping it when he was absent.

... Emptiness more real than the big snoring body. Absence keeping him alive" (126).

Return of the Prenda

Two Cities concludes with a magical box and a chaotic funeral that is simultaneously held for Mr. Mallory and a dead gangbanger. Before this funeral, Kassima roots through Mallory's personal effects, finding his pictures and scrutinizing his negatives. The reader then learns that almost all of Mr. Mallory's shots were unprintable. Kassima laments:

> Nothing on the negatives. Everyone I looked at, and I looked at lots from each box, just blank. All grayed out. He must have ruined them. Accidentally or on purpose. Who knows. Told me he took pictures on top of pictures. Don't make sense to me. I never used a camera much and sure don't understand nothing about them but you take one picture then you have to wind the film right. Well, he said he fixed his camera so he could take a dozen, a hundred without turning the film. Said every picture was there on the film and one day he would or somebody would figure out a way so everything he was photographing could be printed for people to see. All I could see when I held the film up to the light was gray, gray, gray. (211)

In this passage, a spectator responds to the art of Mr. Mallory. Perhaps, here, she speaks for Wideman who anticipates readers who have turned to his work in search of mimetic representations of Black life. For Kassima, the overexposed film represents nothing. It is ruined. It captures nothing. Such an attitude is reminiscent of those reactions to Wideman's turn-of-the-century work, which deem it fragmented, inchoate, and basically inaccessible to the average reader. They may be at a loss to explain how the writer of *Brothers and Keepers* and *The Homewood Trilogy* could write something like *Reuben, Philadelphia Fire, The Cattle Killing*, and *Two Cities*, books that are difficult to read and jam packed with voices, narrative layers, disembodied heads, abandoned plots, disbanding centers, compounded genres, a ragged sense of time, and fragmented, random images. These are unstable and volatile works, where voices mix together and characters lose their individuality, detach from history, time and space, and distill into spirits. The books themselves, thus, have much in common with Mallory's overexposed negatives which nevertheless capture something real; a "flash of the spirt" that cannot be seen, grasped, or illuminated by an imagination constrained by the "fixity of power" and the working of Western knowledge. As they ply their magic on the world, they foreground the question repeated by Kassima. "Who knows?"

At the end of *Two Cities*, Kassima brings a box of Mr. Mallory's printable pictures to the dead photographer's funeral. The box is not unlike, *Two Cities*; a fake book collecting together the stories of two, struggling African American communities—of Pittsburgh and Philadelphia—as jazz heads or as the "spirit embodying material" of a magical Black Atlantic bundle, a minkisi container. It exudes the life force of the living dead animating Monk's "zombie music" or Romare Bearden's collages, work bundled by an artist possessed by this music "whose rhythms guide his eyes, hands" and shuffling feet (Wideman, Shadow 209). As Mr. Mallory struggles to use his "camera in new ways" (81) exploring the bridge between sculpture, collage, music, and photography, *Two Cities* equally alchemizes its words into the snapshots of Mr. Mallory, performing "the trick of remembering and caring" that he envies in others and treasures (85). Through a gaze enlivened by the one-sided correspondence with Giacometti, *Two Cities* transforms the stories and heads of Homewood and Philadelphia into snapshots of a balding, middle aged man still able to play basketball in the "taint time" of a city park; of a grandfather carrying a boy on his shoulders or cooking up a pot of chitterlings; of a group of gangbangers—"blue warriors"—terrorizing the neighborhood where "blues rule"; of a man and a lamenting woman racked with the pain of loss and struggling to recover life; of the final, lonely death of an elderly African American man; and of the love the owner of a corner diner feels for a young man moldering in prison for the crime of trying to hold him up in a knuckleheaded scheme. It even includes nudes—snapshots—of African American soldiers making love on an Italian beach during World War II, and of Kassima, as Mr. Mallory and the text, lovingly pose her and snap pictures.

At one point, Mr. Mallory's letters to Giacometti also channel the thoughts of a writer, simultaneously engaged in a one-sided correspondence with the reader, anticipating the effects of his pictures while ruminating over the power of an art positioned at the crossroads.

> Rather than discomforting me . . . the thought of you somewhere beyond all the reach of words, frees me, puts my project of writing to you in the proper perspective, outside ordinary day-to-day time, into a space where your figures live, fixed and dancing, metal and flesh, entering and leaving time through the needle's eye of each beholder [. . .] I want people to see my pictures from various angles, see the image I offer as many images, one among countless ways of seeing, so the more they look, the more there is to see. A density of appearances is my goal, Mr. Giacometti. So I snap, snap, snap, snap. Pile layer after layer [. . .] If I ever get good, my pictures will remind people to keep a world alive around them, to keep themselves alive at the center of a storm swirling of emptiness. (90–91)

These snapshots capture or save a community, at once lorded over or structured by the "ill chance, misfortune and deliberate, unjust destruction" of Carrefour, where lamentations and "the blues rule," but also one where the twin figures at the crossroads wield the awesome power to modify "the worst of fates," and an ex-con relentlessly hopes "for a miracle, just like the rest of the fools around here" (166). And it happens.

The blues—gangbangers flying their color—irreverently disrupt the coincident funerals of Mr. Mallory and one of their number, spilling the photographer's naked body onto the street where the procession takes place. It is too much. Kassima, whose name evokes the street—the crossroads itself—shouts out. "Stop. Stop, goddammit. Stop [. . .] Don't you see yourselves" (237). She preaches through the text, "From my anger. My hurt. My love for those boys. For him and Mr. Mallory and I don't know what else" (239). She then shakes out the box of pictures, scattering them over the street. The pictures freeze them in their tracks

> Then some of them started coming up, looking at us beside the coffin, looking at the pictures all over the ground, picking up pictures, looking at them, looking at each other, handing them around, talking, walking off with pictures in their hands. Who knows what they were seeing. What they said. Who knows what they thought. And that was the beginning of the end of the worst part of the day. (239)

The pictures charm the community. At least momentarily, they release people from the enchantment of controlling, hostile fictions. These scattered, spirit-embodying materials perform as the text, which equally wields the power of the crossroads and which unravels the fate of what is written in newspapers, but not in the cosmos. And perhaps it works. "Who knows?"

Chapter 5

Fanon and the Art of Spiritualizing Narrative

Toward the beginning of John Edgar Wideman's 2008 work, *Fanon*, a writer figure invokes traditional Igbo cosmology as he describes his creative process.

> The Igbo of Nigeria, a people you no doubt encountered during your frequent diplomatic missions on behalf of Algeria, say a person doesn't die until the living stop remembering, stop telling stories about the person. Also, in Igbo tradition the age-mates or age-set of a freshly deceased peer scour their village, rushing hither and thither, searching for their missing comrade everywhere he once would be sure to have been found, the search increasingly intense and frantic as the age-mates run disappointed, back and forth from one familiar, intimate place to another, and their entreaties, their lamentations fail to coax the missing one from hiding.
>
> I'm not suggesting I consciously mine Igbo lore to organize my project. I cite the Igbo to acknowledge my unanticipated good fortune, my gratitude for the presence of what might be called ancestors (like you) waiting to be discovered. Ancestors who speak, not on demand, but if and when they choose. The simultaneous loss and discovery of their presence defines a space I might inhabit if I learn how, a vast solitude, a space less alone, less silent perhaps because others once occupied it and I've been expected.
>
> Think of me, of Thomas, as your age-mates, Fanon, playing a deadly serious game of chasing your spirit. Think of us hurrying along real streets, knocking on real doors, peeking in real windows, asking real people if they've seen our friend, our brother, visible now only in our search, our hunger for him. Imagine a gang of us, a posse of the bereaved, each person making separate forays or the whole bunch driven by a single thought or stalled, huddling together for mutual comfort, some hopeful, some resigned, some frayed, some disbelieving,

others intoxicated by the effort, every one of us so full of pain, fear, longing, memories that our bodies droop and collapse in a heap like shed costumes or skins at the end of a night of seeking since dawn our lost companion. The one we won't save. Won't let go. Can't. Imagine how deeply we might sleep, how sealed in darkness, oppressed by the weight of our sorrow, how weightless our dreams, as weightless, bodiless, remote and close as we seem to our fellow villagers or a curious stranger passing by who witnesses us, grown men behaving like spooked chickens or a band of orphaned children, noisy phantoms slipping, gliding through the compound's paths and shadows, then fading into the bush, ghosts in pursuit of a ghost, wailing, crying out in tongues, marking our trail with wet, glistening tears, real and far away as stars. (Fanon 8–9)

Like Frederick Douglass, who disavows superstition and dabbling in the black arts before he reluctantly secures a magical root that (perhaps as much as his acquisition of literacy) diverts the direction of his life, the writer figure dismisses knowingly mining "Igbo lore" as he also slips it into his right-hand pocket. Named for Frantz Fanon, the renowned Martinican psychiatrist who charted the pathological structure of international racism, *Fanon* at first seems ambiguous about its own magic and the ability of writing—of words as images or images as words—to change the actual world. The title itself reads like a belated outward turn, anachronistically going back to the constricting prescriptions of the Black Arts era as it summons the guiding spirit of a Black internationalism discredited by the fall of the Soviet Union, globalization, and the reigning neoliberal order of the early twenty-first century and the post-September 11 era. In fact, critical biographer Keith Byerman tempers Wideman's seemingly belated desire to "help cleanse the world of the plague of racism" (147) and write like Fanon, one of the patron saints of Pan Africanism and the Black liberation movement. According to Byerman, Wideman's recovered

> idea of writing sounds more like the Black Arts Movement people that Wideman wanted nothing to do with, precisely because they wanted literature to serve political rather than artistic goals. While his work from that time was "honest," it was also about the private lives of its characters, not their social concerns. He admits that his ambitions changed over time, that he took up different kinds of books, but, even then he "was hoping they didn't dishonor Frantz Fanon nor compromise unforgivably my original project." (147)

Indeed, the work begins with a writer figure in Europe (perhaps more of a Black cosmopolitan than an internationalist), far removed from the besieged African American communities that set Wideman's earlier work, yet still trying to summon the power of the black arts—this time moving between writing and the medium of film—while in search of a functional art that would make an actual difference. While still embracing the powerful, saving structure of the Black Atlantic bundle through its patchwork form, *Fanon* seems equally pessimistic about its own ability to change things and questions the real-world impact of the writer's previous works. The writer figure of *Fanon* seems blocked and despairing. He voices to himself a distressing question as he fuses the intentions of his life's work with those of Fanon. "When I ask myself if your example made any difference, Fanon, ask if your words and deeds alleviate one iota the present catastrophe of hate, murder, theft, and greed, where else should I start looking besides the mirror" (5).

Fanon is a perplexing, densely structured, and sometimes confusing text. Indeed, as with much of Wideman's later works, it is difficult to say clearly what the novel is about. It begins with an author figure in France as he spends the morning writing, which he poignantly translates as "trying to save a life" (3). So, on a basic level it is about the imagination of an aging writer haunted by a host of images from his life, previous fictions, and aborted projects that include a fictional work about Frantz Fanon; the story of Thomas, a man who unexpectedly receives a severed head in the mail; a film project collaboration with pioneering experimental filmmaker Jean Luc Goddard; the unending stories of a brother and son serving out a life-sentences in prison; the devastating impact of a nephew's murder; the desperate hope imbuing a December romance; and an effort to save or capture the rhythms and life force of an ailing mother, who is slipping away from this world.

Woven throughout the work are Wideman's usual preoccupations and philosophical musing on mortality, time, space, movement and the prospect of investing living power in dead words, or, this time, the dead images of film. The Fanon figure of the title, lithely weaves in and out of the text, sometimes rendered and sometimes eluding capture by the fictionalizing imagination of the writer. Stylistically, the work reveals Wideman still at the top of his craft, perfecting a narrative point of view (if it can be called that) which ultimately reveals the superfluous nature of the fictive, unified subject as it toys with the imagination's ability to navigate its way through epistemological uncertainty. It is never certain who or what narrates the work. At first, it is an author figure, who shares much in common with John Edgar Wideman. He shares the same name. He is a writer. He is in his sixties. He is divorced and now married to a French woman and living in Brittany, France. He had a career as a teacher. He has an ailing mother, a nephew who was murdered, and both a brother and son in prison. But this figure is also somewhat interchangeable with Thomas. Thomas is a character from an aborted novel who strangely receives a severed head in the mail. He, too, is a more or less successful writer, who sometimes takes his hand at narrating the work, exchanging places with the Wideman figure. He even seems to have the same unfinished literary project—a "Fanon manuscript" (27)—that melds with that undertaken by the Wideman figure. Even this "aborted" project defies a conventional reading anchored in time and space, cause and effect. On several occasions, the work itself (a project of the text that logically cannot be finished) materializes in the hands of the narrator while he daydreams on a train traveling through the French countryside.

Above all, *Fanon* must be read as a post-September 11 work, written before the 2008-beginning of Barak Obama's hope-filled presidency and from the depths of a despair resulting from the United States' prosecution of its war on terror through a regimen of torture. According to Byerman, this war deeply distressed Wideman, who further emerged as an outspoken public intellectual in 2002, signing an open letter and penning essays critical of the curtailment of civil liberties and the expansion of military power that ravaged the imagination of a nation as it inexorably demonized, tortured and killed people of color (Byerman 93–96). In *Fanon*, the writer figure tells his mother: "*There's a war going on, a war being waged against people like us all over the world*" (62). Produced within this context, *Fanon* queries the role of writing, or engaging in any act of representation in a post-9/11, neoliberal world of bankrupt and enslaved images; images that themselves are "serving power, speaking the master's language, saying and doing what the master orders" (80). *Fanon* underscores this loss of confidence as the author figure's double, Thomas, remembers a lecture to a writing class he once taught. He instructs:

> Words. If you choose to write, words are a necessary evil. And if necessary means, no way round it, then we have the answer to our original question: yes. Your stories are more than words. They are evil. (77)

This suggests further questions. Can a career, books, words counter their own evil and that of a world, in the quoted words of Fanon, "at total war" (190)? Can they reinvigorate images, ignite the imagination, save life, and make a difference?

Fanon's response seems to teeter on the edge of despair. Schemes and dreams are aborted or unfinished. Even the visits to the brother in prison, initiated for readers through the critically acclaimed 1984 work, *Brothers and Keepers*, capture a sense of mourning for lost time that writing fails to save or restore. "Almost thirty years ago," says the Wideman figure, "I tried to write a book I hoped might free my brother from a life sentence in the penitentiary. It didn't work. Everything written after that book worked even less" (52). He disparagingly adds:

> Or maybe he's disappointed less by the slavishness of images than by their refusal to be his slaves. Prospero snapping his wand. Appalled by his career's tail end, the gathering darkness of any career winding down. All those pretty

candles lit one by one with so much care and hopefulness, then one by one they gutter out, and when you peek over your shoulder, the room's just as black as when you started. (80)

Fanon thus seems like the latest installment, maybe the last guttering candle in the darkening room of an ineffectual career of a spent-out writer, of an aging Black wizard finally "snapping his wand."

Read as work of despair, *Fanon* channels the behavior of the Igbo age mates it invokes who behave "*like spooked chickens or a band of orphaned children*," and who, like the writer and his creations, are blocked or "stalled" (9). The text equally overflows with their "pain, fear, longing, memories" for the ones they "won't save. Won't let go. Can't." It wails, cries "*out in tongues*," and marks a "trail with wet, glistening tears" (8–9). The "saving" of the text thus captures the despair of the moment and of imaginations trapped within a closed, dialectical system of thought with no way out—no exit—as summarized by existentialist philosopher, Jean Paul Sartre in his "Preface," to Fanon's *The Wretched of the Earth*. "We [European citizens of colonial nations] find our humanity this side of death and despair; he [Fanon] finds it on the other side of torture and death" (Sartre, Philcox, lvii).

Yet, such a reading of *Fanon* and of an African or Black cosmology as acted out by the Igbo mourners mistakes the tears for dread, fatalism, and despair at the absurdity of life and at the finitude of death. The traditional Igbo world as conjured by the text, however, defies such closure. Instead, within their belief system, there is what one theologian calls an "incessant commerce between" the world of the living and the multiple ones of the dead (Uzukwu 195). The cries and tears of the mourning Igbo agemates do not despair, but ritualistically dispel one of the most dire of Igbo maledictions: "'*ama nna gi chie*': let your father's compound or the road leading to your father's compound be closed—which means a complete obliteration of the memory of the family"(Uzukwu 205). *Fanon* thus catches the mourners (as it does itself) in the act of writing, of signifying, of performing, masking, and masquerading a rite of Igbo "spiritualsation" (Uzukwu 194) or the ritualistic reclamation of an ancestral spirit; assuring their active participation in the material world. Through their frantic search, the mourners uphold the "continuity" between this world and the "other side" (Uzukwu 206). A "human who has been completely spiritualized" has undergone an "initiation" that involves "symbolic death and burial, resurrection from the dead, symbolic recreation of the world, and so on" (Uzukwu 203).

Fanon is thus a functional work that operates in the tradition of the black arts. It rejects closure as it opens the way to the compound. It is not an obituary notice for the dead, locked in, frozen on the page of a newspaper, clipped out, and then entombed in the "morgue" of yesterday's news. Instead, it makes use of those clippings as it engages in the black arts and acts of necromancy. It withdraws the clippings from the death grip of Western notions of "history" and a past inexorably created, modeled, and disseminated by the fictions of the dominant society masquerading through stylized techniques of verisimilitude as journalistic purveyors of truth and the real. Such works invent and pretend to dominate "time" as they shove a date over a homepage or in the upper corner of a front page, imposing the idea that it is ticking, spatialized, measurable, sub-dividable, perishable, and monetizable. *Fanon*—through its fragments, orphaned stories, misguided plans, aborted plots, "false starts," and dead-end plot devices—unravels this dateable and dated fiction of packageable closure.

As a spiritualizing work, *Fanon* comprises a variety of Black American-style explorations of Black or African cosmology that revel in what writer Toni Morison has called the "discredited knowledge" of Black spirituality (Morrison, Rootedness 342). It not only accepts, in the words of writer Ishmael Reed, that "Africa is the home of the loa (Spirits)," but expands the "pantheon" with its own rites that are similar to those of what he labels Neo-HooDoo. "Neo HooDoo," Reed proclaims, "borrows from Haiti Africa and South America" (Reed, Norton 811). It involves "the dance music/ and poetry of Neo-Hoodoo and whatever the ideas the/ participating artist might add" (813). *Fanon* catches this spirit, adding many of its own flourishes as it deploys writing to perform disparate acts of "spiritualization." These include the Black rite of Signifying(g) or conjuring a literary version of musical jazz heads (or standards), repeating them with a difference, and communing with the fixed and finished spirts of the past, giving them new life. It breaks the spell enchanting the post-9/11 imagination ensnared by images—by films and television shows—that sate and produce the inexorable American desire for violence. It further takes the dead, fixated gaze of conventional Hollywood cinema, subjects it to spiritualization, and alchemizes it into a living spirit of connection and empathy. Finally, it performs its own, spiritualizing acts of necromancy and mourning, crossing the boundaries between the world of the living and the dead as it grants reprieves and "saves" the lives of beloved elders and ancestors, clearing a way for their spirits to actively participate in, and penetrate through the boundaries of a closed-off world of despair, torture, and terror that is desperately in need of their guidance.

THE JAZZ STANDARD AND SPIRITUALIZATION

Similar to *Two Cities, Fanon* performs as a collection or bundle of jazz heads, a *fake book*, that deploys the spirit of improvisational performance and does the "deadly serious" work of the Igbo mourners scouring the village shouting out names, coaxing "the missing one from hiding," "defining space" and opening paths. It functions as the spirit of the music to which the writer opens himself as he imagines his "project."

> I prefer conceiving of my project [. . .] as music, finding it, playing it note by note, word by word, trying to teach myself to play and listen at the same time, as if I'm jamming with another player, listening and playing at the same time, listening for notes the other will play, listening to myself play in my mind the notes I'm guessing might sound good with what I guess I'll hear when the other's music rushes at me from the silence, listening to music nobody else hears, there and not there, inside and outside, beyond me, though the music fills me up and I'm playing before I know I'm playing, breaking silence already broken by the other's music not waiting for mine searching for mine. (140)

Fanon thus calls upon on the structures of African American music or what Amiri Baraka once called "the extension chord of blackness" within himself (Autobiography 61) as a link to a ritual of honoring and giving new life to the ancestors, the missing, the disappeared, the dead, and the foreclosed.

In *Fanon*, this music begins somewhat literally with the "haunting" of a "head." The writer figure's double, Thomas, receives what he thinks is a gruesome, severed head in the mail, perhaps channeling Wideman's own stymied reaction to receiving a similarly repugnant package: the military court martial file of the judicially murdered father of an extra-judicially murdered teenage boy—Emmett Till. The packaged head, like the Louis Till file, produces a sense of closure and despair evoking the grip on the imagination of rampaging power engaging in an inexorable cycle of lynching, torture, murder, and the breaking of brown bodies manifested by the hanging of Louis Till in 1945, the lynching of Emmett Till in 1955, and America's war on terror at the dawn of the twenty-first century. On one side, Sartre recalls, lies "despair," on the other "torture and death." This cycle of despair foreshadows the Afropessimism embraced by writer Frank Wilderson in his 2020 book, *Afropessimism* (2020). Wilderson rails against the dominant, European master narrative in which "Blacks are not Human subjects, but are instead structurally inert props, implements for the execution of White and non-Black fantasies and sadomasochistic pleasures" (15). The severed head embodies (if one can use that word for a severed appendage) this despair, which ensnares the aging writer. He announces that he has not only run out of inspiration, but may not even complete his *Fanon* project, asserting: "I won't be writing many more books, if any" (5). He refers to the stymieing head as the "central trope" (84) of the stalled fictional work, and shamefully admits that it is a borrowed metaphor stolen by an author in desperate need of inspiration from an earlier work.

The writer then returns to his young ambitions for the titular work of a 1981 collection of short stories named for the Haitian deity, Damballah, "the good serpent of the sky" (Wideman, Stories 271). He summarizes the story in which "a slave boy on a plantation in the American South rescues the severed head of a murdered fellow slave, carries the head to a river, and tosses it in. A kind of burial. A kind of grim wish for more life" (184). Although the writer of *Fanon* now dismisses the deftly fabricated ending, he performs the same work as the boy by conjuring the earlier fiction and superimposing the head of "Damballah" upon the head that Thomas receives in *Fanon*. The head thus performs as a return—as a jazz head—that enables the despairing artist to improvise upon rhythms, textures, and themes from his earlier work, perhaps as a way of assessing a certain evolution of consciousness and actively responding in the present to a shamefully timeless past that hasn't passed, but continues to structure the "present catastrophe of hate, murder, theft, and greed" (5). The writer figure(s) (as well as *Fanon*) respond to this timeless "catastrophe" as they use their own stories as jazz "standards," which give rise to a new set of improvisations around a theme that are anchored in the moment. The text performs what African Americanist Henry Louis Gates calls the "fundamentally black," (64) rite of Signifyin(g).

> Signifyin(g) turns upon repetition and difference, or repetition and reversal. There are so many examples of Signifyin(g) in jazz that one could write a formal history of its development on this basis alone [. . .] It is this principle of repetition and difference, this practice of intertextuality, which has been so crucial to the black vernacular forms of Signifyin(g), jazz—and even its antecedents, the blues, the spirituals, and ragtime. (64)

In *Epistrophies Jazz and the Literary Imagination*, Brent Edwards further names this practice as an "aesthetics of disposal" (161). He then underscores a "historiographic sensibility" that approaches the past as a *deposit,* and describes it as a "haunting"—of a "spirit" or "passion" that "informs" the methodological approaches of the black aesthetic tradition" (168). So, like the Igbo mourners, this practice and Signifyin(g) ritually excavate and repeat the original, imbuing it with life as it carves out new space for the present or for what literary theorist Walter Benjamin calls the "presence of the now [*Jetztzeit*]" (Benjamin 110). Within *Fanon*, the "head" of "Damballah" also grants a reprieve, opening a path to the past of youth for the aging, despairing writer, who engages in a conversation with (guiding and being guided by) his once lost, younger, "daring" self, "[i]toxicated by possibility, drunk on his talent" (186). So, *Fanon* doesn't just return to the head, it daringly corrects it, cracking open the stylized ending of "Damballah," which now doesn't end. It exposes to revisions the narrative placeholder of the finished and closed as a response to the problems of the now.

This collection of heads also includes a return to the "motif" of the brother in prison most extensively explored in *Brothers and Keepers*, the 1984 work that seems to have propelled the more politicized and functional energy of the longer works that followed. On the journalistic and autobiographical level, *Fanon*, provides a status report to readers. In 2008, the writer figure's brother, Robbert, is still in the penitentiary. "My brother ain't going nowhere. My flying carpet saves neither his time nor mine. I carry around the penitentiary walls everywhere I go" (49). Little seems to have changed between 1984 and 2008 except the passage of time. The writer observes: "my brother's clock ticks at its usual pace, minutes, hours, days bearing good news—more time served, therefore less time remaining to serve, and bad news—more time passed in jail" (49). They get older. Their mother, wheelchair-bound and feeble in 2008, probably won't live to see the son emerge from prison. Yet, this repetition from early works also sounds a difference. The brother's imprisonment resounds with the now of the present moment and the post-9/11 war on terror with "this prison visiting room one of the battlefields" (62) and the setting of the prison itself comprising "brutal, war-torn surroundings" (65). The brother comments on the war: "That's what this terrorism shit is all about [. . .] Stone confusion. People scared of they own damned selves" (177). The now also imposes itself as the immemorial prison visits of other works begin to take their toll on the brother. He says he "couldn't survive without" (55) them but also wants them to stop. "I made up my mind," he tells the writer figure, "to stop visits for me, for my benefit. To save me, bro" (54).

The novel even contains a repetition and pessimistic revision of the magical "Caterpillar Story" performed in *Sent for You Yesterday*, "Lizabeth: The Caterpillar Story," and *Two Cities*. In the original "head" a woman watches through a window as a gunman stalks her husband in the alley behind her home. Although she seems helpless, sitting behind the actual barrier of a glass window, she rejects the assigned role of passive observer, jabs her fist through the window and screams. The husband dashes away to safety and the gunman runs away, dropping his weapon. *Fanon* repeats the story with significant differences as the present moment encroaches on the triangular relationship between witness, perpetrator, and victim constructed by the earlier texts. The woman, unlike the figure of the much younger woman from the other texts, now admits "she's old and can't work miracles" (207). She watches as a shady, unknown shooter takes aim at a teenaged African American. This time, there is no glass for the helpless woman to shatter and only her mind struggles to emit a scream.

> go, go, go young man, go that way please, please run, run away please she begs grandson or great-niece or great-grandnephew whom the streets make strangers

for that instant when they first appear and the shape at a distance could be anyone coming or going down there in the street till the next instant a heartbeat, heart burp, or sigh away when the miracle she's watching for is something else again, not a lost one returning, not one saved, but the same old regular thing again happening. (119)

There is no miracle. There seems to be no saving black magic. Instead, like an experimental film structured around the ragged time of jump cuts—a "heart burp"—the narrative timeline skips and "the boy has moved from the corner and is lying shot to death in the vacant lot" (120). In *Two Cities,* an ex-con living in an African American community hopes "for a miracle, just like the rest of the fools around here" (166). In *Fanon,* the "fools" are replaced by the elderly and failing mother, "sitting alone, crippled in a goddamn wheelchair above those bare streets watching for miracles" (135). It's seems to be the same trap as the false hope evoked by the figure of Fanon himself, a "native doctor administering hope to the natives" (197), who cures torturers so they can go on torturing. He saves men who go on to deploy false hope as a torture technique that makes victims talk because they also desperately want to "save a life"; a life that is their own (192).

The Images of Film and Spiritualized Ancestors

Although it announces a skeptical attitude toward organized religion and the mother's devout Christianity and belief in God, *Fanon* overflows with the spirituality of traditional Igbo cosmology. It openly conveys an all but dogmatic accession to aspects of this belief system as summarized by its version of the proverb, "All stories are true," which resonates throughout Wideman's later writing. It conjures this spirit through an epigraph taken from Frantz Fanon's writing which holds that "the imaginary life cannot be isolated from the real life." *Fanon* then channels this dogma with real life acts of the imagination as it dabbles in the Black arts, dons masks, carves fetishes from words, and imaginatively uses writing to perform acts of necromancy and "spiritualization." Within the text, spirits dance as it revels in their distinct voices and performs its version of the mourning ritual staged by the Igbo age mates. It evokes this practice in the first section of Part III through one of most poignant passages of the work, which ponders the existence of God and the eternal. Indeed, the passage plays as an instrument for bridging the distance between the imagined and the real, clearing a space for the layered perspectives of the ancestral voices of the mother and Fanon, which comes alive through the narrative writing style.

> When I listen closely and listen well what I hear when the best musicians are playing together at their best is give-and-take [. . .] hearing it means something

is being made, being resolved out of nothing, out of a wish to touch [. . .] something's crossing the uncrossable space, a contradiction like the god I don't believe who's also real for me because my mother loves him with an enormous, unconditional love she mistakes for his love for her, and so it serves as such, she's sure his love's reciprocated, no, more than returned, magnified because she believes his love for her humbles her love for him, his love burning a million times brighter than her unbound adoration, his love saving her in spite of her unworthiness, she believes, another proof of his bottomless compassion, a mystery she's content to worship without understanding and her mistake about him, her belief generates an appetite for love, a flickering presence around her and an abundant radiance within her she shines on me, and who needs, who comprehends more reality than that, I wonder, though it's also a reality I do not share, only observe, ponder, enjoy, envy, a reality crossing through the silence of these thoughts I plan and listen to inside, filling in the blanks, reaching out with words. (142–43)

Here, the narrative voice of the text relinquishes control as it listens for, calls upon, and allows the structuring ancestral presences of the mother and Frantz Fanon to "fill in the blanks," cross boundaries and guide the words etched upon the page.

Fanon opens the path to these spirits as it uses writing to engage in Black American necromancy, performing stylistically improvised rites akin to the traditional Igbo process of "spiritualization." These rituals were famously introduced to the Western world by highly influential Igbo writers such as Ben Okri and Chinua Achebe (a writer that Wideman all but followed to the University of Massachusetts at Amherst and whom he repeatedly cites throughout his later work). In traditional Igbo belief, the spirit of a life—like matter itself—can neither be created nor destroyed. No being passes forever out of life. Instead, if the path is properly opened, spirits migrate between the world of the living and "the home of the dead from which all souls come into the world of man," observes theologian Elochukwu Uzukwu in his authoritative, 1982 summarization of Igbo cosmology, "Igbo World and Ultimate Reality and Meaning." For the most part, a person's "soul," Uzukwu observes "is a reincarnation of the soul of the ancestor." They are the worldly vessel of the spirit which includes his or her "personal *chi*," or "'spiritual essence of the living self'" (198) as well as that of the ancestor (*mmuo*), who could be living or dead, including: "ancestors respected by the community, venerable living elders, local spirits, one's dead comrades, and malignant spirits" (197).

Within this cosmology, the spirit of a living elder (or *agu*), such as that of Wideman's actual, ailing mother, who has a "good *chi*" manifested by the "fullness" of her long life (86 years) and copious progeny, may "return" in the soul of a newborn child (197). In *Fanon,* this return is manifested by renderings of the mother's captured voice, and, for instance, by her childhood fear of a long-gone dog that she conveys to her son: "teaching you to look out for something bad not even there anymore" (126). The *agu*'s soul possess the child like the coffee the mother drinks while pregnant, which is, she says, still with the grown man and now "inside him, wherever he's sipping his first cup of coffee this morning." *Fanon* thus performs its own amalgam of the spiritualizing mortuary rites of reclamation for an ancestor, which in the Igbo world, "act out ritually for the dead the role he played in the world of man" (206). The work even presents the dead psychiatrist's daughter engaging in a rite of remembering and thus saving the life-spirit of her father.

From the beginning, *Fanon* deploys the text as a means of rushing about a village—"ghosts in pursuit of a ghost"—"playing the deadly serious game of chasing," and calling out the name of the dead one (9) of the Igbo agemates. Their acts sculpt and define a space for a spirit. Through the written text, *Fanon* claims and carves a likeness *(okpesz)* of the psychiatrist as an ancestral figure, both saving or preserving the essence of his life and exhibiting "gratitude" for his ancestral presence. It similarly saves the life spirit of the mother, communing with her; channeling her voice, and "making up words. Exchanging words with her to teach myself whatever might remain to be said" (134). It invites her to direct the style and flow of words and thought. As a living *agu* the mother's voice animates and engages with the text while it also protects her son's spirit. Finally, the text struggles to performs a ritual that will keep upon the path to her spirit upon her eventual death, spiritualizing her as a *mmuo*, who will then assume "full responsibility" for her progeny, and remain an active force in his life and the world (Uzukwu 198).

Indeed, within *Fanon* it becomes abundantly clear that one of the lives the work sets out to "save" is that of the dying mother, who through her example, works, and enchanting style of speech is also "a life-saver like Fanon" (22). Yet, the actual mother of the actual author of *Fanon* (of John Edgar Wideman) dies the same month that Houghton Mifflin announces the publication of the actual book. According to an obituary saved online by the Pittsburgh Post-Gazette, Bette A. Wideman, died: "Quietly on February 7, 2008. Loving mother of John Wideman, Otis Eugene Wideman, Letitia Charity El, David L. Wideman and Robert D. Wideman. Also survived by 13 grandchildren and 11 great grandchildren" (*Pittsburgh Post-Gazette*). The Pittsburgh newspaper thus performs its own rites of giving notice and inserting the mother and grandmother into the official record of what American newspapermen have famously termed, the "first rough draft of history" (Shafer); pasting her into a column of its own magician's collage; ensconcing her life within its "fictive" ordering of time and space or what political scientist Benedict Anderson summarizes as "the steady onward clocking of homogeneous, empty time" of a narrative that models the dominant imagination. Within that time, observes

Anderson, "'the world' ambles sturdily ahead" (33). Thus, the obituary notice dates and puts a definitive end to her life, leaving her behind in the wake of dominant notions of history through a clipping that can be filed away, along with all the other "dead" clipping in the newspaper library (infamously referred to as the "morgue") of yesterday's news.

Fanon, however, rejects and troubles this representation of hegemonic time, "history," and finalized death as captured within the fictive collage of the *Pittsburgh Post-Gazette,* which dubs itself "One of America's Great Newspapers." Completed before the mother's passing—before the obituary is written—*Fanon* uses the prospect of this future death notice to engage in the black art of necromancy through the type of Neo-Hodoo aesthetic performed by politically engaged Black writers that African American author Ishmael Reed describes in a 1971 interview. "Necromancers" he asserts, "used to lie in the guts of the dead [. . .] The black writer lies in the guts of old America" (Obrien 16). For these writers, the words of dated newspapers serve as the guts of the dead. In the case of *Fanon,* strips of film celluloid also preserve the deceased's body. At one point, *Fanon* conveys this concept as it imagines Frantz Fanon ruminating over film images, tying them to African or Igbo cosmology through the words "as the Igbo insist" (194). Fanon then disparages film as a paltry "trick" (194), a "technique for recording" (195), and a mechanical or "practical means of harvesting and preserving dead images" (194) that nevertheless implicitly engage in a Europeanized version of the black arts. He calls a pair of early French filmmakers "pioneers and wizards and necrophiles" (195) who "discovered how to catch, cook, fast-freeze the dead images [. . .] preserving this stuff on strips of celluloid they shined light through" (196).

Fanon activates its necromancy by presenting the imbedded "Fanon manuscript" as a film script that Thomas plans to (but never does) deliver to the infamous French experimental filmmaker, Jean Luc Godard. Thomas, along with the text, obsesses over "distinctions between literary and cinematic representations of reality" (79) and thinks of Godard as "a director as betrayed by images as I find myself betrayed by writing" (80). Conscious writers and filmmakers, Thomas observes, work "on the same thing. A global commerce in images usurping, colonizing, lobotomizing, digitizing, roboticizing thought [. . .] images are slaves, prisoners [. . .] Images serving power, speaking the mater's language, saying and doing what the master orders" (80). In the wake of 911, these same images give rise to a perverse, imagination-ordering American pastime: the endless consumption of what some media critics call "torture porn" (Edelstein). These filmed and televised fictions cast the torturer in the role of the rescuing hero while fueling a collective desire for hackneyed poetic justice and a sensation of orgasmic release through the penetration of bodies. They perversely organized the imaginations of the public and of public officials during the early 2000s. During this era, fictional figures seemed to step out from films screens and television sets—alchemized into actual people who murder and torture with an impunity granted by power-serving images. Bound within a popular recurrent fantasy of television and film (one being the ticking time bomb scenario), these images became the actual, needed proof that breaking brown bodies helps work against the immemorial clock of fictionalized time, leads to information that saves lives, and assists in the fight against the inexorably ticking bombs known of or put into motion by their suffering victims. "The ticking bomb scenario is the standard justification used by all apologists for torture," argues Hilary Neroni in her book, *The Subject of Torture: Psychoanalysis and Biopolitics in Television and Film* (98). Meanwhile, says media scholar Michael Kerner in *Horror, Exploitation, and the Cinema of Sensation Book*, these fictions and their images unmask "the American sadistic disposition that not only made the War on Terror possible but also desired it" (205).

As a written text, *Fanon* struggles to disarm the power of these Hollywood images that sate and produce sadistic desires. At one point, in a mindstyle conversation between the author figure and Thomas, the text mocks its own lack of Hollywood cachet, or of a financially viable, satisfying and "intricate" plot of "terrorists, torture, [and] sizzling sex" (14). It defiantly disavows having a simplistic "story with an arc and ending. Fanon's story, the one Thomas can't write" (20). *Fanon* pitches its patchwork form against such narratives. This includes correspondence, such as the on-sided conversations the author figure and Thomas launch with Godard on aesthetics and which evoke a similar practice in *Two Cities*. Indeed, *Fanon* extends this practice by not only including imbedded letters, but fragments of the unfinished script which contains conversations between a character with the initials JEW (John Edgar Wideman) and another with the initials JLG (John Luc Godard). "Bet you get off on images the way I groove on words" JEW says to JLG, while they take lunch together in the "setting" of a rundown Homewood diner (109).

Like Percival Everett's 2007 novel, *The Water Cure*, *Fanon* treats any conventional, Hollywood-style attempt to represent torture as a trap that either devolves into a banal rhetoric of conscience-soothing pathos or transforms into a quasi-pornographic vehicle for reinforcing the sadistic appetite for torture by titillating readers with doggedly salacious torture "numbers" featuring images of penetrated and mutilated bodies (Kerner 5–6). In contrast, *Fanon* ensnares readers in present acts of "re-membering" or compelling them to piece together within their imaginations the horror witnessed by Frantz Fanon, who confronted and wrote about torture and the trap of the banal evils constraining a world engaged in "total war" (190) in his book, *The Wretched of the Earth*. Within this work (a likeness of which is pasted into the patchwork of *Fanon*) a torturer seeks out Frantz Fanon to cure him of the mental trauma of regularly spending 10 hours brutally pounding captives with fists turned to pulp so it won't affect the his loving relationship with his family and so he can keep his job and calmly go back to torturing "without any prickings of conscience, without any behavior problems, and with complete equanimity" (Fanon, Philcox, Wretched 268–69). Meanwhile, *Fanon*, explores the issue of torture through a collage of layers. For instance, it captures a fantastic scene of the wheelchair-bound mother of the writer anachronistically wandering the halls of a Bethesda hospital in search of Frantz Fanon, the ailing former therapist-to-torturers. He suffers from cancer and comes to the United States, hoping for a cure. The mother reflects that he must be a "troublemaker big-time" (213) because he is under guard. "You'd think they got Ben Laden himself with those sad pretty eyes up on" the institution's third floor, she anachronistically muses (212). Meanwhile, she places herself in the role of a victim of torture being interrogated for her curiosity about Fanon and swears: "she wouldn't confess anything to them, or yes, forgive me lord if they torture her, she'll tell them, hand on the Bible every barefaced lie she can dream up (202). This is as far as *Fanon* overtly gets to representing the slavish images that normalized torture in the post-9/11 era. Instead, when tackling torture, *Fanon*, works like the later films of Godard, where, according to one critic, the "real story is precisely how to tell the story, or whether if is in fact possible to do so" (Brody).

Fanon thus joins purpose with the later films of Godard, which work to disarm and reverse the spell of caustic Hollywood images; perform necromancy; spiritualize; and open the path for the ancestral dead. For instance, in a film from the 1980s, Godard, disguised as an aging, withdrawn professor resurrects life as he revels in the type of film miracle that once spellbound and transformed the imaginations of late-nineteenth-century and early-twentieth-century spectators who witnessed on screen something they had never seen before or imagined possible. On "Easter Sunday," says film critic Richard Brody, the professor achieves the "ultimate creation" by "reattaching the petals of dead flowers through the miracle of reverse photography" (Brody). Godard works similar magic in a film made ten years after *Fanon*, called, *The Image Book* (2018). In this film, says critic J. Hoberman, more "than once, a frozen still comes to life" (Hoberman). Then, as if describing the overall effect of *Fanon,* Hoberman summarizes the impact of *The Image Book* on the imagination. "How to take the spectacle of all these souls trapped by the camera, preserved on video? [. . .] As close to music as Godard has ever gotten, this is less the book than the conflagration of images" (Hoberman).

Within *Fanon,* the "Fanon manuscript" performs the same musical black magic through the figure of the mother and its repetition and revision of the "Caterpillar Story." The script captures her looking out from a balcony, inverting the traditional cinematic gaze. At first, the mother's gaze works to channel the frustrations of the writer figure and perhaps of John Edgar Wideman who struggle with the false hope and confining structures of Western epistemology and its dependence on signs and symbolic representation. The very "act of representing," says Hoberman, paraphrasing Jean Luc Godard, "necessarily involves violence against the represented" (Hoberman). Indeed, at one point in the script, the JEW figure questions the wisdom of subjecting his mother's stories to cinematic treatment, telling JLG:

> I don't need you to remind me that getting my mother's stories on film next to impossible, Mr. G. I share your pessimism about the limit of cinema about the lost cause of any made-up shit supposed to be representing real shit and I know my mother's old, her stories old stories and who gives a flying fuck these days about old folk's rambling stories. (128)

Indeed, the conventionally rendered, cinematic gaze inexorably projects a primal and patriarchal terror inherent to the threat posed by rupture and brutal excision—by the original cleaving away of the represented from its image (of the signified from the signifier) or of the spoken word from its written imprint. It manifests the "stare that freezes and kills" (Two Cities 118) and captures the original anxiety of writers who represent the living world through the written word, which itself seems lifeless, frozen, and dead. In her landmark, 1988 essay "Visual Pleasure and Narrative Cinema," feminist film theorist Laura Mulvey uses the language of the Medusa story to describe the way "mainstream film coded the erotic into the language of the dominant patriarchal order" (59) producing a "voyeuristic or fetishistic mechanism to circumvent" the anxiety induced by the primal violence of representation (67). "The fact of fetishization," she argues, "freezes the look, fixates the spectator" (68).

Within mainstream film, spectators stare at heroes, who gaze at a figure whose represented body inexorably arouses that original anxiety. The gaze then works to contain the threat as it eroticizes, fetishizes, and objectifies the body, translating primal anxiety into a densely coded source of erotic, cinematic pleasure. It works like the head of Medusa, which encapsulates the betrayal of writing summarized in *Two Cities*, where the hero of the myth: "Chopped off her head and carried it around to freeze his enemies" (118). In the case of the fixating cinematic gaze, says Mulvey: "Erotic involvement with the look is disorientating: the spectator's fascination is turned against him as the narrative carries him through and entwines him with the process that he is himself exercising" (66). The very structure of such representation constitutes a trap or in the words of the gazing mother, "the same old regular thing again happening" (119). Inevitably, the torture victim's body transforms into an object of erotic desire, a plot device that displaces the woman's body of traditional cinema. All get caught up in the same fixation.

Yet, the gaze of the aging, impotent, wheelchair-bound, and "nosey" mother defies these Hollywood codes. Within *Fanon*, the woman, "*approximately eighty years old*" both gazes at and is gazed upon. The script imbedded in the work provides italicized director's cues for representing her face, which should appear as "*monstrously oversized, a wasteland of skin*" (120). The cues offer an example from a Godard film as a model: "The *closeups of elderly faces in* In Praise of Love *could serve as a guide here*" (120). The mother's face and her gaze intend to unsettle—"the viewer doesn't feel comfortable" (120) —rather than arouse desire or project comfort. Her wheelchair and position seem to lock her down in the cycle of impotence, death and despair described by Sartre as she gazes upon yet another of the endlessly repeating scenes of death and destruction.

Yet, this saving or capturing of her gaze doesn't serve to represent and produce the cycle of violence engendered by a closed symbolic system or by the dead images of Hollywood. It does not fetishize, eroticize, objectify, or project and mobilize violent desires. Instead, it is the melding, layering, gaze of an elderly woman whose life experiences place her outside of cinematic time. *Fanon* lavishes this gaze with descriptions of the mother's time-defying, storytelling technique, which the Wideman figure conflates with the collages of Romare Bearden and the stylized writing of Fanon.

> Romare Bearden's collages remind me of how my mother, another one of my idols—a life-saver like Fanon—talks. Her stories flatten and fatten perspective. She crams everything, everyone, everywhere into the present, into words that flow, intimate and immediate as the images of a Bearden painting. (22)

Her stories and her gaze flatten and fatten time. Rather than freeze their object, she directs her look and mind toward the victim, begging him to "please run, run away" (119). Rather than objectify, she empathetically engages the victimized stranger as a fellow human being and a beloved relative: "grandson or great-niece or great-grandnephew [. . .] anyone coming or going down there in the street" (119). Such a gaze releases people—opening a way—rather than fixing or fixating them. *Fanon* weaves the magic of this old woman's gaze and its layering of time into the patchwork fabric of a text that channels her very spirit and is equally crafted like her speech to "flow, intimate and immediate" (22).

Such a gaze helps break the spell as it departs from the traditional Hollywood chronotope (its edited and narrative production of time and space), and deals blows against, what Mulvey calls "the monolithic accumulation of traditional film conventions." For Mulvey such blows involve similar, meta-cinematic or meta-fictional gestures that unmask "the camera" as a "mechanism for producing an illusion of Renaissance space, flowing movements compatible with the human eye, an ideology of representation [that creates] a convincing world in which the spectator's surrogate can perform with verisimilitude" (68). She then invokes work "already undertaken by radical film-makers" (68) such as Godard, who use cinematic techniques that don't produce a "thrill" that comes from voyeurism and quasi pornographic representations but which emanates from "transcending outworn or oppressive forms, or daring to break with normal pleasurable expectations in order to conceive a new language of desire" (59).

The imbedded script hones a similar "new language" and works like a Romare Bearden collage as it defiantly rejects the "Renaissance space" described by Mulvey, or what Thomas and his painter friend Charley deride as "the illusion of space receding" (21). It works to capture or "save" the time-fattening and time-flattening voice of the mother figure. Rather than merely describing this "speech," it allows the voice to seize control over the text. She not only speaks, but her style of talk—the spirit of her thinking—lavishly contaminates the voice of narration and melds with that of the writer characters, JEW, and the author of *Fanon*. This style, states the introduction to Part II of *Fanon*, involves not just "stepping back, standing apart, analyzing, and instructing others." Instead, like the stylized writing of Frantz Fanon, it closely identities with and plunges "into the vexing, mysterious otherness of them" (99). The narrative voice asserts: "I think that's what my mother understands about Frantz Fanon, what she shares with him, something like that anyway expressed in her own words, in the actions of her life" (99).

A section of a script (the "Fanon manuscript") then begins with the words: "Dissolve to" (115). Once again, this script presents cues for directing the scene depicting the murder of a teenager as witnessed by the mother in her wheelchair and subjects it to the time flattening style of the mother's voice, which equally possesses the narrative voice (if it can be called that since the text here occurs as unmediated, mock action cues for a film director). This voice thus masquerades as the objective voice of what linguist Emile Benveniste calls *histoire* or "history" (Benveniste 241) as it first presents, "a young man of African descent standing on a corner." Yet, this fictional, historic voice, like that of the mother of Wideman, of Fanon, and of the author figure(s) of the text, flattens and fattens perspective. It defies the ticking clock, resisting both the renderings of hegemonic time and the "Renaissance space" of the dominant culture. The voice melds with the mind of the mother who looks down from her vantage point on the standing boy, with the cues: "We watch him like my mother watches" (118). The streets below become thick with the time of her long experience. Vacant buildings become once vibrant "department" and "chain stores"; people "disappeared from these streets" walk again (115). For an instant, she muses, the people below "could be a grandchild, a grandniece, a great-grandnephew, could be herself" (118). She could effortlessly "tell you about the shenanigans going on outside and inside" a bar below and within the standing boy's mind "and probably get much of it right" (118). At one point, the mother—"my mother" —contemplates the sky and airplanes as she "tries to think of the doomed boy elsewhere, on a plane headed to a place where he is not dead so soon." Then, through the infinite, connecting, flattening digressions that mark her speech and represented thought, she "wonders who decides who rides [airplanes] and who decided that her old frail body, locked down in a wheelchair, will outlast the boy's" (118). Through its inversive gaze, melding points of view, use of vernacular speech, play with ambiguous possessive pronouns (among other devices that conflate the real and the imagined, characters and people, this world and that one), the imbedded script works like the films of Godard which metafictionally unmask the conventionally invisible camera. Through its slippages and confounding deictic markers it cavalierly connects the actual, historic author, his mother, and Frantz Fanon to a slew of made-up or fictionalized doubles. The words of the text thus scopically perform like the unmasked camera, once again asking the question posed by an Aretha Franklin song and taken up as a meta-refrain of *Philadelphia Fire*: "Who's zooming who?" (Fire 76).

Indeed, inspirited by the work of Godard and Frantz Fanon, Wideman uses all of the stylistic tricks of the trade (which he learned from more than fifty years of writing fiction) to render the mother's voice. It overflows with the conventions he developed for representing the musicality and deep meanings of an African American orality that resist the devaluing frame of standard written English. At one point, for instance, a single paragraph with few standardized grammatical markers flows over the narrative for as many as nine pages (120–28) as the stylistically rendered voice of the mother—of African American Vernacular English—controls the text. To render this voice, the text uses its own stylistic techniques, and some of those garnered from reading Fanon's *The Wretched of the Earth*. Indeed, *Fanon* performs as a collage, pastiche, and vessel of Frantz Fanon's distinctive writing style. It thus provides a reading of *The Wretched of the Earth* as a text overflowing with stylistic flourishes—"shifts, substitutions, translations, denials" (193)— that uses the literary artifice of a brilliant creative writer to craft a politically urgent, documentary work. It conjures this style as it imagines the psychiatrist first orally dictating the book. The scene recalls *The Cattle Killing*, where the blind women dictates her novel to her enslaved woman, Kate, staging both an inversion of the amanuensis theme of the slave narrative and of the capturing of the Black voice by the WPA Slave Narrative Collection that Wideman analyzed in academic articles such as "Charles Chesnutt and the

WPA Narratives: The Oral and Literate Roots of Afro-American Literature" and "Defining the Black Voice in Fiction." In both essays, Black speakers struggle to elude the stranglehold of standard written English and "free themselves from a frame which a priori devalues black speech" (Wideman, Defining 79).

Fanon imagines Frantz Fanon as engaged in a similar struggle. The text characterizes his dictated speech as violent, tactile, and urgent, like Liam's impressionistic brush strokes on the canvas in *Two Cities.* Fanon speaks to a typist "sawing, chiseling, drilling, driving nails" on her machine, producing a "cage erected bar by bar for his words" (188). This violence of written capture evokes Walter Ong's description of this vocabulary of death in his book, *Interfaces of the Word.* He observes:

> the concepts and vocabulary connected with writing often associate the activity itself with activities which are, or can be, lethal, such as cutting and dismembering. The word can be "incised" or cut into a surface (such as marble); the "stylus" means originally a stake, a spearlike instrument; "scribe" connects with the Proto-Indo-European root *skeri*, to cut, separate, the same root that gives us not only "inscribe" (cut into, like "incise") but also "crime," "critic," "crisis," and "hypocrite." The association of writing with death is not total, but it is manifold and inescapable. (Ong, *Interfaces* 240)

Fanon, however, toils to free himself from this "manifold and inescapable" prospect and the inexorably devaluing frame of writing while making the same types of stylistic choices as Wideman, the actual author of the text.

> In this book I want readers to hear precisely the language with which a patient describes his or her situation. Perhaps you could insert an extra space to separate blocks of text when one voice gives way to another [. . .] I don't want to fall into the trap of treating my patients as the *beke* treat me. The proper presentation of these cases is immensely complicated. Perhaps hopelessly compromised by any form of writing [. . .] I also find myself splicing into my account their exact words or words not exactly theirs not mine either, words I try to imagine the patient might employ in a particular situation. An odd, second hand alienated structure's being formed [. . .] A process that controls me as much as I control it. A sort of bricolage of free-floating fragments whose authorship is unsettlingly ambiguous. (191)

Indeed, such fanciful "bricolage," Fanon thinks in another passage, is "as good as it gets, as close as an author gets to character, subject to object, fiction to truth, black to white, representation to reality, as close as many truths get to one truth" (192).

Clearing the Path for Ancestral Spirits

In *Fanon*, words as representations take on the quality of masks, charms, or fetishes. They are spiritualizing "likenesses," an idea repeated by Fanon imaginatively caught in the act of reciting the words of Baudelaire when he repeats to himself: "My brother, my likeness" (220), or when he reads the chart of a patient, and considers for a "millisecond [. . .] how you might feel if you were him" (199). Indeed, the work imagines him mentally offering a gloss on the immemorial Igbo proverb of the text, declaring: "Masks are true" (220). In this light, words wield the power of masks and charms. At birth, the Igbo who embrace traditional religion craft a spirt-saving likeness, *nkpulu chi*, and safeguard it in specialized vessels. At death, they break this charm and produce other likeness that are "carved out by one's progeny" and buried with the body or preserved in the family shrine (Uzukwu 204). Then, at the funeral ceremony, likenesses in the form of spirit-saving masks return to visit grieving family members. Within Fanon, writing performs these functions, as it crosses "the uncrossable space" (Fanon 142) bridging the world of the living with those of the dead through Black American-style acts of necromancy and ritualistic spiritualization.

The text thus captures the undying, indestructible, and "uninventable" (Wideman, *Fanon*164) life force and structuring imaginations of the mother, of Fanon, of a younger brother speaking from the other world of the prison, and of an increasingly distant, ailing community. It opens a path between worlds. The work again expresses this cosmology through the imagined ruminations of Frantz Fanon over the innovations of early French filmmakers in Part III as he tackles the writing of *The Wretched of the Earth*.

> we live in at least two kingdoms, a known and unknown, a visible kingdom and a kingdom we cannot see [. . .] among those kingdoms always traffic [. . .] then the unpredictable returns of people and things so stunningly reconstituted, as the Igbo insist, we're sometimes halted in our tracks and wonder how we'd believed the things or people had departed forever. (194)

The imbedded manuscript channels this belief.

Indeed, through it, one of the departed or disappeared comes to life through the sentence: "I wonder if my nephew Omar, alive again in my thought about the boy on the corner" (116). These ruminations work to save and reclaim Omar's living spirit. Like Godard's "miracle of reverse photography," (Brody) where the filmmaker reverses the process of death as "more than once, a frozen still comes to life" (Hoberman), these ruminations weave a spell of words imbued with Igbo cosmology. The narrative voice of *Fanon* incants: "To be in someone's thoughts or stories keeps the dead alive, the Igbo say [. . .] so if we hold another in our imagination even if we think of them as dead, do we grant them a chance, however slim, a chance, something like a reprieve" (116). Yet, the Wideman figure and Wideman himself, as Omar's actual "elder by three decades" (116), fear they may have lapsed in their protective role as an ancestral *agu*, because (as stated in the dedication of *Two Cities*) he and others "didn't try hard enough," and thus failed to "save" the young man from being gunned down one day in his Pittsburgh home. Yet *Fanon* extracts Omar's life spirit, remembers him, and grants him "a reprieve" removing him from being a variable "in an invariant formula" (50), from the finitude of obituaries, newspaper chronotopes, and the dogmatic "countdowns" produced by the Western imagining of "homogenous empty time." Indeed, *Fanon*, overflows with the time of a commerce of spirits, not only saving Omar, but the figures of the writer himself, of Wideman's beloved mother, and of Frantz Fanon as it spiritualizes them, carving out a space for them and dispensing reprieves that bridge the boundary between the "the imaginary life" and the "real life." It deploys the power of fiction to explore the deep time of traditional Igbo cosmology and present an afterlife where, for instance, the aging, wheelchair-bound mother of around 2008 comforts the dying Frantz Fanon of 1961 in a Bethesda, Maryland hospital while she sits with him, flicking through the channels of a TV, and watches news reports of the Indian Ocean tsunami of 2004. And though they don't speak each other's language—separated in life by the earthly Tower of Babble—they now understand one another.

Jean Paul Sartre reads *The Wretched of the Earth* as a work delimiting a dialectical cycle between despair, death, and torture with no way out. The Wideman figure of *Fanon* reads the work of the Martinican psychiatrist differently. At one point, he defends writing about Fanon and says to his brother in prison: "no way out of this goddam mess [. . .] and Fanon found it" (95). *Fanon* explores the "no way out," or "way out" through cries and tears that do not despair, but ritualistically reject the "complete obliteration of the memory of the family" (Uzukwu 205). It opens the path to the ancestral spirits assuring their active, protective, and saving participation in this world. It channels the possibility of a still hoped-for miracle in an insistently timeless world of false hopes and repeating dead-end cycles, or in the words of the wheelchair-bound mother: "the same old regular thing again happening" (119).

Chapter 6

Writing to Save a Life and the Art of Hagiography as Possessed Text (*Texto Montado*)

Toward the end of John Edgar Wideman's *Writing to Save a Life: The Louis Till File* (2016), the narrator remembers once receiving an unassuming talisman of Catholicism and Caribbean Santeria from a memember of the Chicago Black Panther Party.

> In France beside his dishonored grave I had not spoken to Louis Till about Clement, about my father or mother, nor Latreesha, nor Promiseland. Nor about the statuette of Saint Martin de Porres, patron saint of the poor, the humble, of lost causes according to the elderly woman who took a shine to me and gave me a small wooden figurine as a farewell present in Chicago fifty-some years ago. Thomasina Hawks was her name, Tomahawk her street name, a fierce veteran of Chicago's deadly war on Black Panthers in the sixties. She was as full of stories as *Clement* was full of clamoring silences. Tommie gave me a talisman to keep me safe during my life's journey, she said [. . .] [L]eafing through an account of Pizarro's conquest of the Inca empire in Peru, I came across Figure 10, a photo of a contemporary votive card sold in front of Lima churches. *San Martin in the hospital infirmary with his trademark broom and one of his many miracles.*
>   Saint Martin de Porres, the book would inform me, renowned for piety, modesty, the all-forgiving leniency, mercy of his gaze, had spent most of his life as a lay brother, a nurse and domestic servant inside a Dominican monastery in Lima. He grew up in the turbulent sixteenth century, a period during which the Catholic Church was busy importing African slaves, slaughtering, converting, pacifying, enslaving Indians and *mestizos*, mixed people of color, like the Tills, me. Like Martin de Porres, illegitimate son of a Spanish knight and a Panamanian slave [. . .] Same saint. My pale, lost wooden statuette and the colored San Martin pictured on the card in the book, broom in hand, his face a dark disk framed by a halo and at his feet the humble miracle of mouse, dog, cat,

eating from one dish [. . .]. [H]e wears a flowing black cassock, gold cross on a chain draped from neck to knees. A white dove hovers at Saint Martin's right, and on his left, the sick with tiny crosses above their beds lie in an infirmary behind him [. . .]. I learned the father of Martin de Porres had apprenticed him to the trade of cutting hair and bloodletting and one of the boy's regular chores was to sweep the barbershop floor. (189–91)

Writing to Save a Life is a text of mysteries—*misterios* in the Spanish of Cuba and the Dominican Republic or *mystères* and *mistès* in the French and Kreyòl of Haiti. It works like a small statuette, or a laminated prayer card of the type found in spiritual supply, occult, and *botánica* stores which regularly stock the "iconic" image of Saint Martin de Porres described toward the end of the work. In addition to laminate images, these shops sell other magical, functional things including herbs, candles, beads, "statues, prayer cards, rosaries, [and] medals" (Padilioni 104); the type of items that the enslaved insurgents of the Haitian Revolution, the freedom-fighting maroons of the Caribbean and Brazil, and the rebel army of Fidel Castro—'El Caballo'—used, wore and carried on their bodies for protection. These items are not mere representations or symbols, but working amulets and charms—often inscribed with writing in English, French, Spanish, Kreyòl, Portuguese, and even Arabic—that quilt together powerful belief systems of West Africa and the *mysteries* of the early Christian church through the notion that *real* (as opposed to represented) spiritual *presence* can infuse, transform, and transubstantiate matter.

Writing to Save a Life through its collection of mysteries works as a Black Atlantic *Lives of the Saints* that conjures the transformative power of writing and its inseverable connection to the *saint-cultus* (saint cults), religious relics, icons, and hagiography of the early Christian Church. Much like these original sacred stories, *Writing to Save a Life* challenges the readers thirst for clear facts and record-straightening historiography. Indeed, it reveals that the desire for such finished, closed, comforting, and dogmatically fictionalized records fetishized by the dominant culture are the problem. Like the millennial work of Wideman, many original hagiographies had the "overall effect [of] a patchwork quilt" argues medievalist Julia M. H. Smith, in her article "Oral and Written: Saints, Miracles, and Relics in Brittany" (318). She adds that some experts even "condemned [them] as a worthless historical source because so much of the life is a pastiche" (333) and were written hundreds of years after the death of the actual person. Initially, the hagiographies, like much of African American literature, were intimately connected to oral performance, which once included speech acts, incantatory performatives, exorcisms, prayers, venerations, and functional pedagogical activities such as sermons. For many of the faithful, the written words of hagiographies did not reproduce the Medusa-effect of freezing or killing life often invoked by Wideman, but worked as vessels, capturing, saving, and deploying a living spirit. They replaced and often supplemented the miracle-working saintly body part or religious relic "a physical object which encapsulated both the past event and the present power" (339). In fact, argues medieval theologian, Rachel J. D. Smith, the hagiography of a thirteenth-century Dutch mystic teaches that the "proper reading of the hagiography will allow access to the body of the saint" (154). It affirms the "interchangeability between text and saintly body. . . . Text becomes body, body text" (155). Like the laminated prayer card or statuette, *Writing to Save a Life* invokes this protective power as it performs like the religious icon, which does not only "represent" a figure, but safeguards a living spirit. In Byzantine cosmology, asserts art historian Bissera V. Pentcheva, the "icon was perceived as matter imbued with *charis* (Χάρις)), or divine grace. As matter, this object was meant to be physically experienced" (Pentcheva 631).

Furthermore, as with many hagiographies, the saints of *Writing to Save a Life,* are not all good people. In hagiographies, many of the saints are imperfect, vengeful, and "vindictive" (Julia Smith 340), though they were also magical, mystical, and after death worked miracles of protection and often exacted "divine justice" (340) when properly venerated. Indeed, the saints or mysteries captured by *Writing to Save a Life* are both like the gentle, broom sweeping Saint Martin de Porres and like the man whom the text sometimes uses his geographic birth place to call "Saint Louis Till" (153), who evokes the "bad Negroes" elaborated by Richard Wright's explanation of his novel, *Native Son.* These were "the only Negroes I know of," he says, "who consistently violated the Jim Crow laws of the South and got away with it [and] were shot, hanged, maimed, lynched, and generally hounded until they were either dead or their spirits broken" (Wright 437). They are the haunting and haunted writer figure of the work; his ancestors; his mother; Emmet Till and his father, Louis Till; a disabled barbershop broom sweeper; and the battling, battering male figures from the narrator's childhood community and of his family, who define themselves through a toxic masculinity that places them out on the street, doing their "dirt" (169), which then lands them in trouble, in prison, dead in a river, or at the end of a hangman's noose. *Writing to Save a Life* does not excuse or vindicate these figures. Thus, as an exploration or capturing of the "Louis Till File," the text does not present a simple moral vindication of the life and death of Louis Till, a chronologically coherent history, or an unambiguous explanation of events. An American soldier during World War II, Till was executed by the U.S. military for the murder of an Italian woman and the rape of two others in Civitavecchia, Italy in 1945. "No doubt about it, "the narrator of *Writing to Save a Life* cryptically observes, allowing his observations to semiotically flow in multiple directions over the text, "Some brutal, ugly shit went down in Civitavecchia" (103). Instead, the text performs as an icon, hagiography, Black Atlantic talisman, and literary charm that abstracts, preserves, and safeguards living spirits of figures such as Till. In Black Atlantic cosmology, says one theologian, these spirits "are collectively called *misterios* (from Haitian Kreyòl *mistè*); *santos*, and the variants *sanes/sanses* ('saints'); or *luá* ('spirit', from Haitian Kreyòl *lwa*)" (Padilioni 95).

WRITING TO SAVE A LIFE

Writing to Save a Life through the stories of Till and its collection of saints—the memories of dead and dying relatives and of a dead and dying community—confronts the urgent issues of the second decade of twenty-first century America: the fetishistic structures of institutionalized racism; the inner-workings of toxic masculinity and violence against women; and the progressive agenda of reclamation and restorative justice invoked by the Black Lives Matter movement and its calls to defund the police and end extrajudicial executions, unjust courts, and a societal ethic of violent retribution. The work, therefore, engages many of the themes of Wideman's other work involving the relationship between Black American fathers and sons, innocence and guilt, truth and fiction, history and myth, art and propaganda, silence and sound, absence and presence, and existence and non-existence.

On the final page of the book, Wideman (as author) describes the text as "an amalgam of research, memoir, and imagination." As such, its eclectic aesthetic form extends and performs the ongoing conversations Wideman has held with artists in other media, such as the American photographer, Edward Muybridge in *Reuben* (1987); anatomical illustrator George Stubbs, in *The Cattle Killing* (1996); the Swiss sculptor Alberto Giacometti, painter Romare Bearden, and jazz pianist Thelonious Monk in *Two Cities* (1998); and filmmaker Jean-Luc Godard in *Fanon* (2008). Ultimately, through its investigation, of "The Louis Till File," the work responds with its own fictionalized bundle to the aesthetic organization of power that depends upon an endlessly repeating American narrative of White over Black. Like Wideman's other millennial works, this involves a "patchwork" or collage form embedded with newspaper stories, fictionalized correspondence, citations from official documents, and personal memories that is grounded in African American literary tradition and the functional black arts of what one theologian refers to as the "the folk hagiographic and iconographic conventions" (89) of various forms of Black Atlantic cosmology.

Although published in 2016, the work struggles to breathe life into the deeply disturbing story of the 1945 court martial and hanging of the father of

Emmett Till for war crimes allegedly committed toward the end of World War II. Yet, the work also seems to function as the most deeply intimate memoire that Wideman has attempted. It is a first-person story of a narrator who almost shares Wideman's age. Yet, there are some minute differences. For instance, the narrator of the novel is born on June 10 (71), while Wideman is born on June 14, 1941. Indeed, it never lends the name John or John Wideman to the narrative voice. This narrative seems cut off from that particular historic mooring, which often invades his other work. Yet, the writer figure does seem to extract life from the same (or a very similar) family as that of Wideman. Some family members have the same names. Both the narrator and Wideman have grandfathers named John French and Hannibal and a great-grandfather named Tatum. Other family members have different names but a similar biography, such as the narrator's "youngest brother Rakhim," who like Wideman's youngest brother, Robert, is still serving a life sentence in prison for murder in 2016. And like Wideman, the first-person narrator says he works "for an incarcerated son and brother. They are locked inside me, I am imprisoned with them during every moment that I struggle with the Till file" (164). Both have three brothers and a sister. Both grew up in the same community. Indeed, they have the same memory of once riding the shoulders of their mother's father, John French, as the pair wended its way "through the streets of our colored community Homewood in Pittsburgh, Pennsylvania" (3). They also have fathers from a village near Greenwood, South Carolina. The narrator's father is from Promiseland (142), while Wideman's actual father is from Promised Land. Finally, both are married to a French woman from Brittany, France. She has a brother, Antoine, who like the figure of Antoine in the text makes glass art objects with a mystical iconic power that the narrator admires.

In some ways, *Writing to Save a Life* is similar to *Fanon*, where the writer figures of that text use the life and work of Frantz Fanon as a jazz head or a starting point for improvisation and personal reflection as they reject engaging in conventional biography, or what has come to be formally known as hagiography. Yet, *Writing to Save a Life* is, in many ways, a more structurally stable text, mostly arising from the first-person observations of a single narrator who, this time, indulges the imagined reader, telegraphing his metafictional strategies and openly describing the intricacies of his craft.

> As a writer searching for Louis Till, I choose to assume certain prerogatives—license might be a more accurate word. I assume the risk of allowing my fiction to enter other people's true stories. And to be fair, I let other people's stories trespass the truth of mine. (34)

The work thus presents the structuring consciousness of this narrator as an aging, roving writer, investigating the life and execution of Louis Till, the father of Emmett Till, the 15-year old boy lynched in Mississippi, whose brutal death helped ignite the Civil Rights Movement. During the trial of the boy's murderers, the public first assumed that his father died a War hero. The details of his death had remained a classified secret. Initially, the U.S. government even considered pressing further charges against the boy's two brazen murders, who had been exonerated by an all-White jury. Then, according to the narrator, a "redneck senator" pressured the military to declassify and leak the father's ignominious court-martial file to the newspapers (97). Suddenly, the federal government reversed course, all but exonerating the murderers. The narrator bitterly observes: "two weeks before a Mississippi grand jury was scheduled to convene [. . .] Louis Till, was conjured like an evil black rabbit from an evil white hat" (11). In this way, the court martial and hanging of the father were used to deny justice to the son. Within the text, the narrator originally pursues his investigations while conducting research for a stalled and eventually aborted work about Emmett Till. He requests and receives the once "conjured" file. He visits Louis Till's unmarked grave in France; takes trips to Italy where the military hanged Till; drives to the American South on various abandoned, truth-finding missions; and solitarily pours over the file through a storm of his own resurgent memories.

Meanwhile, he also revisits many of the stories and urgent themes of Wideman's earlier work, communing with and sometimes overwhelmed by family ghosts and those from works once firmly rooted in the Homewood community. Now, the narrator lives a Mandarin life, shuttling between the United States and France with time and space removing him from his once more fixed communal moorings in Pittsburgh and Philadelphia. He hauls around his memories and scraps from earlier texts like ghostly fragments that block his efforts to write in the present. These assume the aura of the "plague of dead jellyfish"—washed up by the Atlantic Ocean—that he toes as he wanders a beach in Brittany, France. Like them, the once concrete communities become ghostlike and translucent—"you can peer through their skin at an odd conglomeration of pastel-hued pipes, valves, pumps, viscera" (158). They seem useless and dead, divorced from living urgency. They take on the unsettling shape of "roadkill" or something "randomly, violently emptied of life" (175) that he encounters on other meanderings and about which he tries and fails to write a meaningful essay.

The narrator, like the writer figures of *Fanon*, confesses that he is "adrift" and blocked in his work. Indeed, his voice is that of a man in his seventies, who feels the "rest of my life undreamed, a life that's much closer to over now" (70). Haunted and cut off, his voice seems to resonate more from the saintly, other world of the dead than from the living present. He confesses:

The Till project has stalled. I'm adrift. Probably on purpose. Probably conscious flight. Running. Hiding. As if I can close the distance between whatever it is I possess and what I've lost. Running. Hiding. South to collect villains and family stories. France to find a grave, jellyfish, a dead uncle's shoes, talking stones, glass sculptures. Nowhere to put it all, no way to connect, bind together scattered bits and pieces [. . .] Free the power of those gleanings, details, remains [. . .] Do words have power to create more life. To reach back far enough or forward enough and help me enter Louis Till's silence. Mine. Words on these pages. My file, my story. These words I chase to represent a life. Who will open the file. Read the words. What will they make of me, us, after I'm silenced, like you, Louis Till. (176–77)

The work thus abounds with discomforting and intimate confessions about the narrator and people he loves. And though its title evokes the family name of a central spirit of the Civil Rights Movement, it at first seems to embrace the "inward," more intimately aesthetic, and less outwardly functional turn that critics have observed in the writing of the later part of the twentieth and early part of the twenty-first centuries. At one point, the narrator admits his heart is "too full of things I wasn't prepared to deal with" (176).

The Lives of the Saints

Within *Writing to Save a Life,* the military court-martial file of Louis Till functions as a meticulously bundled fetish disguised as an objective legal process that not only rationalized Till's hanging but was later "conjured" (11) to deny justice once again and further absolve the murderers of his son. *Writing to Save a Life* pits itself against this sorcery as its own functional work of the black arts. Since the late 1980s, the 25-years-to-life sentence for murder handed to Wideman's teenage son had entangled him in Kafkaesque legal processes. Within Wideman's work, such entanglement unveils the ruthlessness of legal processes that use the bewitching "spells" of performative legal documents to cavalierly and inexorably consume Black life in America. *Reuben* engages this process through an eponymous figure, who embodies Papa Legba, a spirit of Black Atlantic cosmology who wields the power of "word magic" to "untangle people from the negative effects of the dominant culture" (*Reuben* 151–52). For Wideman, the formal and aesthetic possibilities of this power wielded in the form of a book seem to come largely from his reading of anthropologist Robert Farris Thompson's book *Flash of the Spirit* and its *"exposition of Kongo cosmology"* that he credits in *Reuben's* epigraph. In this work, Thompson explores the Black Atlantic arts of African American Voodoo, Haitian Vodun, Cuban Santeria, and Brazilian Candomblé connecting them to the cosmology brought to the New World by enslaved Africans.

These religions drove successful Black liberation struggles throughout the Caribbean and Latin world.

In his landmark book, *Black Jacobin*, C. L. R. James observes that during the Haitian Revolution, "Voodoo was the medium of conspiracy." It organized the masses after all traditional measures had failed (86). Afro-Cuban religion also played a powerful role in the Cuban Revolution, argue historians Dick Cluster and Rafael Hernández in *The History of Havana* (2018).

> The rebel troops had entered Havana wearing not just crosses but the beads of *santería*. For many believers in the "people's faith"—blacks and whites living in those barrios that had once been Havana outside the walls—the top leaders of the revolution were illuminated and protected by the *orishas* of the Yoruba pantheon [. . .] Among Fidel Castro's popular nicknames was "El Caballo," the horse [. . .] There were those who felt he had been bathed in the virtues of the Three Warriors of *santería*—the strength and battle spirit of Changó, the tenacity and will of the blacksmith Oggún, and the ability and vision of Elegguá, lord of the roads and opener of doors. It was well known that some of his closest collaborators [. . .] were hidden believers who consulted with distinguished *babalawos*. (252)

According to Thompson, the charms and talismans of Vodun and Santeria originate in powerful objects of Kongo cosmology or "[s]spirit-*embodying* materials" that the possess the ability to divert the power of a soul and use it for healing, divining, locating, protecting, binding together loved ones, or arresting "enemies in their tracks" (131). The eclectic or amalgamated aesthetic form used by Wideman and by such authors as Ishmael Reed and Toni Morrison links their work to the "functional" quality of African and Black Atlantic craft embraced by writers of the Black Arts Movement. In their hands, the novel itself becomes [s]pirit-embodying material," or a concrete, literary fetish through the act of writing and the preservation or saving of stories that work to capture the spirit of a life. "A man's story is his gris-gris," writes a character in Reed's 1976 novel, *Flight to Canada* (8). "His writing was his HooDoo" (89).

The quilted together stories of *Writing to Save a Life* thus aesthetically resemble and function much like the *minkisi container* of Kongo cosmology, the *pacquets congos* of Haiti, the *punto de segurar* of Cuba, or the "bundle" of African American Voodoo. The work equally functions as a Black Atlantic, *Lives of the Saints*, a text evoked by the narrator's conflation of the sweeping figure of San Martin de Porres with the disfigured shape of Clement (the barbershop errand boy who haunted his childhood) and the brutalized, dead face of Emmett Till, who still haunts his adult ones. So, through its evocation of Saint Martin, saving of the story of "Saint Louis Till," and capturing of other ancestral figures, the text equally functions like an original hagiography, which also arrests or saves a living spirit, investing writing and representations with the power wielded by religious relics and icons.

Saint Martin de Porres

In his evocation of Saint Martin, the narrator says that he first received a statuette of the Saint—"a talisman to keep me safe during my life's journey" from "a fierce veteran of Chicago's deadly war on Black Panthers in the sixties," who had the street-name, Tomahawk (189). It is a story of loss, recovery— "Found and lost, found again, lost again (192)—, of revolutionary power, and of mystical reclamation densely associated with the Black Liberation movement and its literary expression in the Black Arts Movement. Yet, many critics traditionally isolate Wideman from this aspect of the 1960s counterculture. Wideman and other contemporary writers, says critical biographer Keith Byerman, "not only felt that the Black Arts Movement restricted their artistic freedom, but that the Black Power philosophy behind it was socially dangerous" (15). Yet, within *Writing to Save a Life,* Chicago's "deadly war on the Black Panthers," like the Till File, evokes just another dominant and dominating "version of the script altered but not enough to obscure its resemblance to the original." The narrator avows it is "getting even worse day by day it seems when I pay attention—one more colored victim declared guilty without a trial falls, fallen, falling dead, here, there, everywhere" (16). As for Chicago's "deadly war"; it came to a horrific head in 1969, when city police brazenly murdered the twenty-one-year-old Chairman of the Chicago Black Panther, Fred Hampton, and his twenty-two-year-old aid Mark Clark. They were among the nearly thirty members of the party killed in the United States within a little over a year. Even mainstream newspapers such as *The New York Times* observed that law enforcement had declared an "open season" on Black Panther Party members (Kifner E3). Indeed, the American "law and order" response to the Black Panthers, Black radicalism, and the countercultural movements of the 1960s and 1970s initiated the militarization of police and helped launched the mass incarceration epidemic denounced by Black Lives Matter protesters in the second decade of the twenty-first century.

So, a "fierce veteran" of this "war," with a nom de guerre that recalls indigenous American genocide, gave the narrator a "talisman"— a statuette of Saint Martin de Porres—that she said would protect him. Over the years, he loses and then recovers it while reading a book. At first glance, the scene seems to overflow with a cognitive dissonance that questions why a committed Black revolutionary named Tomahawk would possess a "wooden figurine" of a pious, gentle, modest, "all-forgiving" and broom sweeping Catholic Saint, canonized in 1962 by Pope John XXIII. Yet, this dissonance only has meaning if one knows nothing about San Martin de Porres, whose "presence" asserts theologian James Padilioni, "radiates from the center point of the cosmic mysteries one encounters at the crossroads of Catholicism and Vodú" (111). In other words, Saint Martin is also a Saint—a *misterio*—of one of the world's most vilified religions—a religion of resistance and revolution. Because of his transformative power, the humble San Martin is a "bad Negro." Indeed, like the writers of the Black Arts Movement, described by Ameri Baraka, the very Blackness of this literally "iconic" figure defies the "twisted racism of Europe and America where everything Black was bad" and uses this energy to "turn their Evil backward." As a Black "misterio," San Martin is "Badder dan Nat" (Baraka, Movement 499). Baraka uses this phrase to describe Black Arts Movement writers, rendering it in "bad" African American Vernacular English as he conjures the spirit of Nat Turner, the deeply religious enslaved preacher, who lead a violent insurrection against slavery in 1831 that killed at least 51 White people and ended with his hanging. Still, Saint Martin de Porres is also "bad." though for other reasons.

The Catholic Church canonized him amid the anti-racist struggle of the American Civil Rights Movement, and in the wake of the anti-imperialism struggle of the Cuban Revolution. In 1959, Fidel Castro's troops entered Havana, many of them adorned with the protective talismans of Santeria, a syncretic, Afro-Cuban Religion. Soon afterward, in 1962, the Church began "to engage the movements for anti-colonialism, anti-imperialism, and human development" (91), leading Pope John XXIII to canonize San Martin as "the patron saint of social justice and racial harmony" (86), says James Padilioni in his article "A Miami Misterio : Sighting San Martín de Porres at the Crossroads of Catholicism and Dominican Vodú." This process of canonizing what seemed like an inexorably servile Black man, argues Padilioni, renders "the historical life and supernatural charisms of San Martín into an idealized image of, first, colonial racial hierarchy, and, later, racial democracy" (88). Yet, in canonizing Blackness, the Church could not control or contain the flow of its own mystical aporias. According to Padilioni:

> The supernaturalism of San Martín de Porres, when refigured within the folk hagiographic and iconographic conventions of Dominican Vodú, Blackens the spiritual lineages of his transnational devotees and provides them with a source of ancestral power from which they challenge elite, authorized, and white-dominated narratives of [their] Catholic history and identity. (89)

So, when Tomahawk presents the statuette to the narrator, she offers him a protecting, White-narrative-challenging, "spirit-embodying" icon of Black Atlantic Santeria. Indeed, the icon not only contains the power of a bad, Black spirit of resistance, but conjures the memory of solidarity with the Cuban

Revolution and anti-imperial internationalism evinced by Black activists of the 1960s and early 1970s such as Baraka, Assata Shakur, and Kwame Turé (Eldridge Cleaver), who took an interest in Afro-Cuban culture and religion.

The San Martin charm and even his hagiography (works within which text and saintly body become one) challenge a basic aporia of modern Catholicism. When Padilioni invokes the "supernatural charisms of San Martín" he fundamentally links the "flash and arrest of the spirit" (Thompson 118) or the mysteries (*misterios*) of Black Atlantic cosmology to the Catholic notion of *charis* (Χάρις) and its "open potential for divine immanence, such as the indwelling of the transubstantiated Eucharistic host, the supernatural radiating through saints' relics and sacramentals, and the holy emanating from the mouths of the Virgin Mary, saints, and the spirits of the dead" (Padilioni 87). Statuettes, prayer cards, and hagiography safeguard the protective power of the saint's spirit. Meanwhile, often discredited oral testimony witnesses the saint's miraculous visitations. And while Catholics may venerate San Martin as a figure of "social justice," the practitioners of Santeria await and expect his powerful intervention in their lives through charms that save his "real presence."

Indeed, practitioners of Santeria and others follow San Martin because he is a powerful, miracle-working, "bad negro" and not just a good man or caring ally of the poor. During his life, he was what Padilioni calls a "mystical" African (88). He exhibited supernatural powers such as the one's described by Liam in *The Cattle Killing*. Liam says he was destined to become "a holy man, a healer of soul and body," like his Igbo father. He adds: "My father was a renowned wizard [. . .] I recall [. . .] fear and respect for my father's powers. How he could change his shape or disappear instantly. How he could be many different places at once" (104). San Martin could also be in two places at once as well as levitate, fill a room with saintly light, know things he hadn't learned, and heal the sick (Franciscan Media). Also, like the bad man, John Africa, the charismatic leader of MOVE who materializes in *Philadelphia Fire* and *Two Cities*, San Martin had a respect for all of life and protected, whispered to, and even trained the vermin infesting his monastery.

As a *misterio* or loa *(lwa)*, San Martin often has the immensely powerful role "of *centinela* (sentinel), a spirit who attends the more prominent *misterios* in their dealings with humans" observes Padilioni (109–110). His spirit often invigorates *mambos*, or the songs that conjure spirits (Thompson 110). In some groups, he is closely associated with the powerful spirits of the crossroads which go by different and related names: *Gedé Carfú* (*Ghede and Carrefour*), *Eshu-Elegbara*, Elegba, and Papá Legbá. Indeed, one popular *salve-palo*, a central American and Caribbean musical chant, titled "Saint Martin de Porres Throw Me Some Water" ("San Martín de Porres, Échame Agua"), functions as a *mambo* and conjures the saint's spirit (Padilioni 108).

These songs work equally like original hagiographies, or, according to one musician, as "possessed texts" (*textos montados*), says Padilioni (107). The incantation of "San Martín de Porres, Échame Agua" opens the way, compelling listeners first to "dance dance dance" while conjuring the presence of *Papá Legbá* and the powerful, wise, African spirit, *Candelo* (Padilioni 108).

In the portrait captured in *Writing to Save a Life*, Saint Martin wears "a gold cross on a chain" (190). Yet in the iconography of the Black Atlantic, this cross does not bind him to the Catholic Church, observes Thompson. In Kongo Cosmology, the cross, "has nothing to do with the "crucifixion of the Son of God" (108); instead it conjures the crossroads, or a sacred "point of intersection between the world of the ancestors and the living" (109). The image from the prayer card abounds with other powerful icons wielding Black Atlantic power. For instance, a "white dove hovers at Saint Martin's right" (190). This may symbolize peace for some, but it confers power in the cosmology of Santeria. "In the Roman Catholic Church," asserts cultural historian Ivor L. Miller in his article, "Religious Symbolism in Cuban Political Performance," doves sometimes represent the Holy Spirit; in Santeria doves represent "Obatali" (38). Obatali is the manifestation in Santeria of Damballah. So, for instance, when a dove alighted on Fidel Castro's shoulder during his first speech as president, for many people in Cuba it performed a benediction protecting him and giving him the power to carry forth the revolution. Even the "broom in hand" (190) of the picture, which signifies for many the humble servitude of menial labor, also confers power and perhaps helps *Writing to Save a Life* perform its own ritual against the spells cast by deadly official documents such as the Louis Till File. According to Padilioni, "this icon intended to depict Martín's lowly place in the racial hierarchy of the colonial church is transformed into an object of power, as his devotees sweep their brooms across Martín's statue before offering them at the saint's feet or using them to perform *barradas* (sweepings) and other magico-ritual cleansings" (102).

Finally, the image of San Martin de Porres empowers the text to unravel and deploy some of the tensions between oral and written testimony that has preoccupied the writing of Wideman since the 1960s and which is a major trope of African American literature. Indeed, the syncretic religions of the Black Atlantic world are driven by relentlessly discredited oral testimony, music ("possessed texts"), and the real-life experience of people who participate in religious rituals and submit their bodies to possession by the spirit as they witness the visitations and miracles of agentive saints like San Martin de Porres who protect them. Nestled "in oral history," accounts of San Martin's power present a radical "challenge both to Western Enlightenment metaphysics and traditional conventions of historiography, because Martín de Porres emerges as an agentive person, though he had been dead for centuries before these events transpired" (86). Original religious hagiographies also present this challenge as they overflow with *charis*, displace relics and icons, and function as equally "possessed texts" that save, capture, and actualize the spirit of an oral transmission that often predates them by hundreds of years.

Saint Bigger Thomas

As a twenty-first-century hagiography, *Writing to Save a Life* also challenges and breaks the spell of the official, written, historical record, which it treats as a fetish of the dominant culture. The hostile charm of the Louis Till File, for instance, harvests and deploys Till's bad spirit to maintain racial hierarchy, propagate lies, and disseminate a racial allegory with a plot anchored in the logic of "southern lynch law" (107). As a response to similar fetishes, *Writing to Save a Life* begins with eighteen actual "newspaper excerpts" taken from the narrator's "notebook" (11). These imbedded excerpts once formed a part of the powerful, magical collage that American newspapermen have famously termed the "first rough draft of history" (Shafer). They bear witness, and enable the text to perform acts of necromancy, extracting renewed life from yesterday's news by exhuming the clips from the newspaper archive; a place that American journalists once called "'morgues' because the libraries contain dead stories" (Fedler 155). Cut out, clipped, extracted, and pasted onto a different context—a different magical collage—the amalgamated excerpts also respond to discussions of the left and of the right in contemporary America, which have used terms such as "fake news" and idealized a more reliable, more objective journalistic past that has never existed for enslaved Africans and their descendants. They tie *Writing to Save a Life* to the aesthetics of a protest tradition in African American literature. This includes works such as Harriet Jacob's, *Incidents in the Life of a Slave Girl* (1861), in which she imbeds excerpts of her own runaway slave advertisement; Claude McKay's *Banjo* (1929), which contains an untranslated clip from a French newspaper about an actual Senegalese soldier who commits mass murder; Ishmael Reads, *Mumbo Jumbo* (1972), which overflows with photographs and facsimiles of newspaper stories that translate the coded language of the mainstream press's reporting on the Black Panthers with sentences such "self-styled," and "band of freaks" (123); and, of course, Richard Wright's *Native Son* (1940), which almost functions as an early, magical template for *Writing to Save a Life* and its treatment of the fetishes of White supremacy.

Indeed, *Writing to Save a Life* reads backwards, toward *Native Son*. In many ways, Louis Till becomes its protagonist, Bigger Thomas, a bad Black spirit who migrates to Chicago from Mississippi before murdering and sexually assaulting two women—one White, one Black. Through Bigger, Wright like Wideman confronts Western constructions of history, "fake news," and its lies, silencing, and deadly effect on Black life. Through this text, Wright works to unmask, disarm and then harvest the power of the American newspaper as both script and fetish, redeploying it to work against the racial hierarchy that uses the spirt of bad negroes to maintain a script that justifies lynchings, extrajudicial killings, and the legalized executions of Black Americans. In his essay on *Native Son,* "How Bigger was Born," Wright calls this script a "plot [. . .] that I knew by heart" (455). He then imbeds the novel with faithful facsimiles of actual *Chicago Tribune* newspaper stories, ensconcing the crafted fictions of the daily news within his own fiction. It is powerful, demystifying magic that threatens the aesthetic ordering of society that the newspaper works so hard to uphold with mastheads, headlines, datelines, pasted stories on pages, and other conventions that produce in readers a sense of who they are, where they are, and what's important as they concoct a role for them in the world. Imbedding these fictions within a fiction works much like staging a "fake holdup" instead of a real one as described by Jean Baudrillard in his essay, "Simulacra and Simulations." A "real hold up" Baudrillard says, "only upsets the order of things [. . .] whereas a simulated hold up interferes with the very principle of reality" (180).

Many early reviewers of *Native Son* believed Wright had staged a "real holdup" through his necromantic deployment of newspapers within the novel. Critics of Wright, such as James Baldwin, in his essay, "Everybody's Protest Novel," denounced aspects of the novel that seemed to lack literary craft, and were too journalistic, too timely, and simply ripped, lock stock, and barrel, from yesterday's news. Margaret Walker reports that while writing *Native Son*, Wright asked her to send him copies of the *Chicago Tribune*, which he "spread over his nine-by-twelve bedroom floor" and then read "over and over again" (Walker 123). Even Wright seems to support this criticism in his description of his method. "Many of the newspaper items and some of the incidents in *Native Son* are but fictionalized versions of the Robert Nixon case and rewrites of news stories from the *Chicago Tribune*" (455).

Yet, Wright does not use "the Robert Nixon" case to simply add a layer of journalistic verisimilitude to the text. His novel reveals that when he reads the *Tribune,* he understands it as a fetish that captures or conjures Nixon's spirit and impresses it in the service of the same old "plot" that told readers why Black lives don't matter and why they need to be policed, caged, shot down on the streets, or snuffed out in the electric chair. *Native Son,* however, reclaims this same spirit, deploying it to break the spell as it reworks the story of Nixon through the character of Bigger Thomas. Nixon was an 18-year-old migrant from Mississippi and probably a petty criminal. In 1938, a White woman was found beaten to death with a brick on Chicago's south side. Police cast a dragnet over the Black Belt, snagged Nixon (an idea conjured by the nickname of "Snag" imposed on Louis

Till while he awaited execution), and extracted a confession. He then was accused of a string of rapes in Chicago and California, where he also had lived. Thereafter, a court judged him guilty and a state executioner quickly ended his very short life.

From the beginning, the *Chicago Tribune* frames the case as a racial allegory—an immemorial sex crime committed by a Negro against a White woman in fulfillment of the running American script that embraced Social Darwinism as truth. Indeed, before police find the culprit, the front page of the paper (using its own stylized language) runs the inflammatory headline: "Sift Mass of Clews [sic] for Sex Killer: Chief Suspect Baffles Police By Mixed Tales: 15 Seized in Slaying of Mother" (*Chicago Tribune*). Yet, beyond the headlines, none of the stories about the crime provide any indication that the accused had actually raped the victim, observes Keneth Kinnamon in his fairly definitive, 1969 exploration of the novel's context, "Native Son: The Personal, Social, and Political Background" (68). Then, in the words of the narrator describing events leading to Louis Till's execution in *Writing to Save a Life,* "the plot thickens" (111). The *Tribune* augments the intrigue of Nixon's story in a June 5, 1938 profile providing readers with background that should normally boggle the imagination. As a fetish, it cavalierly cobbles together fictional tropes taken from the Black-face minstrel show and Hollywood films such as *King Kong* (1933) that connect Blackness to savagery as it also underscores the infinite expendability of Black lives and the inherent superiority of White ones. It begins with the headline: "BRICK SLAYER IS LIKENED TO JUNGLE BEAST: Ferocity is Reflected in Nixon's Features." It then described Nixon as: resembling an "ape," suggesting "an earlier link in the species," being "very black," and lacking "the charm of speech or manner that is characteristic of so many southern darkies." It ends by quoting a Southern sheriff who says: "Only death can cure him" (Leavelle). In *Native Son*, Wright confronts this assembled fetish of death and White supremacy with an equally powerful charm. Bigger, confined to a jail cell, asks for a copy of the *Tribune*. There, he reads a story that repeats the incantation of the *Tribune* work. It bears the headline: "Negro Rapist Faints at Inquest." He reads the words: "'He looks exactly like an ape!' exclaimed a terrified young white girl [. . .] his skin is exceedingly black . . . he seems a beast utterly untouched by the softening influences of modern civilization. In speech and manner he lacks the charm of the average, harmless, genial, grinning southern darky so beloved by the American people." In the place of the Southern sheriff, Wright's amalgam even includes the words of an "Irish police captain" who proclaims "with deep conviction [. . .] death is the only cure for the likes of him" (279–80). Through the novel, Wright thus saves and then redeploys the spirit of Robert Nixon arrested within the pages of the *Chicago Tribune*. Such work captures the rhythms of American life and pits

its narrative magic against the seemingly timeless "plot" or "script" of White supremacy.

When confronted with Wright's acts of literary necromancy and resurrectionist trips to the "morgue" of the American news, early reviewers found themselves forced to read the novel as African Americans had read American newspapers since the days when they ran commonplace advertisements for slave auctions and runaway slaves. His craft works to dismantle what contemporary activists would call the lack of "self-awareness" of "white privilege" as maintained by the pages of the American newspaper. It stages a "fake holdup" as it interferes with their sense of superior White identity; with their understanding of space and time; with their inherent feeling of benign innocence; with their notion of truth, and (in Baudrillard's words) "with the very principle of reality" (180). Reeling from such confusion, Southern writer Hubert Creekmore, in a 1941 review of the *Native Son* attempted to restore narrative order. He denounced Wright's faithful capturing and redeployment of the scripted American fetish as inflammatory, distorted, and "exaggerated ridicule" that turns "the usefulness of a documentary story into an impassioned romance" (137). "Mr. Wright," he proclaims, "is trying to dramatize an editorial rather than present *his story* . . . human nature and fact are distorted into a cartoon" (139).

Wright's work had expose the concocted "plot" of American newspaper stories and unmasked them as aesthetically crafted fetishes, destined to use the spirit of people such as Nixon, just like the narrator of *Writing to Save a Life*, says a "redneck senator" uses the Louis Till file to conjure "an evil black rabbit from an evil white hat." *Native Son* reverses such White magic. Indeed, in 1963, in the midst of the Civil Rights Movement and not long after the canonization of Saint Martin de Porres, essayist Irving Howe famously said the following about Wright's saving of the life and spirit of Robert Nixon, an otherwise forgotten 19-year-old bad negro, who was snagged, judged and executed in 1930s Chicago. Howe observes:

> The day *Native Son* appeared, American culture was changed forever. No matter how much qualifying the book might later need, it made impossible a repetition of the old lies [. . .] Richard Wright's novel brought out into the open, as no one ever had before, the hatred, fear and violence that have crippled and may yet destroy our culture. (354–5)

Saint Louis Till

The narrator of *Writing to Save a Life* pours over the Till file and tries to pick apart its cabalist seams with the same intensity of Wright who read the hateful, spell binding stories of the *Chicago Tribune* "over and over again"

(Walker 123). The documents tell the same immemorial story. As he reads, the narrator finds himself relentlessly "mocked by power. Power that controls the record [. . .] Power putting words in Louis Till's mouth" (98) and the mouths of everyone associated with the young man's court martial and hanging.

> Spoken words have been reduced (CID agents' term of art) to typed summaries. Translation. Conversion. Reduction. Each process transforms a witness's words. Each creates a step away, further and further away, from the words of live encounters between CID agents and witnesses. (102)

The narrator thus struggles with the Till File, which overflows with "unreliable, corrupted representations of conversations" (102). These distorted records of speech preoccupy the narrator, much the same way that written representation of African American speech had preoccupied Wideman in both academic articles and his writing since the late 1960s. Indeed, for Wideman, a major characteristic of African American literature relates to the way that writing captures the struggle of Black Americans to "free themselves from a frame which a priori devalues black speech" (Wideman, Defining 79). This is also a significant characteristic of original hagiography, which attempts to safeguard the spirt of centuries-old oral testimony that bears witness to miraculous events, visitations from spirits, and in which representational text works as icons imbued with a spirt. It is equally a characteristic of the discredited religions of the New World, inspired by African cosmology. "African-derived religions in Cuba," says Ivor Miller "are based on oral traditions" (30). Although official documents attempt to frame and discredit this oral base, these spoken events, rooted in Black power, challenge and disrupt the ordering power of conventional historiography and of the official written record. While official documents, such as the Till File, frame and mock such speech, as they belittle, disavow and contain its Black power, they also capture that power and impress it into service.

The narrator of *Writing to Save a Life* attempts to free the oral voice of Louis Till from this official record. In fact, he does not reproduce the original betrayal of written words, or imagine and allow Till to speak in his own defense and enter into the distorted record. As he reads the file, he observes:

> Till remained adamantly silent, offering no information about the crimes being investigated [. . .] Breaking his silence once in response to the agents' repeated demands for a statement, Louis Till allegedly said to [an informant], "There's no use in me telling you one lie and then getting up in court and telling another one," a remark that clearly conveys to me and should have conveyed to Rousseau [an informant], Till's Igbo sophistication, his resignation, his Old

World, ironic sense of humor about truth's status in a universe where all truths are equal until power chooses one truth to serve its needs.

Louis Till, thus manifests the indomitable spirt of High John de Conquer, as described by novelist and African American folklorist, Zora Neale Hurston as he "'wages a mighty battle' [. . .] 'without outside-showing force'" against the capturing and sinister deployment of his voice by the official document— The Louis Till File. Instead, like High John, he "choses to win his war 'from within'" (70).

Within *Writing to Save a Life*, Till fights this battle with a miraculous silence that brazenly defies capture, summary, translation, conversion, and reduction. Nevertheless, this "stubborn" (22) or bad silence overflows with an unrepresentable spirit of Black Atlantic orality. For the narrator, it demonstrates that Till, like Saint Martin, knows things he hasn't learned and renders him privy to the type of cultural retention that animated the religions of enslaved Africans throughout the Americas.

> All stories are true. As far as I've been able to glean, Louis Till possessed no knowledge of that particular Igbo proverb [. . .] In the only direct quote attributed to him by army officers in the entire Till file, Louis Till articulates a very Igbo understanding of the predicament in which he found himself. (21).

Meanwhile, Till says nothing else that the file includes. Such recalcitrant silence resounds with the *charis* of saintly relics. Jesuit theorist Walter Ong, who coined and elaborated the term "orality," not only associates such silence with eternal truth, but with the actual word of God. He asks: "Is not what we have called the moment of truth, the instant when we savor the truth or falsity of an utterance, a kind of silence?" He asserts that "encounter with God is even more encounter with silence" (161).

Saint Ezra Pound

Still, it is possible that Till wasn't entirely silent; that he did actually confess to the crime of rape—just not in a prosaic official document. On the written record contained by books, Till confesses in one of the most brilliant and influential works of American literature: Ezra Pound's long poem, the *Pisan Cantos*. Pound was an inspired and perhaps dangerous poet. Indeed, in his autobiography, Black Aesthetic writer Amiri Baraka refers to Pound as "the scientist of poetry, the translator, the mover and shaker (and fascist)!" (234). Pound's fascism and his adoration of Benito Mussolini landed him in prison for the crime of treason in 1945. He and Till occupied the same U.S. compound in Italy at the same time. While there, Pound wrote the *Pisan Cantos*.

Within the poem, the speaker locates his own broadly associative consciousness within that particular place and time, describing the "smell of mint under the tent flaps" (120) and the drift of a conversation between a "nigger murderer" (whom Pound scholars say was Till) and "his cage-mate/(cdn't be sure which of the two was speaking)" (86–87).

Still, something about the orality of Till, must have profoundly affected Pound, who included him in some of the most evocative and affecting passages of the poem. Indeed, he seems to figure Till as a fellow poet who places his art above morality, law, and the petty affairs of mortals. For him, Till evokes the bad Black spirit of Gassire, the progenitor of West African griots, whose story was captured and published for Western readers by an infamous German anthropologist, Leo Frobenius. Frobenius summarized, translated, reduced, and amalgamated the oral epic as sung by "a Soninke bard living in northern Dahomey" says Alta Jablow, in a 1984 analysis of the work (520). Though this amalgamation "is highly dubious" (520), says Jablow, the epic emerged for Western artists in the twentieth century as an African counterpart "to the Romantic Western notion of the artist, with the world well lost for art" (527). Within the story, an African prince murders his children, forsakes his worldly possession, and decimates his kingdom so he can become the original poet of his people. The "dubious" rendering of the tale by Frobenius ultimately commandeers Gassire's spirit and uses it to convey a story embodying the aesthetic value of "art for art's sake;" an idea embraced by mid-twentieth century writers and excoriated by Black Aesthetic artists and their ethic of functional art. Pound (who read the German anthropologist's version of the tale long before his confinement) equally uses Till's voice to affirm this moral in one of the most significant and sonorous passages of the text, which evokes Till, Gassire, Zeus, and the lost kingdom of Wagadu, the land destroyed by a poet's pursuit of art.

Indeed, Pound links his own poetic spirit to that of Till and seems to record the doomed man's words in the *Pisan Cantos*. The high-art poem captures and frames Till's speech—perhaps among his last words—through the low-art eye-dialect, mispronunciations, malapropisms, postures, and racist tropes of the Black-face minstrel show, America's first distinct form of popular entertainment. The speaker of the *Pisan Cantos* eavesdrops on a conversation between the "nigger murderer," and "his cage-mate." A man named "Snag" (whom Pound scholars says is Till) seems to delineate a Zip Coon-like figure, the incorrigibly immoral dandy, whom a minstrel show scholar describes as "high- stepping stutterer with a mismatched vocabulary" (Lemons 102). "'Hey, Snag, wot are the books ov th' bibl''/ 'name 'em, etc/ 'Latin? I studied latin' [. . .]/ 'c'mon, small fry,' sd/the smaller black lad/ to the larger/ 'Just playin' ante mortem no scortum" (83–90). The literally gallows humor of the sad Latin punchline, "before death no prostitute" (and where "no scortum" also has the phonic and visual resonance of scrotum, which evokes castration and lynching) is summarized by a joke bitterly remembered by the narrator of *Writing to Save* a life as he remembers a conversation between his mother and father. "Where there's life, there's hope, my mom used to say, even though my father [. . .] would always interject: And for every tree, there's a rope [. . .] it was the punch line of a joke making fun of a southern darky ha-ha-ha obsessed with copping him a taste of white pussy ha-ha before he dies" (20).

Finally, in one of its most influential passages, the *Pisan Cantos* ruminates over and mythologizes the crimes of Till, weaving Till's hanging into images from Greek mythology while also conjuring the spirits of Gassire and Wagadu. It likens Till to the Greek god Zeus, the infamous ravager of the nymphs. Although the court-martial file records no confession from Till, in the *Pisan Cantos* he seems to confesses to the rape of a young Italian girl through a voice at once his own and that of a Greek immortal with the lines: "the ewe, he said had such a pretty look in her eyes." Yet, *Writing to Save a Life* openly ignores the transcribed confession within the poem, or perhaps imbeds some aspect of it in a conjecture that Louis Till—"Snag" in the poem—got snagged for paying to have sex with a young girl refugee (the "ewe"), sold him by the disreputable owner of the house, Ernetto Mari.

> A hunch the file doesn't confirm. Or negate. If Elena Lucretzia, a juvenile, had been raped or bought or both wouldn't army agents welcome that information as one more evil deed to pin on Till and McMurray [. . .] the army's case is messy, all soft, gooey circumstantial evidence. Problematic at best. (162)

So, for the most part, *Writing to Save a Life*, performs the same work on Pound and the *Pisan Cantos* that the Louis Till file performs on Louis Till. It translates, summarizes, and reorders his words to suit different ends. It contains made-up letters from Pound revealing his cavalier racism and mining of African and African American thought, a practice of cultural appropriation by modernists that was later excoriated by writers of the Black Arts Movement such as Amiri Baraka and African intellectuals, such as Nigerian Writer, Wole Soyinka. In a 1986 essay, Soyinka, denounced modernist Europeans that "sniffed at, delicately tested, swallowed entire, regurgitated, appropriated, [extolled], and damned," what he called "the reality that was Africa" (Soyinka). And in *Writing to Save a Life*, Pound, "listens to colored prisoners talk" as he "pilfers. Collects. Savors. Mimics" (65).

Indeed, the narrator also seems to collect the flash of Pound's spirit as one of the text's saints. He calls Pound "an endangered soul I must rescue, bring back alive as a witness for the defense" (146). In contrast to the confession of the *Pisan Cantos,* however, the narrator's facsimile of the poem infers that

Till may have only confessed to the guilt of committing minor infractions by disobeying orders, being in the wrong place at the wrong time, or breaking the law in a scheme to steal sugar. In this version of Pound's poem, Till defends his innocence of the crimes of rape and murder. For this declaration, the narrator cuts and pastes words from the beginning of LXXX of the Pisan Cantos, taking them out of order and context.

Ain' committed no federal crime
jes a slaight misdemeanor (LXXX)

This confession occurs in the original *Pisan Cantos*, but many pages and sections after lines that directly quote and represent judgments on the guilt of Louis Till—the "nigger murder" who ravaged a "ewe." In fact, the confession to misdemeanors cut and paste by *Writing to Save a Life,* lies much closer in the *Pisan Cantos* to the lines, "the greatest is charity /to be found among those who have not observed /regulations," which seem to refer to the acts of another Black prisoner, named by Pound, "Mr. Edwards." Pound's poem images Edwards as "a jacent benignity, /of the Baluba mask," who disobeys orders when he kindly crafts a small writing table for the poet's use. This act in the poem also gives rise to the narrator's own translation, summary and poetic rendering of Pound's work within *Writing to Save a Life*:

> Luminous traces of dark speech, dark faces, dark music, the dark generosity of kind acts that dark hands dared to perform. Africa surviving but only if, like the poet, you paid attention, looked around yourself, inside yourself, and knew how to look. The poet's desk a gift from an African spirit disguised as a colored prisoner. A writing desk ingeniously fashioned from a packing crate just appeared one morning, no warning, in the poet's bare cell, compliments of quiet fellow prisoner Saunders, whose gleaming, bronze forehead, the poet wrote, belonged on a Benin mask.

Despite the wistful production of Till's confession misdemeanors in his reworking of the *Pisan Cantos*, the narrator of *Writing to Save a Life*, like Pound grasps Till as embodying the spirit of a bad man; a figure who does not observe regulations on both human and cosmological terms.

In fact, the narrator does not translate Till into a "good man" nobly speaking out in his own defense. Instead, Till relentlessly defies authority. He "Breaks rules," says the narrator, "because if a prisoner doesn't break the rules, rules break your heart, my brother, my son, all the colored prisoners I know and have read about assure me" (63). The narrator captures Till insistently doing bad acts: rowing out of rhythm; rebelling against the authority of military officers; battering his wife; ending the Jim Crow policies of a soda shop owner by sneering at him; and doing whatever "brutal, ugly shit" he may have done in Civitavecchia, Italy (103). In addition, he boxes like Mohammad Ali, who resisted the American draft during Vietnam and embraced the radical Muslim leader, Malcolm X or like Jack Johnson, who openly flouted segregation in the 1920s and married White women. "Jack Johnson [. . .] was the baddest fighter in the world (I'm the baddest man that ever lived)," Ali said in a 1970 interview (35). When Till trains at the sport, he even flies, like Saint Martin who levitates or the Africans of Black American folklore. As he skips rope, his feet "don't hardly touch the ground—he's flying" (23). In all, Till's captured story embodies the ancestral spirit of the bad negro and the other disobedient patron saints of African American lore and literature. He captures the spirit of the lackadaisical murderer Stackolee, of oral "prison toasts"; the infanticidal Sethe of Toni Morrison's *Beloved* and the murderer and rapist Bigger Thomas, of *Native Son*. The text crafts a talisman of Louis Till, deploying his bad, Black power—a power beyond the official historical and conventionally narrative judgments of good and evil—and that of its other saints.

In the *Pisan Cantos*, Pound likens Till's spirit to a "diamond" that withstands an "avalanche" and does not die. Similarly, for the narrator of *Writing to Save a Life*, the light or "flash" of Till's spirit—amid the "avalanche" of the Poet's and the Till File's summaries, translations, conversions, reductions, transformations, and his "stubborn silence" (22)—becomes a light saved by a "possessed text" that conjures the power of a religious relic. Indeed, in reclaiming Till's spirit, the narrator goes back to the flash of "light" animating the statue of San Martin de Porres.

> I will invent ways, Louis Till, to tell you Tommie Hawks bestowed a gift upon a young man, a gift she hoped would protect, guide, and light the long life she wished for him [. . .] Light I lose, forget, remember, dream. Found and lost, found again, lost again [. . .] Light in the watchful eyes of my people, living and dead just yesterday, and many, many years before. Luminous eyes I searched in the colored face of Saint Martin de Porres on a votive card reproduced in a book. The book I opened on a flight to find your grave in France. (191–92)

The narrator of *Writing to Save a Life,* captures these flashes of the spirit, producing a protecting and saving hagiography as he reclaims and saves his own family stories layering them onto the lives of the Till family.

Family Saints

Much of *Writing to Save a Life* is unpleasant and revolves around the complicated relationships between Black men and women, Black fathers and sons.

Emmett Till's mother, Mamie Till, a battered woman, immemorially waits for (waits on) her husband and his return from a night out or from the war and she also waits for a train bringing back the brutalized body of her murdered son from Mississippi. Similarly, the narrator's mother waits for his angry, sullen, stubborn, hard, "selfish" and constantly absent father who batters her after three successive nights "out." A strong, recurrent, soothing presence in Wideman's other work, the mother now has died, yet she remains close to him through the ebb and flow of the French coastal water: "The sea far away though it's close. Inside me like my mother now, invisible, seachanged. As close as I'm ever going to get to having her" (165).

Ambiguous memories of his father also haunt the work, which layers the execution of Louis Till and the murder of his son Emmett Till onto the continuing specter of police shootings, the ubiquitous miscarriages of justice, and the consciousness-raising, 2014-police killing of eighteen-year-old Michel Brown in Ferguson, Missouri. Indeed, as a struggle with the nature of the relationship between Black fathers and sons, the work enters into a subtle dialogue with (perhaps ceding ground to) Ta-Nehisi Coates 2015 book, *Between the World and Me*. "All the words that follow are my yearning to make some sense out of the American darkness that disconnects colored fathers from sons, a darkness in which sons and fathers lose track of one another" (17). So, in his saintly bundle, the narrator also strives to save the spirit of his flawed, unfaithful, and distant father, who stubbornly gave bad advice and failed to protect a son from serving a life sentence in prison. He laments: "Oh, my good black man, Daddy. Lover man, loser man, Oh, my good, honest, cheating father" (75). The narrator's father, like Louis Till, also boxes. He is saved as a "bad" Black man, who is "good with his hands," and goes to jail, one day after deciding "to give Big Jim Saunders a whipping [. . .] My father marked him. Split his lip. Bloody nose. Eye swole up. Big Jim never had a chance" (74).

Meanwhile, the narrator further explores his absent father's notion of Black masculinity as a particular form of social construction. "If he believes he's a man, he's going out. And do what he has to do to survive. Do his dirt. His selfish things" (169)

> Once he leaves the space they are struggling to secure for their mutual benefit, for the benefit maybe of their children, once *he's* beyond the door and out in a world which does not love him, there are no guarantees. Except shit will cross his path. Deep shit that won't make it easy or simple for a colored *him* to come back clean, in one piece [. . .]. To stay alive he becomes very, very selfish. Very silent. As if nothing can touch him or hurt him or ever will [. . .] Hardness and selfishness a means of survival once *he* steps out the door. *Out*. (168–9)

Yet the narrator, is also "out," isolated, and far from home. And according to his mother, he is also "Selfish. Just like him. Just like your father" (165). So, in saving his father he is also saving aspects of his own bad spirit, struggling to take it on a detour and prevent it from doing further harm, as Louis Till's had been used to harm his dead son.

Writing to Save a Life does not attempt to justify or rationalize these qualities so much as it formally saves the spirit of their badness by conjuring an African American version of "possessed texts"—the blues. The narrator explores this notion as he remembers hearing the words his father uses while battering his mother:

> I was old enough to understand nearly everything. It was all in the music. In the talk in Henderson's Barbershop. Woman who's a wife and mother got no damned business out in the street [. . .] Did I hear those particular words that night or are they blues words, gospel words, barbershop words dreamed, heard before the fact or after the fact of my mother's body striking the floor. (30)

African and Haitian cosmologies, like the "profane" spirit of the blues, often do not make the moralistic and non-violent distinctions often associated with the "sacred" aspects of the spirituals and conventional ideas about African American religion. Vodun, says Thompson, has two sides: *Petro* and *Rada*. "*Rada* [. . .] is the "cool" side of vodun, being associated with the achievement of peace and reconciliation. *Petro* [. . .] is the hot side being associate with the spiritual fire of charms for healing and for attacking evil forces" (164). And like the imperfect saints of original hagiographies who were often vengeful, and "vindictive" (Julia Smith 340), the spirits of *Writing to Save a Life* have this kind of hot "power." At one point, the narrator makes a guilty confession when he witnesses the toxic control his father wields over his mother. He admits: "in my most secret places, I envied, coveted my father's power" (166). Such power can be harvested and deployed to take life, as in the case of the Till file and racial allegories of Black inferiority, or saved and bundled into charms of protection, as in the case of the statue of Saint Martin de Porres or possessed texts such as *Native Son* and, if it has been properly crafted, *Writing to Save a Life*.

Transubstantiation

In a search for the proper method, *Writing to Save a Life*, like *Reuben*, *Philadelphia Fire*, *The Cattle Killing*, *Two Cities*, and *Fanon* meditates over other media that seem to have successfully overcome the deadening effects of representation inherent to that of writing. This time, the narrator wonders at the *pâte de verre* aesthetic of glass sculptures made by his

French friend, Antoine, who owns the cottage the narrator occupies while in Brittany, France. He marvels at the, "Transparent cubes, globes, chunks of glass with all sorts of unpredictable things displayed inside [. . .] I'd always been intrigued by my friend's work, its roots in ancient Egypt, necromancy, alchemy, and family tradition" (174). He even admits he envies Antoine's success (176). In an essay for a 2007 book about French artist Antoine Leperlier, Wideman also attempts to describe what mystifies him about these works. He concludes by intimating that the only language that would enable him to convey the powerful effect of these objects originates in pondering the mysteries—*misterios*—of saints, relics, icons, hagiography, *charis*, and transubstantiation.

> He's desperate now for a sentence . . . to jump start the stalled essay . . . as if corrupted flesh could return as bread and wine. (Glass 84)

Writing to Save a Life works as a similar object. It functions as a possessed text—a text where body becomes text and text becomes body.

Conclusion
A "Very Igbo Understanding"

Few things can be more damning than denouncing a respectable, octogenarian, African-American writer as a superstitious witch doctor dabbling in the black arts. It places him in the company of the crazy and shunned as it also locates him in a tradition, cosmology, and system of knowledge that is inexorably "discredited." Discredited, Toni Morrison affirms, "only because Black people were discredited therefore what they knew was 'discredited'" (Morrison, Rootedness 342). Indeed, the Western world used the seemingly non-Christian belief systems of many African peoples as an original justification for their enslavement. The enlightenment thought of European Christendom concocted the notion of the civilized Human against it. This ordering system of knowledge—and its imposition of the Human over the savage; of light over darkness; of white over black—presented itself as the sole means of legitimately casting a thin light into the dark unknown and transforming it into the known, producing (through rationality and the scientific method) the working wonders of technology and concocting the idea of progress. These marvels manifested tangible and unimpeachable proof of European superiority. The mindset of such a system seemed to have no use for that benighted consciousness that lay outside the light. It recoiled at and suppressed the emanations from "the dark at the bottom of the stairs" (Fernandez 215) or that inchoate non-being that instills terror and dread as it looms with its switchblade in the shadowy background. Suppressed, it hides out in the gaps and interstices of the parasitic fields of knowledge and the knowable, which are little more than the "narrative modes" decried by Afropessimism and which also rely on its inchoate form to produce the superior white identity. This all-embrasive, Western way of knowing inexorably discredits any other way of coming to terms with the world and, as Morrison observes, those associated with it. Indeed, as Afropessimist Frank

Wilderson avows, this system of knowledge fundamentally disavows Black people as persons, subjects, beings, and Humans. It unrelentingly dooms them to "social death," placing them beyond any true act of redemption that the Western world could pretend to offer.

Still, this system doesn't *know* everything. By its very nature, it can't *know* anything about the discredited and constitutive darkness.

In 1965 New York, a group of Black artists staged a parade in celebration of that darkness. They were marking the beginning of the Black Arts Movement. Amiri Baraka describes the event in his 1983 work, *The Autobiography of LeRoi Jones*.

> One of our first official actions was a parade across 125th Street. With Sun Ra and his Myth-Science Arkestra leading it [—this was] the core of us, as it had grown, some other black artists from downtown and those in Harlem who'd now begun to come in, plus Baba Oserjeman and his Yoruba Temple. We marched down the street holding William White's newly designed Black Arts flag. I've seen one photo that survives of this (in a magazine put out by Asian activist, Yuri Kuchiyama, *North Star*). A small group of sometimes comically arrogant black people daring to raise the question of art and politics and revolution, black revolution! (Baraka, Autobiography 299)

This parade brazenly embraced "discredited knowledge" or the "superstition and magic, which is another way of knowing things" as embodied by people from the Yoruba Temple and, of course, the Myth-Science Arkestra of pianist and teacher of Black American cosmology, Sun Ra.

Sun Ra was a star, affirms Baraka. The Black people of mid-1960s Harlem "dug" his music demonstrating that the critics who "put down" the "avant and super new" music "as inaccessible were full of shit" (308). "We had huge audiences, really mass audiences," Baraka says. "People danced in the street to Sun Ra" (308). Nevertheless, observes journalist Graham Lock in his book, *Forces in Motion: The Music and Thought of Anthony Braxton*, Sun Ra "never judged his music in terms of commercial appeal or hi-tech fetishism . . . Sun Ra has said that each of his records is an issue of a cosmic newspaper" (16). Yet, many have derided these types of other-worldly pronouncements and disparaged Sun Ra with words similar to those used by the Homewood community as it laughed Ruben "out of existence" and derided him as a "Mountebank. Charlatan. Fool. Witch Doctor [. . .] Their voices taunting him" (71). Sun Ra bore similar taunts. Originally from Birmingham, Alabama, he went by the name of Herman "Sonny" Blount, until "Sun Ra from the planet Saturn" took "over his body," contests Lock (14). Yet, Ra, Lock observes, "is not a freak, a con-man, a madman, or even a singular genius: genius he may be, but he is part of a black historical continuum that reaches back through the blues and slavery to an Egyptian civilization that began 5,000 years ago and lasted for nearly three millennia" (Locke 23).

Sun Ra asserts that Black people who accept the Western way of knowing, "Live lies" (quoted in Locke 22). According to Lock, Ra's distinct African American cosmology espouses "black nationalism" critiques "black Christianity," and exalts "ancient Egypt," as it reminds Black people "of their heritage of 'truly natural Black beauty' which Sun Ra felt the big bands in particular represented" (22). Indeed, Ra's thoughts have more in common with the twenty-first-century idea of Blackcentrism than Black nationalism, as described by theologian Donald Matthews in his 2020 book, *Blackcentricity: How Ancient Black Cultures Created Civilization. Revealing the Truth that White Supremacy Denied.* Matthews reclaims discredited Black knowledge as the matrix that gave rise to the civilization of ancient Egypt. In his music and cosmology, Ra revels in "discredited knowledge," rejecting the Western "narrative mode" and its inexorable figuring of knowledge as light. Instead, he embraces the unknown and what he calls "dark" tradition. In his liner notes to the 1992 album, *Destination Unknown*, he asserts: "The unknown is great, it's like the darkness, nobody made that it just happens. Light and all that someone made that, it's written that they did. But nobody made the darkness" (Ra). Sun Ra plays in the dark, like the basketball players of *Philadelphia Fire* who continue the game after nightfall. He possesses the spirt of Frantz Fanon that Wideman's eponymous work presents playing soccer past dusk and deploying similar power as he writes *The Wretched of the Earth.* "Fanon's been here and gone. Played the game till it was too dark to see the ball. You can't touch that" (164). Ra, Locke maintains, "is both serious and magical—perhaps, serious *because* he is magical" (23). His "entire career can be seen as an attempt to make the impossible happen, to make the world change" (15).

The later works of Wideman relentlessly engage such magical playing in the dark—deploying the spirit of àshe—"the power to make things happen" (Thompson 5)—which defies the trope of en-light-enment. Indeed, *Philadelphia Fire,* manifests such play; nearly offering an early manifesto of Afropessimism, as it explores the "social death" of the Western "narrative mode" through a lesson taught schoolchildren by a dreadlocked amalgam of Caliban from Shakespeare's the tempest, John Africa from the streets of Philadelphia, the spirit of James Brown resonating from African American music, and even the writer himself stepping away from the real world and his position as "fabulator" of the text (132).

> And one of my jobs as model and teacher is to unteach you . . . to remove de tail. Derail the tale. . . . That the tail was a tale. Nothing more or less than an ill-intentioned big fat lie. And that when all is said and done, sound and fury

separated with Euclidean niceness, with Derridian diddly-bop from the mess that signifies nothing, what you discover is the one with the tail was old mean landlord [. . .] without thought of God or man the merry ole cat-o'-nine tails unmercifully whupping on your behind and still would be performing his convincing imitation of Simon Legree, of the beast this very moment in this very classroom, cutting up, cutting down, laying on the stripes, if it weren't for me, girls and boys. (Philadelphia, 131)

Sun Ra engages in similar acts of "unteaching": "I teach my musicians not to know things and that's a totally different thing." he asserts. "They don't teach that in schools" (Ra)

These are dangerous lessons, fraught with the peril of being laughed "out of existence" through the serious invalidating charges of suborning foolishness, superstition, and black magic. Yet, these charges place Wideman in the tradition of master Black American artists, who often have the luxury of working in less representational media than writing, an art that seems confined to working with what Saint Paul calls the letter that kills. Throughout the works discussed here, Wideman struggles against such death and tries to make words do more. Although read words inexorably represent something, they also have the power to extract and save something of actual human life that is indestructible, or, in the words of *Fanon,* "uninventable" (164). Each of these works enchants the word, impressing it into service, and forcing it to function like the matter of other media—as the icon and religious relic; as hagiography where the body becomes a text and the text becomes a body; as life capturing film images; as sculptures in space; as time and space defying collage; as spirit channeling painting; as motion freezing photography, and, of course, as great Black music. The force or *àshe* of these works not only aligns them with twenty-first-century Afropessimism, but with Afrofuturism (Black Speculative Fiction) and the Afro-mysticism of musicians such as Sun Ra. Yet categorizing them is a dead end. According to Robert Farris Thompson, a "thing or work of art that has *àshe* "transcends ordinary questions about its makeup and confinements: it is divine force incarnate" (7).

On some levels, it seems fitting to link these later works of Wideman to the music of his near age mate; the experimental alto-saxophonist Anthony Braxton. Born in 1945, Braxton has also been figured as an esoteric, stridently independent artist who often seemed to accept and then resist the limiting prescriptions of the Black Cultural Nationalists of music as he voraciously located his work in a variety of cultural traditions. In his description of Braxton's use of pictogram titles for his work, Graham Lock instructs readers to "Imagine a very personal mystery system that draws on, say, Egyptian hieroglyphics, astrological correspondences, druidic runes, and voodoo *vèvè* and you may have some idea of the kind of areas to which (I guess) Braxton's titling systems are related" (10). Although he openly owns European influences, Braxton, says Lock, "like Sun Ra, aligns himself (at least in part) to a black spiritual lineage that reaches back through African history to the mystery systems of ancient Egyptian civilization" (13). And like Wideman, he engages in the practice of crafting functional art. "My music, my life's work," he asserts "will ultimately challenge the very foundations of Western value systems" (quoted in Lock 163). He similarly refuses to stay within his medium, sometimes working with sound like a visual artist and producing "collage improvisation, thinking in terms of collage" (quoted on 203). He, too, plays in the darkness, rejecting the "narrative mode" as structured by conventional notions of melody, harmony, and rhythm. In fact, he says he has produced for music his own "100 plus languages" (quoted on 103). Locks calls him a "meta*physician* writing [. . .] prescriptions" (quoted on 10).

In these "prescriptions" for an art that *"will"* (future tense) alter "Western value systems" (quoted in Lock 163), Braxton, like Louis Till in *Writing to Save a Life,* "articulates a very Igbo understanding." This understanding, which inveighs against the "Euclidean niceness" and "Derridian diddly-bop from the mess that signifies nothing" described by *Philadelphia Fire*'s amalgamated Caliban, manifests Wideman's version of the Igbo proverb "all stories are true." It embraces the spirit of the Frantz Fanon quote, captured in *Fanon's* epigram, which asserts that the "imaginary life cannot be isolated from the real life." Along with Fanon and the Igbo, Braxton insists that the art of "music can permeate into the greater culture and [. . .] through the understanding itself" (quoted on 201). He asks:

> What's wrong with the idea of establishing a universal composite information base that can help us better to sustain and appreciate physicality? With this information it might be possible to heal the planet—a music to heal deserts [. . .] You know, music as a practical tool to help create planets and states of being, so, since we've made this planet unhealthy, we can go to another planet. Or if we can heal this planet, we might still want to go to another planet just because it exists. (quoted on 209).

He insists that the "challenge of creativity, as far as I'm concerned, is to move toward the greatest thought that you can think of [. . .] I'm saying that whatever you think can be manifested. And whatever that is can be generated" (quoted on 211).

Through embracing similar cosmology in his later works, Wideman inserts himself onto the company of practitioners of the black arts. And like them, he established a significant body of work that may or may not be understood in conventional terms. This is not a problem within the matrix of a "very Igbo understanding" exhibited by Braxton. Says Braxton: "It's funny. When you establish a consistent body of work it makes its own reality, and there's no way it can be put down or put up: it becomes something that exists for human beings, a body of musics that will help people on the planet" (quoted on 154). Still, the question remains of whether Wideman's bundles of spirt-embodying material in the form of novels actually function to protect people and perhaps even "help people on this planet." When asked during the interview that concludes this book if his work had changed the practices of the Pennsylvania penal system and altered its attitude toward mass incarceration, Wideman projects a very Afropessimist attitude toward any system of knowledge that could produce the type of consciousness that would proffer a tidy answer. Indeed, he responds much as Frederick Douglass did, after taking a magical root from an "old advisor" in the woods, battling a slave-breaker, and initiating a "turning-point" in his "career as a slave." From "whence came the spirit I don't know—I resolved to fight," Douglass says (393). In a similar response, Wideman transfigures into Kassima of *Two Cities* reacting to Mr. Mallory's "ruined" film negatives with the type of Wideman question, "Who knows," that Bonnie TuSmith calls a rhythm and "incantation" that "often doubles as a thoughtful statement due to the use of a period rather than a question mark" (TuSmith X). The markers separating question from statement fall away and Wideman responds to the inadequacy of Western knowledge and its ability to provide any kind of meaningful answer about the efficacy of his work. "Who knows," he concludes. "Who knows."

Works Cited

Achebe, Chinua. *Things Fall Apart*. 1959. Ballantine Books, 1984.
Alexander, Michelle, and Cornel West. *The New Jim Crow: Mass Incarceration in the Age of Colorblindness*. New Press, 2020.
Ali, Muhammad. Interview. "*The Black Scholar* Interviews Muhammad Ali." *The Black Scholar* 1, no. 8 (1970):32–39.
Anderson, Benedict. *Imagined Communities: Reflections on the Origin and Spread of Nationalism*. Verso, 1991.
Anderson, John and Hilary Hevenor. *Burning Down the House: MOVE and the Tragedy of Philadelphia*. W.W. Norton and Co., 1987.
Armah, Ayi Kwei. *The Beautyful Ones Are Not Yet Born*. Houghton Mifflin Harcourt, 1968.
Baker, Houston, Jr., *Blues, Ideology, and Afro-American Literature*, Chicago: University of Chicago Pries, 1987.
Baraka, Amiri. "A Post-Racial Anthology?" *Poetry* 202, no. 2 (2013):166–173.
———. *The Autobiography of LeRoi Jones*. 1984. Lawrence Hill Books, 1997.
———. "Black Art," *The Leroi Jones/Amiri Baraka Reader*. Ed. William J. Harris. New York: Thunder's Mouth Press, 1991, pp. 219–220.
———. "The Black Arts Movement," *The Leroi Jones/Amiri Baraka Reader*. Ed. William J. Harris. Thunder's Mouth Press, 1991, pp. 499–506.
———. "The Changing Same (R&B and New Black Music)." *The Leroi Jones/Amiri Baraka Reader*. Ed. William J. Harris. Thunder's Mouth Press, 1991, pp. 186–209.
———. Letter to Robert Duncan, April 24, 1963. Box 1. MSS037. Robert Duncan Papers 1955-1971. Department of Special Collections, Washington University Libraries, University City, MO. 4 Nov., 2016.
Barnhurst Kevin G. and John Nerone. *The Form of The News: A History*. Guilford Press, 2000.
Berben, Jacqueline. *La Communauté et la communication dans L'univers fictif de John Edgar Wideman*. 1987. Thèse, Doctorat de 3ᵉ Cycle. Université de la Sorbonne Nouvelle, Paris III.

———."Mother Goose and Brother Loon: The Fairy-Tale-in-the-Tale as Vehicle of Displacement." *Callaloo* 22, no. 3 (1999):594–602.

"Bette A. Wideman" Obituary. Pittsburgh Post-Gazette. 9 Feb 2008, obituaries.post-gazette.com/obituary/bette-wideman-1078630025. Accessed: August 13, 2020

Baudrillard, Jean. "Simulacra and Simulations." *Jean Baudrillard: Selected Writings, 2nd Edition.* Ed. Mark Poster. Standford University Press, 2001, pp. 169-187

Benjamin, Walter, and Hannah Arendt. *Illuminations.* Mariner Books, 2019.

Benston, Kimberly W. "The Black Arts Era." *The Norton Anthology of African American Literature. Third Edition. Vol II.* Eds. Henry Louis Gates and Valerie Smith. New York: Norton 2014, pp. 533–561.

Benveniste Émile. *Problemes De Linguistique Generale.* Gallimard, 1966.

Birkerts, Sven. "The Fever Days: John Edgar Wideman re-creates the chaos of an 18th-century epidemic." *New York Times Book Review,* 3 Nov., 1996, p. 20.

Brody, Richard. An Exile in Paradise: How Jean-Luc Godard disappeared from the headlines and into the movies." *New Yorker,* 13 Oct. 2014, newyorker.com/magazine/2000/11/20/exile-paradise. Accessed 15 Aug. 2020.

Brokaw, Tom. *The Greatest Generation.* Random House, 1998.

Byerman, Keith Eldon. *John Edgar Wideman: A Study of the Short Fiction.* Twayne Publishers, 1998.

———. *The Life and Work of John Edgar Wideman.* Praeger, 2013.

Casmier, Stephen. *L'esthetique du jazz dans l'oeuvre de John Edgar Wideman.* 1998. Thèse de doctorat en Études anglaises. Université de Nice-Sophia Antopolis.

———. "Did I Get James Baldwin Wrong?" *NPR,* NPR, 5 Feb. 2017, www.npr.org/sections/codeswitch/2017/02/05/513144736/did-i-get-james-baldwin-wrong. Accessed 31 Jan. 2021.

———. "The Funky Novels of John Edgar Wideman: Odor and Ideology in *Reuben, Philadelphia Fire* and *The Cattle Killing.*" *Critical Essays on John Edgar Wideman.* Eds. Bonnie TuSmith and Keith Byerman. Knoxville: University of Tennessee Press, 2006, pp. 191–204.

———."Rising from the ashes." *The Times Picayune,* 21 Oct. 1990, p. E-8.

———. "Two distinct voices make sweet harmony." *The Times Picayune,* 14 Jan. 1990.

Chicago Tribune. "Sift Mass of Clews for Sex Killer: Chief Suspect Baffles Police By Mixed Tales: 15 Seized in Slaying of Mother," *Chicago Tribune,* 28 May, 1938, p. 1.

Clausen, Jan. "Native Fathers." *The Kenyon Review* 14, no. 2(1992):44–55.

Cluster, Dick, and Rodríguez Rafael Hernández. *The History of Havana.* OR Books, in Partnership with Counterpoint Press, 2018.

Coates, Ta-Nehisi. *Between the World and Me.* Random House, 2015.

Coleman, James. *Blackness and Modernism: The Literary Career of John Edgar Wideman.* University of Mississippi Press, 1989.

———. *Writing Blackness: John Edgar Wideman's Art and Experimentation.* University of Louisiana Press, 2010.

Cone, James H. *Black Theology and Black Power.* Orbis, 1997.

Crapol, Edward P. *John Tyler, The Accidental President*. The University of North Carolina Press, 2012.

Creekmore, Hubert. "Social Factors in Native Son," *University of Kansas City Review* 8 (1941):136–143.

Currey, James. "Literary Publishing After Nigerian Independence: Mbari as Celebration." *Research in African Literatures* 44, no. 2 (2013):8–16.

Davis, Charles T. and Henry Louis Gates, Eds. *The Slave's Narrative*. Oxford: Oxford University Press, 1985.

Davis, Miles, and Quincy Troupe. *Miles: the Autobiography* Simon & Schuster, 1989.

Deren, Maya. *Divine Horsemen: The Living Gods of Haiti*. 1953. McPherson 1983.

Domke, David. *Journalists, Framing, and Discourse About Race Relations*. Journalism & Mass Communication Monographs, 164, 1997.

Douglass, Frederick. *Narrative of the Life of Frederick Douglass*. *The Classic Slave Narratives*. Ed. Henry Louis Gates. Signet Classics, 2002, pp. 323–436.

Edlestein, David. "Now Playing at Your Local Multiplex: Torture Porn." *New York*, 2 Feb 2006, nymag.com/movies/features/15622/. Accessed 14 Aug 2020.

Edwards, Brent Hayes. *Epistrophies Jazz and the Literary Imagination*. Harvard University Press, 2017.

———. "Wideman's Breadth." *Regards Croises Sur Les Afro-Americains/ Cross Perspectives on African Americans*. Presses Universitaires François Rabelais, 2003, pp. 199–204.

Ellison, Ralph W. *Invisible Man*. Vintage International, 1995.

Everett, Percival L. *The Water Cure*. Graywolf Press, 2007.

Fanon, Frantz. *Black Skin, White Masks*. Translated by Richard Philcox 1952. Grove Press, 2008

———. *The Wretched of the Earth*. Translated by Richard Philcox. 1963. Grove Press, 2004.

Fedler, Fred. *Reporting for the Print Media 3rd Edition*. Harcourt Brace Javanovich, 1984.

Franciscan Media, franciscanmedia.org/saint-martin-de-porres. Accessed 23 August 2020.

Gates, Henry Louis, Jr. Ed. *The Classic Slave Narratives*. Signet Classics, 2002.

———. *The Signifying Monkey: A Theory of African-American Literary Criticism*. Oxford University Press, 1988.

——— and Valerie Smith. *The Norton Anthology of African American Literature*. *Third Edition. Vol II*. Norton 2014.

———. "The Two Nations of Black America: The Best of Times, the Worst of Times." *The Brookings Review* 16, no. 2 (1998):4–7.

Giacometti, Alberto. "A Letter from Alberto Giacometti to Pierre Matisse, 1947." *Alberto Giacometti*. New York: The Museum of Modern Art, 1965.

Gillespie, Dizzy with Al Fraser. *To Be or Not to Bop: Memoirs of Dizzy Gillespie*. DaCapo, 1979.

González, Juan and Joseph Torres. *News for All the People: The Epic Story of Race and the American Media*. Verso, 2012.

Gossett, Thomas F. *Race: The History of an Idea in America*. 1963. Oxford University Press, 1997.
Guzzio, Tracie Church. *All Stories Are True: History, Myth, and Trauma in the Work of John Edgar Wideman*. University Press of Mississippi, 2011.
"Harriet Jacobs." *The Norton Anthology of African American Literature. Third Edition. Vol I*. Ed. Henry Louis Gates and Valerie Smith. New York: Norton 2014, pp. 221–224.
Holloway, Karla F. C. "*Beloved*: A Spiritual." *Callaloo* 13, no. 3 (1990):516–525.
Howe, Irving. "Black Boys and Native Sons," *Dissent* 10 (1963):353–368.
Hughes, Langston. "Harlem." *The Norton Anthology of African American Literature. Third Edition. Vol I*. Ed. Henry Louis Gates and Valerie Smith. New York: Norton 2014, p. 1319.
———. "The Negro Artist and the Racial Mountain." *The Norton Anthology of African American Literature. Third Edition. Vol II*. Ed. Henry Louis Gates and Valerie Smith. New York: Norton 2014, pp. 1320–1324.
Hurston, Zora Neale. "High John De Conquer." *The Sanctified Church*. Turtle Island, 1981.
Jablow, Alta. "Gassire's Lute: A Reconstruction of Soinke Bardic Art." *Research in African Literatures* 15, no. 4 (1984):519–529.
Jacobs, Harriet (Linda Brent), *Incidents in the Life of a Slave Girl. The Classic Slave Narratives*. Ed. Henry Louis Gates. Signet Classics, 2002, pp. 437–668.
James, C. L. R. *The Black Jacobins: Toussaint L'Ouverture and the San Domingo Revolution*. 1938. 2nd edition. Vintage, 1989.
James, George. "Newborn is thrown in Trash and Dies." *New York Times* 14 Aug. 1991, B-3.
Joyce, James. *Portrait of the Artist as a Young Man*. 1916. Penguin Books, 1976.
Karenga, Ron. "Black Cultural Nationalism." *The Black Aesthetic*, edited by Addison Gayle, Jr., Doubleday, 1971, pp. 32–38.
Kendrick, Walter. "A Voodoo Guide to the Marginal." *The New York Times Book Review*. 8 November 1987, Sec. 7, p. 3.
Kerner, Aaron. *Torture Porn in the Wake of 9/11: Horror, Exploitation, and the Cinema of Sensation*. Rutgers University Press, 2015.
Kifner, John. "The 'War' Between Panthers And Police." *New York Times*, 21 Dec. 1969, p. E3.
King, Author Don Roy. "SNL Transcripts: 10/03/81: 'Prose and Cons'." *SNL Transcripts Tonight, 3* Jan. 2019, snltranscripts.jt.org/81/81aprose.phtml. Accessed 20 Sept. 2020.
Kinnamon, Keneth. "Native Son: The Personal, Social, and Political Background." *Phylon* 30, no. 1 (1969):66–72.
Lacey, Steve. "Thelonious Monk's Advice to Steve Lacy." *Ramsey Castaneda, DMA: Performance, Education, and Scholarship*, ramseycastaneda.com/resources/thelonious-monk-advice-steve-lacy.html?fbclid=IwAR3IHkBp6mCBzJ6euW1BLtxIx2_esXDQYUnDS2p7yMI8N4bvnP3furlAOHQ. Accessed 4 Sept. 2020.
Leavelle, Charles. "BRICK SLAYER IS LIKENED TO JUNGLE BEAST: Ferocity is Reflected in Nixon's Features." *Chicago Tribune* 5 June 1938, p. 6.

Lemann, Nicholas. *The Promised Land: The Great Black Migration and how it Changed America*. Vintage, 1992.

Lemons, J. Stanley. "Black Stereotypes as Reflected in Popular Culture, 1880-1920." *American Quarterly* 29, no. 1 (1977):102–116.

Lewis, George. *A Power Stronger than Itself: the AACM and American Experimental Music*. University of Chicago Press, 2009.

Lock, Graham. Forces in Motion: *The Music and Thoughts of Anthony Braxton*. New York: DaCapo Press, 1988.

———. "Introduction." *Mixtery: A Festschrift for Anthony Braxton*. Ed. Graham Lock. Stride Publications, 1995.

Lodge, David. "Mimesis and diegesis in modern fiction." *After Bakhtin: Essays on Fiction and Criticism*. London, Routledge, 1990.

Lott, Eric. "Love and Theft: The Racial Unconscious of Blackface Minstrelsy." *Representations* 39 (1992):23–50.

Lyotard, Jean-François. *The Postmodern Condition: A Report on Knowledge*. Trans. Geoff Bennington and Brian Massumi. University of Minnesota Press, 1989.

Mackey, Nathaniel. "Baraka in Bohemia." *Novel: A Forum on Fiction* 14, no. 2 (1981):184–187.

———. *Bedouin Hornbook*, University of Kentucky, 1986.

Mbalia, Doreatha Drummond. *John Edgar Wideman: Reclaiming the African Personality*. Associated University Press, 1995.

Malraux, André. *La Tête d'obsidienne*. Gallimard, 1974.

——— *Picasso's Mask*. Trans. June Guicharnaud and Jaques Guicharnaud. Holt, Rinehart and Winston, 1976.

Matthews, Donald. *Blackcentricity: How Ancient Black Cultures Created Civilization. Revealing the Truth that White Supremacy Denied*. PARE (Program Against Racist Education), Createspace, Tacoma, Washington, 2020

Meese, Edwin. Interview. *Frontline,* 8 Jan. 2007, pbs.org/wgbh/pages/frontline/newswar/interviews/meese.html. Accessed: August 22, 2020

Miller, Ivor L. "Religious Symbolism in Cuban Political Performance." *TDR* 44, no. 2 (2000):30–55.

Mingus, Charles. *Beneath the Underdog*. 1971. Vintage, 1991.

Mississippi Madam: The Life of Nellie Jackson. Dirs. Mark Brockway and Timothy Givens. 2017. Film Documentary.

Morrison, Toni. *Beloved*. New York: Alfred A. Knopf, 1987.

———. "Rootedness: The Ancestor as Foundation." *Black Women Writers (1950–1980): A Critical Evaluation*. Ed. Mari Evans. Anchor, 1984, pp. 339–345.

———. *Playing in the Dark*. Cambridge: Harvard University Press, 1992.

Mulvey, Laura. "Visual Pleasure and Narrative Cinema." Feminism and Film Theory. Ed. Constance Penley. Routledge 1988, pp. 57–68.

Napier, Winston. "From the Shadows: Houston Baker's Move toward a Postnationalist Appraisal of the Black Aesthetic Black Aesthetic." *New Literary History* 25, no. 1 (1994):159–174.

Neroni, Hilary. *The Subject of Torture: Psychoanalysis and Biopolitics in Television and Film*. Columbia University Press, 2015.

Nielsen, Aldon Lynn. *Black Chant: Languages of African-American Postmodernism.* Cambridge University Press, 1997.

Okunoye, Oyeniyi. "The Critical Reception of Modern African Poetry." *Cahiers D'études Africaines* 44, no. 176 (2004):769–791.

Ong, Walter, S.J. *Interfaces of the Word: Studies in the Evolution of Consciousness and Culture.* Cornell University Press, 1982.

———. *Orality and Literacy: the Technologizing of the Word.* Routledge, 2012.

———. *The Presence of the Word: Some Prolegomena for Cultural and Religious History.* 1967. University of Minnesota Press, 1981.

Ouattara, Tiona Ferdinand. Afterward. Susan Elizabeth Gagliardi and Constantijn Petridis. *Senufo Unbound: Dynamics of Art and Identity in West Africa.* The Cleveland Museum of Art, 2015.

Padilioni, James Jr. "A Miami Misterio : Sighting San Martín de Porres at the Crossroads of Catholicism and Dominican Vodú." *U.S. Catholic Historian* 38, no. 2 (2020):85–111.

Pentcheva, Bissera V. "The Performative Icon." *The Art Bulletin* 88, no. 4 (2006):631–655.

Pinckney, Darryl. "'Cos I'm a so-o-oul man': The back-country blues of John Edgar Wideman." *Times Literary Supplement.* August 23, 1991, pp. 19–20.

Prokopow, Michael J. "Material Truths: The Quilts of Gee's Bend at the Whitney Museum of Art: An Exhibition," *Winterthur Portfolio* 38, no. 1 (2003):57–66.

Puckett, John and Devin DeSilvis. "MOVE on Osage Avenue," *West Philadelphia Collaborative History,* collaborativehistory.gse.upenn.edu/stories/move-osage-a venue. Accessed 8 Sept. 2020.

Ra, Sun. *Destination Unknown.* Aarburg, Switzerland, 1992. Compact Disk.

Rampersad, Arnold. "The Literary Blues Tradition." Review of *Blues, Ideology, and Afro-American Literature: A Vernacular Theory*, by Houston A. Baker. *Callaloo,* No. 24, 1985, pp. 498–500.

Read, Ishmael. "Neo-Hoodoo Manifesto." *The Norton Anthology of African American Literature. Third Edition. Vol II.* Ed. Henry Louis Gates and Valerie Smith. Norton 2014, pp. 808–813.

———. Interview with John O'Brien. "Ishmael Reed." *Conversations with Ishmael Reed.* Eds. Bruce Dick and Amritjit Singh. UP of Mississippi, 1995, pp. 14–24.

———. *Mumbo Jumbo.* 1972. New York: Scribner, 1996.

Reynolds, David, writer and narrator. *Long Shadow.* Clearstory, 2014.

Rhodes, Jane. "Fanning the Flames of Racial Discord: The National Press and the Black Panther Party." *The Harvard International Journal of Press Politics* 4, no. 4 (1999):95–118.

Richard, Jean-Pierre. "John Edgar Wideman: A Bibliography of Primary and Secondary Sources." *Callaloo* 22, no. 3 (1999):750–758.

Rose, Christopher. "Death of madam ends era in Natchez." *The Times-Picayune,* 15 July 1990, 1–2.

Schmidt, Klaus. "*John Edgar Wideman: Reclaiming the African Personality* by Doreatha Drummond Mbalia: *Langston Hughes and the* Chicago Defender: *Essays on Race, Politics, and Culture, 1942-62* by Langston Hughes and Christopher C.

De Santis." *Amerikastudien / American Studies*, Vol. 43, No. 3, The American Sublime (1998), pp. 538–542.

———. "Reading Black Postmodernism: John Edgar Wideman's *Reuben*." *Flip Sides: New Critical Essays on American Literature*. P. Lang, 1995.

Senghor, Léopod Sédar. *Selected Poems by Léopod Sédar Senghor*. Trans. John Rede and Clive Wake. Oxford University Press, 1964.

Seymour. Gene. "Dream Surgeon." *The Nation*. 28 Oct. 1996.

Shafer, Jack. "On the Trail of the Question, Who First Said (or Wrote) That Journalism Is the 'First Rough Draft of History'?" *Slate*, 31 Aug. 2010, slate.com/news-and-politics/2010/08/on-the-trail-of-the-question-who-first-said-or-wrote-that-journalism-is-the-first-rough-draft-of-history.html. Accessed 18 Aug 2020.

Smith, Julia M. H. "Oral and Written: Saints, Miracles, and Relics in Brittany, c. 850-1250." *Speculum* 65, no. 2 (1990):309–343.

Smith, Rachel J.D. *Excessive Saints: Gender, Narrative, and Theological Invention in Thomas of Cantimpré's Mystical Hagiographies*. Columbia University Press, 2019.

Smith, Valerie. "Emmett Till's Ring." *Women's Studies Quarterly* 36, no. 1/2 (2008):151–161.

Snead, James A. "On Repetition in Black Culture." *Black American Literature Forum* 15, no. 4 (1981):146–154.

Soyinka, Wole, "This Past Must Address Its Present. The Nobel Prize in Literature 1986. *NobelPrize.org*, nobelprize.org/nobel_prizes/literature/laureates/1986/soyinka-lecture.html. Accessed 18 Sept. 2020.

Stamelman, Richard. "The Art of the Void: Alberto Giacometti and the Poets of "L'Ephémère." *L'Esprit Créateur* 22, no. 4 (1982):15–25.

Staub, Michael E. "Black Panthers, New Journalism, and the Rewriting of the Sixties." *Representations* 57 (1997):52–72.

Stepto, Robert Burns. "I Rose and Found My Voice: Narration, Authentication and Authorial Control in Four Slave Narratives," in Charles T. Davis and Henry Louis Gates, eds. *The Slave's Narrative*. Oxford University Press, 1985, pp. 225–241.

The Times-Picayune. "Two badly burned in former brothel." *The Times-Picayune*, 7 July 1990, p. B-5.

Thompson, Robert Farris. *Flash of the Spirit: African & Afro-American Art & Philosophy*. Random House, 1983.

Ture, Kwame, and Charles V. Hamilton. *Black Power: The Politics of Liberation*. 1967. Vintage 1992.

TuSmith, Bonnie. "The Value of Reading Wideman." *Critical Essays on John Edgar Wideman*. Eds. Bonnie TuSmith and Keith Byerman. Knoxville: University of Tennessee Press, 2006, pp. vii–x.

Uzukwu, E. Elochukwu "Igbo World and Ultimate Reality and Meaning." *Ultimate Reality and Meaning* 5 no. 3 (1982):188–209.

Wagner-Pacifici, Robin Erica. *Discourse and Destruction: The City of Philadelphia Versus MOVE*. University of Chicago Press, 1994.

Wahlman, Maude Southwell. "African Symbolism in Afro-American Quilts." *African Arts* 20, no. 1 (1986):68–76+99.

Walker, Alice. *In Search of Our Mothers' Gardens*. HarcourtBrace, 1983.
Walker, Margaret. *Richard Wright, Daemonic Genius*. Warner Books, 1987.
Wall, Cheryl A. "The Contemporary Period." *The Norton Anthology of African American Literature. Third Edition. Vol II*. Ed. Henry Louis Gates and Valerie Smith. Norton 2014, pp. 913–929.
Webster's II: New Riverside Dictionary. New York: Berkley Books, 1984.
West, Cornell. Preface. Michelle Alexander. *The New Jim Crow: Mass Incarceration in the Age of Colorblindness*. New Press, 2020.
Wideman, John Edgar. *Brothers and Keepers*. New York: Holt Rinehart, 1984.
———. "Between the Shadow and the Act." The Romare Bearden Reader. Ed. Robert G. O'Meally. Duke University Press, 2019, pp. 209–216.
———. *The Cattle Killing*. Houghton Mifflin, 1996.
———. "Charles Chesnutt and the WPA Narratives: The Oral and Literate Roots of Afro-American Literature." *The Slave's Narrative*. Eds. Charles T. Davis and Henry Louis Gates, Jr. Oxford University Press, 1985, pp. 59–78.
———. "Damballah." *The Stories of John Edgar Wideman*. Pantheon Books, 1992, pp. 275–284.
———. "Defining the Black Voice in Fiction." *Black American Literature Forum* 2, no. 3 (1977):79–82.
———. "Doc's Story." *The Stories of John Edgar Wideman*. Pantheon Books, 1992, pp. 145–153.
———. *Fanon*. Houghton Mifflin, 2008.
———. *A Glance Away*. 1967. Holt, Rinehart and Winston, 1985.
———. "Glass Eye." Andrew Brewerton, Pierre Ennès and John Edgar Wideman. *Antoine Leperlier La métaphysique Du Verre*. Trad. Catherine Nédonchelle. Musée National De Céramique, 2007, p. 84.
———. *Hurry Home*. 1970. Henry Holt, 1986.
———. Interview with Charles Rowell. "An Interview with John Edgar Wideman, Charles Rowell/ 1989," *Conversations with John Edgar Wideman*. Ed. Bonnie TuSmith. University of Mississippi Press, 1998, pp. 86–104.
———. Interview with James Coleman. "Interview with John Edgar Wideman, James W. Coleman/ 1988," *Conversations with John Edgar Wideman*. Ed. Bonnie TuSmith. University of Mississippi Press, 1998, pp. 62–80.
———. Interview with Wilfred Samuels. "Going Home: A Conversation with John Edgar Wideman, Wilfred Samuels/ 1983," *Conversations with John Edgar Wideman*. Ed. Bonnie TuSmith. University of Mississippi Press, 1998, pp. 14–31.
———. *The Island of Martinique*. National Geographic Society, 2003.
———. "Lizabeth: The Caterpillar Story." *The Stories of John Edgar Wideman*. Pantheon Books, 1992, pp. 301–317.
———. *Lynchers*. Lulu Com, 2010.
———. "Malcolm X: The Art of Autobiography." *Malcolm X: In Our Own Image*. Ed. Joe Wood. St Martins Press, 1992, pp. 103–110.
———. "Newborn Thrown in Trash and Dies." *The Stories of John Edgar Wideman*. Pantheon Books, 1992, pp. 120–128.
———. *Philadelphia Fire*. New York: Henry Holt and Company, 1990.

———. *Reuben*. New York: Henry Holt and Company, 1987.
———. *Sent for You Yesterday*: Houghton Mifflin Company, 2006.
———. *The Stories of John Edgar Wideman*. Pantheon Books, 1992.
———. *Two Cities*. Houghton Mifflin, 1998.
———. *Writing to Save a Life*. Scribner, 2016.
Wideman, Robert. "Robert Wideman: I Would Have Died in Prison without Commutation." *Pittsburgh Post-Gazette*, 16 Sept. 2020, post-gazette.com/opinion/Op-Ed/2020/07/09/Robert-Wideman-prison-commutation-life-without-parole-death-by-incarceration-Pennsylvania/stories/202007090036. Accessed 2 Sept. 2020.
Wilderson, Frank B. *Afropessimism*. Liveright Publishing Corporation, 2020.
Wilson, William J. *The Truly Disadvantaged*. University of Chicago Press, 1990.
Wise, Christopher. "Nyama and Heka: African Concepts of the Word." *Comparative Literature Studies* 43, no. 1–2 (2006):19–38.
Wolfe, Tom. "Radical Chic: That Party at Lenny's." *New York*, 8 June 1970.
Wright, Richard. "How 'Bigger' Was Born." Richard Wright. *Native Son*. Harper Perennial, 2005.
Wright, Richard. *Native Son*. Harper Perennial, 2005.
Yellin, Jean Fagan. Editor and Introduction. Harriet Jacobs. *Incidents in the Life of a Slave Girl, Written by Herself*." Harvard University Press, 1987.

Appendix

Keeping the Language of Fiction Alive: Interview with John Edgar Wideman, June 2019

> *Surrounded by field and woods, the cottage near the Gulf of Morbihan sat private and isolated, a fort-five-minute walk from Arradon, the closest town. Arradon a town where years later my wife and I would buy a house. Train from Paris to Vannes bus Vannes to Arradon, taxi from town to cottage.*
>
> (Writing to Save a Life 136)

The house John Edgar Wideman bought with his wife, Catherine Nedonchelle, sits on a winding street lined with an occasional, thatched, gray-granite farmhouse and cream-colored stucco houses crowned with black slate roofs. Their home is a two-story cottage with working, blue shutters and a small enclosed front garden. Wideman had just celebrated his seventy-eighth birthday but had changed little in the twenty years since I first met him at a conference. He stood straight, tall, a little thinner than before, but carefully athletic and still able, he later told me, to carry his three-year old granddaughter on his shoulders through the French village and adjoining forest the way his grandfather carried him through the streets of far-off Homewood—an act he often writes about. He seemed at ease and at home, barefooted and casually wearing black shorts and a black T-shirt when I arrived. He took me inside, guiding me through a narrow foyer toward the back of the house and into an immaculately kept, surprisingly sparse and tastefully decorated living and dining space. We entered the kitchen which held a small, European refrigerator and where a well-used, six-cup espresso percolator sat alone on the discreet stove as if it were a treasured work of art. At first, Wideman seemed somewhat bewildered about why I had come as if questioning which hat he needed to wear for the occasion. He formally offered me something to drink before we walked out of a sliding glass door and onto the tidy wooden deck lining the back of the house and facing the enclosed back yard—the site, perhaps where a writer figure sat drinking a glass of red wine and spent a summer "trying to save a life" in *Fanon*. We sat down on white wrought-iron chairs around a matching table. A blue patio umbrella, a color that matched the shutters, shielded us from the June sun. We started the interview, sometimes being interrupted by the odd suburban racket of a gas-powered lawn, or hedge-grooming machine. But mostly, the almost throaty cooing of doves, that Wideman generically called *tourterelles*, and the sound of children playing at a nearby primary school colored the background. Once finished, we took one of his habitual walks through the village and the pine woods surrounding a bay off the Gulf of Morbihan.

CASMIER:

Has living here in Brittany, France affected your work?

WIDEMAN:

Well, I came here because it's relaxing; it's beautiful.

And I'm not surrounded by the distractions of family and things I like back in the city, things I have fun with. A long time ago, I decided and made my life choices based on not necessarily making myself comfortable, per se, but clearing out as much as I could space so I could sit and think and have a chance to think my own thoughts without a lot of interference. And so, I've always looked for that spot. I thought I could find that in academia. And to a certain extent, I did. It was useful and I don't regret it at all.

I'm not connected here. I'm not tied down here by some immediate set of requirements. People see me wondering around. They look at me. They don't exactly know who I am. What it gives you is the opportunity to play. I can freeform. I can invent. I can imagine who I want to be. If I put on my best suit and went downtown to dinner, they would think of me as one kind of person.

CASMIER:

Where's the downtown?

WIDEMAN:

[laughter] Not only would I have to put on a suit, but then I would have to invent downtown, which means that probably the restaurant I went to likes to think of themselves as downtown. They want people to come in suits. They charge you so much money that you feel like you're in Paris because you're paying Paris prices. So, I would be part of that masquerade, which is the way it is back in the world, too. But it's not as complicated here. It's a little more easygoing. Fewer rules. Fewer constrictions. When I take my walks (and that's what I do most, walk) I might not see another person for two hours. If I see them, they don't know me. I don't know them. There's no compulsion to speak, no compulsion to figure out anything about the other person. They just pass on by.

CASMIER:

How long do your walks usually last?

WIDEMAN:

A quick one might be an hour and a half. A long one might be close to three hours. On a three-hour one, I might go somewhere and sit down and cop some rays for half an hour and walk back. I can walk to the deep water. We can walk around a corner where you'll see the bay. You'll see the bay and more beyond. It will look like the sea. You'll think you're in the sea. It has a tide and it's salty. You know, when my daughter was here, my granddaughter was only three and we took great walks together and I wound up carrying her some.

CASMIER:

When people discuss your work, they discuss it in terms of place. They discuss it in terms of Pittsburgh, and they discuss it in terms of Philadelphia. Do you feel, now that you live here, that you have entered into, at least mentally, a different kind of space?

WIDEMAN:

I think you have to invent a language to float or make any space real. Part of that job, that very difficult job, is to somehow find the language. Now, for African American writers, that often means in the South—and the kind of vernacular of accuracy and power and discovery. But I think that's the challenge. That's the challenge I took and it's one I still feel: to create a language. And then through that language, creating a place or people. Or, start from the other side: take the people or place and distill it into a language.

CASMIER:

Has that changed because of your being here? Is it more difficult? Can you figure this place? Do you have a language for this place as much as you had? In *Writing to Save a Life,* the author figure is here to a large extent, and the other places are sort of becoming distant.

WIDEMAN:

Time has passed. People are dying. But I think it's the same.

When the language is powerful enough, it both includes dimensions of time and place, but it transcends those. For instance, I've been rereading *Blood Meridian* and *Suttree* by Cormac McCarthy and one novel is about the West; the other is about Tennessee. That's where they take place. But what is so absolutely powerful—absolutely breathtaking—about both books are the words on page, the language that he creates to make those places real. I mean, he's talking about the American West in the 1880s and he has clearly gone to school in terms of the geography and the rock formations and the earth and the mountains. You could spend your whole day just looking up words on ten pages. It's incantatory. And these guys are doing nothing. They get on their horses and they go travel. Then, they kill a bunch people. They either run away or they get chased and they go some other place. And that's all that happens.

But the whole American West, the idea of the West—the myths of it, the history of it, the languages that converge in it—they're all captured on the page. That's what I wanted to do. That's what I do want to do, and I think, when I write best, I do it. The American West doesn't in a sense exist. Yes, on a map. But it's a question of really transforming it into words and talk.

CASMIER:

In your work, you create such a space for conceptualizing certain aspects of the American experience and the African American experience.

WIDEMAN:

We'll talk about politics. We both agree that space is an arbitrary concept and it's invented over time, but it also gets standardize. It also gets full of clichés or it gets Hollywoodized, or it gets legislated. Mississippi is Mississippi because of courts and because of organized violence and because of other institutionalized ways of changing that space. Now, the challenge for an African American writer born in Mississippi might be to compete with a definition or a version of that space that is convincing to somebody; that is freeing to somebody. You know, writing a book about a guy in jail, you might just repeat the sort of understood logic of a prison. That guy's a convict. He's a bad guy. There are other mean motherfuckers around and they kill each other, and they are all in crime, and watch out! And, where is it? It's over here. It's a space beyond that wall, hedgerow, or whatever it is. And you wouldn't want to go there. And we don't want them coming here. But another kind of novel might make that space something entirely different, maybe not entirely different but it would have to compete.

CASMIER:

What else do you think the novel does in terms of creating our understanding of time and space versus that which is full of clichés, Hollywoodized, or legislated?

WIDEMAN:

Get out of the trap. You're not as good. You are inferior, you colored people, to White people. If you have problems, that's why you have them. Your inferior. You're in that bag, OK?

And maybe you don't like it, but you look around you and it's reinforced by everything you see. You live in a shitty place. Your friends don't make it to school. So, you're there. Okay. You work your ass off. You become a novelist, or you become a butcher, or you become whatever and you get yourself gone a little, you know, and you get out of that terrible neighborhood. You don't commit a crime. You become middle class. You have a decent suit. You have a decent car. You take care of your kids. What has happened? Are you out of the trap? It would seem like it, wouldn't it?

But everything you've done gets re-interpreted and re-introduced into the trap. Well Steve's a pretty good guy. He has a decent house. But where's all this decent coming from? It's that you have sort of replicated on another level, on the Black level, what were the givens of that society and what were the givens of success that you weren't supposed to have matched up to. And you busted your ass; you kind of matched them. And somebody says, yeah, he's pretty good. He's a pretty good old boy. But what have you done? Have you really upset the apple cart? Have you changed the notion of difference? Have you changed the notion of color? Have you changed the notion of how these two groups relate to one another?

CASMIER:

You don't identify yourself as an activist, but you're actually describing another kind of activism, because the trap is an aesthetic trap. We're living inside of somebody else's fictions.

WIDEMAN

Always. I'm reading the huge book by David Blight on Frederick Douglass. It's a fascinating book. Douglass was a slave. He frees himself. Then he lives through that whole period of emancipation, sees emancipation come, "thank the Lord," or whatever. But then he also sees reconstruction and all the things he's been saying about America have to be re-figured because the South, though it lost the war, is now winning the battle. And it's the same kind of thing. Whose standards are being applied and to whom are they applied? Who has a right to apply them? And who has the authority to applaud them? And it became quite dicey for him because he was moving up. They criticized him because he had a government job. They criticized him at the end because he had a White wife. You know, all kinds of things. He was split up.

He spent a lot of time and energy making that fight, but he kept giving the same old speech: It's not about Black people or White people. It's about living in a country that has a government that claims that that doesn't matter; that difference doesn't matter. But yet it keeps mattering. It keeps mattering. It keeps mattering. So, the trap is set by the way America treats race, thinks of race and thinks of Black, thinks of color. That trap is the one that I want my fiction to get us out of.

CASMIER:

I saw some news in the paper a few weeks ago about your brother and the possibility that he'll be paroled.

WIDEMAN:

It's too scary. There was a time once before when he was supposedly going to be released. We had a big family party in Pittsburgh and then it all got turned around at the last minute. That was heartbreaking for everybody. I don't know how he survived it, but he did. And so, I'm very conservative.

And the governor of Pennsylvania has attempted—is attempting, according to lots of people—to institute a more humane regime of prisons, and parole and probation. He has a new guy as a director of prisons. He has a new guy, actually a Black man who was in prison, as secretary of the parole board. All this is good. But Pennsylvania is still a lock him up and throw away the key state.

CASMIER:

I've been working on your stuff all of my adult professional life. And so, there's a question now of whether there is a cynicism creeping into your work. But if Pennsylvania has changed, part of that is your doing as well, right?

WIDEMAN:

Who knows? Who knows?

But I will say in advance that in terms of my relationship to the press and me saying anything in public about what's going on, that it's all off the record until he's actually out, because not only is he going through this kind of rigmarole, but my son also was paroled more than a year ago. And the people who still want a piece of his flesh in the family of the victim— very, very influential, very rich, very powerful—they managed through collusion with government people in Arizona to get my son reinterred after he was released. And that's a bizarre and Byzantine story, and most of it I don't even have the details about. But as a result, he was put back in the clink, back in prison. His parole was revoked. And since that happened, because it happened under some crazy circumstances, and I'll just say one: one is that his phone was tapped and conversations that he had with various people became part of the parole board hearing; that his home—he has a wife—was raided more than once. They never found anything. They never were doing it. But they were under the most strict kind of observation. There was a private detective following him, dogging him. This wasn't the state. This is the money of the victim's father.

And so, they managed to put together a sort of jerry-rigged case and have a hearing and put him back in jail. The proceedings—what happened—was so questionable that we are in the midst of what's called a "Special Action." That is, we've sought relief in terms of violation of my son's rights—constitutional rights—by this board, by private detectives, by etcetera, etcetera, etcetera, so that we want to reverse the parole board's decision. We want to show in the law through a judge that what happened to my son was illegal. And that's called a "Special Action." There have been hearings, and filings, and the state has fought it all the way, but we finally got it before a civil judge. And we're waiting as we speak for a pronouncement from that judge. But it's an Arizona judge and Arizona and Pennsylvania might be the two worst places in the country.

CASMIER:

You saved your brother in a way that many of us have not been able to save other people. Most people go to prison and they disappear.

WIDEMAN

Well, I owe him because he changed my life. And it's still happening. It ain't over. And Michelle [Alexander], writing that book about *The New Jim Crow*. All this stuff isn't a lie. They don't usually take it all the way back—she would—but the people who write about it don't take it back to *Brother's Keepers*.

CASMIER:

She even acknowledges that when she was first dealing with mass incarceration. The people, who were out there were people like Angela Davis and Amiri Baraka who were seen as extremists. So, they were no longer part of the discourse. You're one of the people who could be part of that discourse because somehow you escaped being seen as an extremist, I guess, from your first novels. You escaped being lumped in with the "political" writers.

WIDEMAN:

But that is beyond—was beyond—my control then and still is . . . the representation. Literature itself is a representation. And then the sort of ephemeral stuff, or epiphenomenon of culture and absorption and dispersion of ideas and language, that's another layer of artifice, another layer of things that the writer really doesn't control. You let the thing; you let the image go. You let your love for your brother go. You tell everybody why he is the kind of person he is. Another person comes along, they read it and they take what they can out of it. They may also see places where you were you were lying, where you were being a hypocrite, where you were talking about poor Black people and how terrible it is, but at the same time, you had this university professorship, you were unavailable on the phone and nobody ever saw you set foot outside your own interest once. So, you know, they figure out, well, this guy is a good talker, and maybe that's a good idea, but he also used the language in other ways.

We haven't spoken of Jimmy Baldwin. He became a saint. He is still a saint for many of the young Black writers today. But I think their comprehension of him is kind of rote, is kind of automatic. Jimmy Baldwin took an awful lot of chances. Jimmy Baldwin changed the language. What he wrote became part of American speech, became part of American thinking.

He really did transform the playing field. And that's what I mean when I say I change the language. You use it for something besides lying, which is not to say Jimmy didn't make a lot of mistakes.

CASMIER:

When I spent my junior year abroad in the South of France I wanted to meet James Baldwin. He lived in St. Paul de Vence. *This* is a different part of the country from St. Paul de Vence, though.

WIDEMAN:

One of the reasons I went to Amherst is because Baldwin was there and [Chinua] Achebe was there at the same time. They were adjunct. And [Ekwueme] Michael Thelwell, a Jamaican guy, was very, very good friends with Jimmy. So, it was usually the three of us. We were hanging out, Michael, myself and Jimmy. And it was just casual . . . social. But he liked Michael. And I was in his inner circle. I sang with him because he loved to drink, and when he got loaded, he would always want to sing hymns and to sing gospel. He was very good at it; knew all the songs. I knew him when I went to Amherst. He was around for a year or so, and then he died not too long after.

It was '86. That's when my son got in trouble. Seventy-six is when my brother got in trouble. Jacob got in trouble in the summer of 86. I was on my way to change jobs, but Jake never made it because that summer he killed a kid while in Arizona and he never joined us in Massachusetts. And that's when I knew Jimmy. So, like I said, I was really busy; a lot of things on my mind. I wasn't cultivating friendships. I was back and forth. It looked like they were going to try to kill my son—capital punishment. A lot of that time is a haze.

CASMIER:

That's weird how Americans are so bent on revenge. When you talk about the West, that's all the Western narrative is about to some extent, revenge. African Americans don't seem to have that as much as Americans in general.

WIDEMAN:

Well, we've been Americans a long time. Look at the gangs, they have taken it and run! My brother's son was a revenge killing—Omar. He got in a fight, kicked some guy's ass, and the guy happened to be a big-time gang banger. And he sent his boys and they went up to Omar's house and blew him away, standing right next to his wife with their two-year-old. Guys came up in the apartment and then: pow, pow! And that was a while ago.

CASMIER:

How did your family react? Did they want the person who did that to die?

WIDEMAN:

Well, we weren't in that culture and in the revenge culture. But I'm saying that the gangs have adopted it to the nth degree, so much so that we were afraid to bury my nephew because not only did they kill you, but to continue the revenge they would fuck up your funeral. And that was just standard procedure. They'd come in the funeral home, tear it up, terrorize people, beat them up. And the only reason that didn't happen is because a friend paid cops to sit outside. But even now, you know—Crips and Bloods, man—yes, we have picked up a few things. The whole power of the gang culture, not only on the gang members, but then in movies and in rap records. You know that was one of the terrible things about the 80s and 90s that these values, which did seem rather foreign to the to the culture—that mainline African American culture—were being infused. I think Bill Cosby was sort of fussing about it in his own knuckleheaded way.

CASMIER

How does your work relate to the work of the Black Arts Movement? There is this line drawn between contemporary writers and writers of that period. In the division, Black Arts Movement people were involved with urgent art, political art and the people who come afterwards are involved with mostly aesthetic issues.

WIDEMAN:

It's a vexed, vexed issue. And the stakes in it are sometimes academic, sometimes labels of books, labels of groups and competing theories and critics. But it's also very much a living issue. People make friends in one or don't like people in the other group. Judgments are made based on stereotypes and misunderstandings. History moves on. Time moves on. Baraka is dead. A lot of people are dead. And then there's a revisiting and recalculating of it all.

So, "A" it's time for that. But it's almost impossible for that to happen, because it's just like you say, "Black Arts." What the fuck does Black mean in that context? The word itself has been so stretched and politicized and popularized that to get on an even playing field; to begin to think clearly about what the issues are, you almost have to start at the level of: OK, what does it mean that people came to this country—a lot of them as slaves—, entered a segregated society, were pushed to the margins yet in spite of that were also incorporated into the country, developed cultural habits and languages, went to different parts of the country, and had different professions? You have to have to almost start there to clean up so that you're starting with something that has some truth in it and some sort of understanding of what actually happened.

CASMIER:

When you talk about getting at the truth, you need to somehow deal with ideology, right?

WIDEMAN:

Give it a fair reading and an accurate reading of what was actually happening. What were the forces? What was conspiring? How did a word like Black get captured? Remind people that it is a stipulating term. Remind people of what it means to even try to say: "Well, what are we? Are we colored people? Are we African American?" and all that stuff that's heaped up around that. Those are peripheral, but you can't get to the other stuff without going through it.

CASMIER:

Getting back to what you were saying earlier, one of the things that I found is that writers of your generation had personal interactions, particularly with Amiri Baraka. Black Arts and Amiri Baraka became the same thing for people and a lot of young writers of your generation were hurt by him, and it became a very personal thing.

WIDEMAN:

I can give you examples, also, of him being very hostile and being very dismissive. I didn't pay that much mind to it, but it was political. He could get you outed. He could get you just removed from what was then the ongoing discussion. He was a gatekeeper. No matter how Black you want to call it; it was also about access to White reporters and White media and White scholars because their approach was through the most well-known folks who were the Black Arts people. And so, they became kind of the gatekeepers to what African American artists were doing. [Imitating a reporter's voice] "Well, Mr. Baraka, what do you think of the work of John Wideman? [Imitating Baraka] Well, I don't think, much of it at all." Now, what's that guy going to then write about me; the guy who just heard that from "the man"?

CASMIER:

Afterward, the cultural firmament changed. What happened in the 1980s was a reaction. It was the era of mass incarceration and a kind of conservatism. In terms of the study of African American literature, it was the distancing of radicals. It was the "not-Baraka" era, and one of creating a space for serious study of the literature using the same kinds of tools that you use to study European literature. So, this is the dividing line between the Black Arts Movement and the contemporary era, even though Baraka is three years older than you or almost about the same age.

WIDEMAN:

Almost the same age. Well, see, I've been around a long time, so already I'm a hard case just because I have outlasted things, because the work responds, like anybody else's work, to its era, to the voices that are out there, to the forces that are out there. So, I've learned. Look. Women. I think I have had pretty reasonable, rational, loving thoughts about women my whole life because of my mother and a female-centered culture. But in terms of actual ways that I perceive women, and really examined, really thought about women and where they fit in my novels and how I used them there and in my own life. All of that changed. It changed radically. It changed dramatically over time. That's just one aspect.

CASMIER:

You came of age as a writer at a moment when there was an explosion of Black women's writing as well.

WIDEMAN:

You said '80. Well, that's Tony [Morrison]. That's Tony and Toni Cade Bambara and Gayl Jones, and Alice. I should have put Alice first. Yes, in a way, she emerged first. Just by coincidence, her editor was my editor. That's how I met Alice the first time through Hiram Haydn. You know who else Hiram Haydn connects to? Charles Waddell Chestnut. They lived on the same street in Cleveland, Ohio. This is my editor. When he was a boy, this guy comes into his father's house complaining about Charles Chesnutt living in the block, living in the neighborhood. And according to Hiram, Hiram's father stood up and said to the man, "Be gone, you whited sepulcher!" That was the beginning of Hiram's acute interest in people of color. Alice Walker and myself were Hiram's authors. Then there's a continuity, because sooner or later, Alice gets in the business of sponsoring people and getting people published and that connects back to Hiram.

CASMIER:

How did the Black Arts Movement affect you? I find it interesting that part of your strength is your independence. Baraka would say things and you say that you were not really bothered by that.

WIDEMAN:

Number one, I always believe in having a day job. I was poor. I didn't ever want to be poor again. I didn't ever want to be under some boss. That's why I wanted to be a ball player or writer because in my juvenile brain, I thought those were very, very independent things. I thought they were about the same. In writing and ball playing, you're your own person. They were adventurous. They were fun. But it all came down to having a day job. So, I made quite an effort to be a college teacher. I got degrees. I worked my way through the system. So, I always had a job. I didn't have to depend on whether my books sold or not in order to eat, in order to feed my family. That's very important because it goes back to independence, financial independence. That kind of self-sufficiency is crucial to me.

Then you can see that I could have very ambivalent attitudes about Baraka and Black Arts. It scared me. I knew people were talking about things I wasn't doing. I wasn't out there in the street. I had gotten away from that stuff as quickly as I could. I lost most of my connections with it. I was not an activist. I was in the university. And that was very, very important distinction. But I also knew that that was a good idea because that gave me my living and I had some independence. It took me a while before I began to figure out and really fully understand how the academy compromises you. The first thing that helped me realize that is the fact that somebody still was speaking for me and that the academy had its prejudices.

CASMIER:

What do you mean by somebody was speaking for you?

WIDEMAN:

Reviews. Essays that interpreted my work. And so, I had not exactly escaped into some sort of idealized world where were things depended on reason and argument and logic. That was my kind of naive sense of what Academia was all about—about issues, about thinking, about tying you up with a great tradition. Early in my career, people asked me, which American I want to be, which American writer is my favorite. I wouldn't blink an eye. "I don't want to be a great American writer. I want to be a great writer." And I really believed that. To a certain extent, I believe that now. I no longer have the notion of being great. But I want to be in that world of writing. And American writing is a very specific kind and it has a great variety of different voices and some tremendous, tremendous work. But it's also been filtered, and channeled and organized to fit the university.

CASMIER:

One of the questions sometimes asked about you is why don't you write about other things, your marriage and stuff like that?

WIDEMAN:

Sometimes I'm very envious of books that I read that permit the writer to think deeply or to think primarily about his relationship to men or his relationship to women, romance, change, adultery, etc. You know, I feel very envious. I don't think I have that privilege yet. I don't think I'm free. I am free, but I have to keep in mind always that not everybody believes that.

CASMIER:

That sounds like the description of the contemporary writer, concerned with issues of intimacy and stuff like that, versus that of the Black Arts Movement writer just concerned with functional art. And so, one of the things that you're saying is that you don't feel free not to engage that script. And the question is, when you say that you envy people who write like that, aren't they engaging the script, too?

WIDEMAN:

I think it's always best to talk about a particular book or particular person because we groupthink too much. And that's what newspapers and Internet allow you to do, groupthink. In fact, that reinforces groupthink because it gives you more material, more statistics, more numbers and we're stuck with that. We're stuck with more and more without cases. We have numbers instead of instances. We concern ourselves with how many Black people are in prison rather than with what it would be like for anybody to be in a fucking cage 24 hours a day, and what that might do to their mom, etc. That individual case gets swept up in what seems to be another kind of scenario.

CASMIER:

There's a bunch of stuff out there that works on this level of trying to try to humanize the person in prison. That's not the level on which you engage people is it?. Aren't you engaging our imaginations and what constructs that person?

WIDEMAN:

I didn't always understand what I was doing. I'm always asking questions. I'm always asking questions. So, then I started to understand better what I was doing. That's what's so fascinating about Douglass. He didn't lose sight of the fact that the enemy was the South. The slave needed help. But if you just let the ex-slave alone, he would probably take care of himself. All right. The government should be concentrating on making the Constitution and the rules that the country goes by serve all people equally. Then you've got an even playing field. Some people will fall, some people won't fall. The bottom will be Black people who fall until they get their shit together. But as long as you have hypocrisy, as long as you have pity, as long as you have condescension, as long as you have abolitionists who don't want to live next door to colored people; then you're not going to solve it.

CASMER:

So how can you even start talking about love if you're already entrenched or engaged in all these constellations of free and unfree that we live with? Is anybody really free to talk about love? Is anybody free?

WIDEMAN:

Well, no, we're not. Because I think the world I tried to describe in 24 words or less just a minute ago in which there is such "A" economic power, and "B" technical power and "C" instant exchange and leveling of difference; in that world, to have a moment in which you are not inundated, in which a script is not being provided for you, or multiple scripts—it doesn't have to be one—; to be outside of that is a very, very rare circumstance. And most people don't have that option, just like most people don't have a lot of time to sit down and read a book.

CASMIER:

Do you accept a division between functional art and sort of aesthetic, non-functional art or art for art's sake?

WIDEMAN:

Well, there's always been a suspicion. In every culture, every society that I've ever read about, there's always a suspicion of people who are different, particularly of people who break the rules. And why is that? Why is that the case?

Because any society and any culture and any little village has a set of rules that it runs by and if you throw wrenches into that by your behavior, or the way you speak, or how much you drink, or whatever, then you're suspicious. There's that real suspicion. "Artist" is an artist/witch, artist/snake, artist/different gods—dealing with different gods. There's always that suspicion, which is funny because we're kind of tied up with outside powers and maybe malevolent powers, but powerful ones. Art is also treated as a kind of escape from responsibility. You're not really holding down a job or you're sitting around blowing that flute or horn. You're not doing your share. Yet, now, you want a place. You want to eat, don't you? You want a roof over your head. So, the artist is lazy. The artist as escapist.

CASMIER:

In *Writing to Save a Life*, the author figure was looking at these glass objects made by a friend. He describes them as a mixture of alchemy. What does that mean?

WIDEMAN:

One reason people are scared by art—the idea that the artist is connected with demons or some sort of separate power—is because effective art can take your breath away. You know, you suddenly as a spectator, or hearer, or watching a dance, you realize, you know, that you don't have it all figured out. That whatever protective covering this society or this village or this race gives you; there is other shit going on. Woah! And if you don't attend to that, you're going to pay. Something tells you you're going to pay. And so, you get that sort of mystery. Mystery.

CASMIER:

You said in an interview with James Coleman about *Reuben* that every writer is somewhat of a shaman or a priest.

WIDEMAN:

I think there's no doubt about it. Because what are you doing? You're creating a competing reality; an alternative reality. And if you're good at it, it does creep in.

But you see this face of a woman and one eyes is up here, and one eyes is down there . . . "Is that my mother? Is that my mom? That is a mouth, isn't it? You're trying to do that?" You know, that's the competing reality—to disarranged somebody's sensibility. And art has that capacity, unless that capacity is sort of filtered and neutered. You know, when I talked about people speaking for me earlier. Well, I can do that woman with two eyes.

But if people only hear: "Well, we saw this painting by Wideman with a woman with an eye in the head, an eye on the bottom of her chin. But that was done already by Mr. X and that was done by another culture. So, you don't have to pay much attention to that. That's just imitative. That's a riff that's old. People don't have eyes in their chin, so why even bother with it?" You know, it's another critical response to say, "Yeah, that's kind of interesting, but let's go back to the hands of this character, this painting." You see what I mean?

CASMIER:

What do you want to hear the response to be?

WIDEMAN:

I'd like to write well enough that there's a residue or there's a at least part of what I'm doing, which comes across as different or other than the usual response that the reader has to these things. It's the opposite of impeachable. The virtue of impeachable is that it keeps reminding you that, OK, these people are . . . oh, they're beautiful. They have lots of money. They're rich. They murder each other. They get away with it. They eat with forks. They do this. We know about it. We have all the information. This is just kind of exotic. They're different. So, you keep reading and reading and reading because you're being reinforced that yes, it's different, but not really that different. So, you can hear nothing. You're kind of charmed by it or seduced by it. The difference is illusory difference; bullshit difference that allows you the confidence and the interest to keep reading about them because they're like you. But it doesn't really challenge, the reader to say, "But they're also not like me. They've nothing to do with me."

CASMIER:

Is there anything in your work that you really like the best, are really proud of?

WIDEMAN:

I can say pretty clearly that the most joy is doing it. And so, whatever I'm working on is what I like best. If somebody says "Well, I have not read your work, but I'd like to read your work." My answer would all depend on what I know about the person. I might say *Brothers and Keepers* simply because that's a very accessible book. It's not even fiction—I mean, not ordinary fiction. But I might say start with stories. If you like them, then learn a little bit about the work and go to other books. But I really have no idea. I think more in terms of passages. I think of things that I'm still kind of happy with. And that might be just a moment in *Philadelphia Fire* when a guy is walking through Clark Park or it might be where I think I really have gotten it right. And that just comes to me at that moment and certain things float and I think they were done well. But an entire book? Something that did what I wanted it to do? I was absolutely serious. Whatever I'm working on; it intrigues me most. And I don't have a lot of energy. I don't reread things. I don't even remember some stuff. I couldn't tell you the characters in all my books because I don't reread them. The whole point is to learn and go ahead. Learn something and go ahead. If I didn't feel there were things I needed to learn and big spaces or something I want to try to do that I haven't done, I really would just wear my laurels and say, OK, I'm a writer. I did this badass book. Forget about it. Why should I worry about anything else?

CASMIER:

What would you like to say is your contribution or *this* is what I did?

WIDEMAN:

The idea that I have kept the language of fiction alive and challenged it and that the challenge comes recognizably from a person like me, a person born in an African-American community, raised in an African-American community and family; that the person like that, somebody like that did something that changed the collective language and pushed it further. What I was saying about what I admire so much about Cormac McCarthy, the two books I'm reading right now, is that they pushed the language forward. They changed it. That's what Shakespeare does.

You know Frederick Douglass—I just have Douglass on the brain because I'm reading the book—but he went from being a slave kid, having to teach himself to read. He just loved it. He loved talking and he loved writing. And he loved performing the language. And he changed it. And he got so good at it, and, you know, he talked to people like Lincoln and Harriet Beecher Stowe and they heard him and then they had an audience.

When I say the language, I don't mean the language of advertising. I don't mean the language of lies. I don't mean the language of repetition. I mean the language that we use for thought. That's what I love about Achebe. That's what I love about Conrad when he's on. That's not distinct from the ideas and the politics. You know, I've been asked that question. What do you want to do? What's your goal? And I said, well, I'd like to keep alive the idea that language can do something other than lie. I don't think all language is a lie. I don't think art is a lie in those senses, because some people use it that way. But it has intrinsic power to go in the other direction, to create things.

CASMIER:

I think it's harder for a writer. You talk about the visual artist, but the struggle of the writer seems removed from that.

WIDEMAN

It's a long haul. One is always defeated by trying to bring into life a piece of the world as you see it, as you represent it. You are always defeated by that task. But you can try again, and you can try again. And maybe in some of those tries, you got some of it right.

Index

Achebe, Chinua, xi, 20, 38, 39, 121
advanced scholarship, xvi
aesthetic approach, 72, 73
aesthetics of disposal, xviii–xxi, xx, 106, 107, 118
Africa, Birdie, 58
Africa, Ramona, 62
African: cosmologies, xx, 4, 21, 27, 46, 115, 123, 156; diaspora, 19, 20, 25; sculptures, 21, 25, 26
African American, 74; ceremony, xxi–xxii; community, 16; cosmology, 161; expressivity, 61; identity, 3; oppression and violence against, 36; orality, 16, 28, 62, 129; tradition, 105; Voodoo, 30, 140; writing, 2
African American Vernacular English, 129
African Motherland, 31
Afro-American oral performance, 86
Afrocentrism, xiii
Afro-Cuban religion, 140, 142
Afrofuturism, 162
Afro-mysticism, 162
Afropessimism, 13, 17–20, 47, 54, 117, 159, 161, 162
Afropessimism (2020, Wilderson), 17, 117
Alexander, Michelle, 8–9, 11–13, 15, 35–37, 43, 57, 63, 73, 81, 87

Ali, Mohammad, viii, 154
American: darkness, 32; dream, 80; fetish, 54; identity, 36, 37, 54; imagination, 51; racism, 37; slavery, 73–74
The American Fugitive in Europe (1855, Brown), 75
American media, in nurturing racism, 36
Amerikastudien/American Studies, xii
ancestral figures, 31–33
ancestral spirits, 131–32
Anderson, Benedict, 122–23
Andrade, Heather Russell, xiv–xv, xix, xxi
antebellum slavery narrative, 75, 76
anthologies, 6–7
anti-imperialism, 142, 143
anti-racism, 142
Armah, Ayi Kwei, 13
Armstrong, Louis, 19
Asante, Molefi Kete, xiii
Attitudes of Animals in Motion (Muybridge), 40
authenticating documents, 71
authenticating machinery, 71
The Autobiography of LeRoi Jones (Baraka), 160
"avant-garde or free" music, 106

"bad Negroes", 135
Baker, Houston, xiii, xiv, xvi, 99, 100
Baldwin, James, vii, 18, 146
Bambara, Toni Cade, 6, 8, 12
Banjo (1929, McKay), 145
Baraka, Amiri, xvi, xvii, xx, xxii, 2, 6, 12, 19, 91, 97–98, 106, 107, 117, 142, 143, 150, 152, 160
Barnhurst, Kevin, 37
Barthes, Roland, xi
Baudrillard, Jean, 52, 146
Beard, Romare, xviii
Bearden, Romare, 27, 92, 101–5
The Beautiful Ones Are Not Yet Born (1968, Armah), 13
Bedouin Hornbook (Mackey), viii
Beloved (Morrison), viii, xi, xxii, 32, 50, 53, 154
Beneath the Underdog (1971, Mingus), 99
Benjamin, Walter, 53, 118
Benston, Kimberly, 52
Benveniste, Emile, 128
Berben-Masi, Jacqueline, vii, xv, xvi, 67
Between the World and Me (Coates), 155
Birkerts, Sven, 74–75
Birth of a Nation, 55
Black(s), 2, 3, 5, 8, 10, 17–19, 21, 117, 160, 161; authenticity, xiv; cosmology, 115, 116; degeneracy, 57; diaspora, 19, 20; discredited knowledge, 159–61; identity, 2; internationalism, 112; microcosm, 16; middle class, 3, 11, 12, 27, 35, 50; nationalism, 161; oppression of, 51; orality, 16, 28, 61–62; postmodernism, 16–18, 25, 29; power, 149, 154; radicalism, 141; slavery and violence against, 70; spirituality, 116; writers, 123
The Black Aesthetic (Gayle), xvii, 9
Black Aesthetic movement, xx, 4, 19–21, 24, 61
Black Aesthetic period, 46
Black Arts, 4, 6, 9, 14, 17–18, 20, 21, 51, 52, 120; aesthetics of, 106; ceremonial acumen, xxi–xxii; characteristics, 20; deculturation, xxi–xxii; of necromancy, 49, 123; role of, 19; tradition of, 105
Black Arts Movement, xiii, xv–xvi, 3, 6–9, 15, 26, 46, 98, 141, 152, 160
Black Atlantic (Gilroy), xx
Black Atlantic bundle, 26, 30, 45–48, 65, 92, 113; *minkisi of*, 70, 72; spirit embodying material, 109
Black Atlantic charms, 29, 44–46, 58, 91, 93, 103
Black Atlantic cosmology, xxi, 4, 21, 25, 46, 139, 143
Black Atlantic craft, xxi, 16, 26, 29, 33, 39, 76, 82, 91, 102; power of, 73
Black Atlantic orality, 150
Black Atlantic power, 144
Black Atlantic structure, 102
Blackcentricity: How Ancient Black Cultures Created Civilization. Revealing the Truth that White Supremacy Denied (Matthews), 161
Blackcentrism, 161
Black Chant: The Languages of African-American Postmodernism (Nielsen), xiii, xvi–xvii, 61
Black communities, xi, xii, xiv, 13, 27, 33, 64, 92; disintegrating, 33–35
Black Cultural Nationalism, xii, 7, 12, 20, 25, 68
"Black Cultural Nationalism" (1968, Karenga), 9
Black-face minstrel, 151
Black Jacobin (James), 140
Black Liberation movement, 91, 112, 141
Blackness, 51–52, 54, 57, 142; canonizing the, 142; liberated, 44, 48
Blackness and Modernism: The Literary Career of John Edgar Wideman (Coleman), 16, 50
Black Orpheus, 20

Black Panthers, 56, 57, 98, 133, 141, 145
"Black Panthers, New Journalism, and the Rewriting of the Sixties" (Staub), 56
Black Power, 2, 6, 26; *Minkisi* of, 57–58
Black Power (Ture and Hamilton), 51
Black Power Movement, 7, 51
Black prison population, 13
Black Skin White Masks (Fanon), 20
Black speakers, written English of, 129–30
"Black Stereotypes as Reflected in Popular Culture, 1880-1920" (Lemon), 56
Bowie, Lester, 19
Braxton, Anthony, 101, 162–64
Brody, Richard, 125
Brokaw, Tom, 96
Brothers and Keepers (1984, Wideman), vii, 4, 15, 23, 34, 108, 114, 119
Brown, James, xxii, 58–60, 98, 161
Brown, William Wells, 75
The Butler, 7
Byerman, Keith Eldon, xxi, 9, 10, 14, 23, 26, 35, 39, 64, 112, 114, 141
Byzantine cosmology, 135

Cabrera, Lydia, 30
Candelo, 144
Candomblé, 139
canon-producing anthologies, 6–7
capturing fetish, 54
Castro, Fidel, 134, 140, 142, 144
categorical panic, 58
Catholic Church, 142, 144
The Cattle Killing (1996, Wideman), xxi–xxii, 4, 5, 21, 27, 32, 67–71, 103, 108, 129; aesthetic structure of, 72; eclectic slavery narrative, 70–77, 84; Kate's story, 83–87, 129; Liam's story, 76–81, 86, 87, 97, 98, 143; Philadelphia, 79–80; prophecy, 87–88; quilted narrative, 74–76; slavery narratives, 70, 72–73, 75, 82, 83, 85; Xhosa cattle killing, 68, 70, 81–82
ceremonial acumen, xxi–xxii
Chesnutt, Charles, 103, 129
Chicago Tribune, 146–48
Civil Rights, 51
Civil Rights Movement, 138, 139
civil rights nightmare, 11
Clark, Mark, 141
class, 11
The Classic Slave Narratives (Gates), 68
Clausen, Jan, 62
Clinton, Bill: drug war, 73
Cluster, Dick, 140
Coates, Ta-Nehisi, 155
coded antiblack rhetoric, 35, 36
Coleman, James, x, xii, xiv, xx, 14–17, 50, 64
The Color Purple (Walker), vii, 73, 102
confession, 152–53
conventional narrative capture, 64
Corregidora (Jones), 62, 103
The Cosby Show, 55
Crapol, Edward, 83–84
Creekmore, Hubert, 148
crime of rape, 146–48, 150, 152; and murder, 153
Critical Essays on John Edgar Wideman (TuSmith and Byerman), xxi
"The Critical Reception of Modern African Poetry" (Okunoye), 20
Cuban Revolution, 140, 142–43
cultural immobility, xiii
cultural terrorism, 51
Currey, James, 20

Damballah, 118–19, 144
"dark" tradition, 161
Davis, Angela, 8, 12
Davis, Miles, viii
"death by incarceration", 4, 14, 32, 39
Debord, Guy, 52
de Conquer, High John, 150
deculturation, xxi–xxii

Dedalus, Stephen, 10
"Defining the Black Voice in Fiction" (Wideman), 62
de Porres, Saint Martin, 133–35, 140–45, 148, 154, 156; as bad Negro, 142, 143; hagiography, 143; power, 144; supernaturalism of, 142, 143
Deren, Maya, 58, 65, 89, 106
DeSilvis, Devin, 98
Destination Unknown (Ra), 161
Discourse and Destruction: The City of Philadelphia versus MOVE (Wagner-Pacifici), 43, 54
discredited knowledge, 18, 19, 72, 76, 116, 159, 160
disintegrating communities, 33–35
Divine Horsemen: The Living Gods of Haiti (Deren), 58, 89
documents, 48
Domke, David, 35–36
Dorsey, Henry, 39
Douglass, Frederick, 112, 164
dream deferred, 51, 65, 66
dreams, 51

eclectic slavery narrative, 70–77, 84
Edwards, Brent, xi, xix, xx, 106–7, 118
effect healing, 21
El Caballo. *See* Castro, Fidel
Ellison, Ralph, ix, 105
enslaved Africans, 80, 83
enslaved women, 72, 73, 86, 87
ephemeral temporality, 53, 54
epistemological crises, 55, 56
epistolary form, 101–8
Epistrophies Jazz and the Literary Imagination (Edwards), xx, 106, 118
Equiano, Olaudah, 72, 77, 79
Eshu-Elegbara, 91, 92, 97
Everett, Percival, 124
exorcism, 26, 107; painting, 15, 26, 37, 40
extrajudicial murders, 70

Fabre, Michel, vii
fake book, 92, 106, 109; of heads, 98–101
fake holdup, 146, 148
fake news, 80, 83, 85, 145
"Fanning the Flames of Racial Discord: The National Press and the Black Panther Party" (Rhodes), 57
Fanon (2008, Wideman), 4, 5, 21, 23, 27, 61, 64, 99–101, 111–16, 139, 162, 163; African American music, 117; ancestral spirits, 131–32; Black American necromancy, 121; Black or African cosmology, 115, 116; Black spirituality, 116; Igbo cosmology, 111–12, 120, 121, 123, 128, 131, 132; Igbo mourning rites, 115; images of film and spiritualized ancestors, 120–30; jazz standard and spiritualization, 116–20
Fanon, Frantz, xvi, 16, 18, 20, 40–41, 61, 112, 113, 120, 121, 123, 124, 128–32, 137, 161, 163
"Fanon manuscript", 123, 125, 128
fatalism, 55
Feith, Michel, x, xiii, xv, xviii, xix, xx, xxi
Fernandez, James W., 54
fetish of narratological re-enslavement, 53–57
Flash of the Spirit (Thompson), xxii, 21, 25, 30, 39, 45, 46, 72, 73, 91, 139
Flight to Canada (Reed), 140
Forces in Motion: The Music and Thought of Anthony Braxton (Lock), 160
The Form of the News (Barnhurst and Nerone), 37
Franklin, Aretha, 17, 129
Frobenius, Leo, 151
functional art, xiii–xv, 9, 10, 12, 25, 26, 46, 71, 78, 90, 113, 151, 163,
functional unruliness, 57
funerals, 108, 110

gangsta rap, 81
Garner, Margaret, 53
Gassire's spirit, 151, 152
Gates, Henry Louis, xiii, 3, 4, 28, 68, 71, 72, 77
Gayle, Addison, xvii, 9
ghettos, 2, 3
Giacometti, Alberto, xviii, 27, 101–9
Gillespie, Dizzy, 99
Gilroy, Paul, xx
A Glance Away (Wideman), 8, 12
Godard, Jean Luc, 27, 113, 123–29, 131, 139
Gonzalez, Juan, 36, 54
Gossett, Thomas, 36, 54
govi, 65–66, 68, 76
Grandjeat, Yves-Charles, xix
*griot*s of Sahelian Africa, 76, 78
Guzzio, Tracie Church, ix, xi–xii, xiv, xv

hagiographies, xx, 134–35, 143–45, 149, 162
Haitian cosmology, 97, 107, 156
Haitian *govi*, 65–66, 68, 76; prophecy of, 88
Haitian Revolution, 140
Haitian Vodun, 5, 46, 58, 139
Hamilton, Richard, 51
Hampton, Fred, 2, 141
Hancock, Herbie, viii
Harlem Renaissance, 51
Henderson, Stephen, 9
Hernández, Rafael, 140
historiographic sensibility, 118
The History of Havana (Cluster and Hernández), 140
Hoberman, J., 125, 126
Holloway, Karla F., 53
The Homewood Trilogy (Wideman), 28, 78, 93, 108
homogenous empty time, 53, 54
Hoop Roots (2001, Wideman), 61
Hopkins, Gerard Manley, x

Hopkins, the Self, and God (Ong), x
Howe, Irving, 148
Hughes, Langston, 51, 52
Hurry Home (Wideman), 8, 12
Hurston, Zora Neale, ix

identity, 35–37; extracted, 63–66
ideology, and Afro-American Literature (1984, Baker), 99
Igbo, 163; belief, 121; cosmology, 111–12, 120, 121, 123, 128, 131, 132; mourning rites, xviii, 5, 115, 118; spiritualsation, 115
The Image Book (2018, Godard), 125
incarceration, 3–5, 11, 14, 15
Incidents in the Life of a Slave Girl (1861, Jacob), 82, 145
In Search of Our Mothers' Gardens (Walker), 73
Interfaces of the Word (Ong), 130
intuitional racism, 12
Invisible Man (Ellison), 105

Jablow, Alta, 151
Jackson, Jesse, 2
Jacobs, Harriet, 82–84, 86, 145
James, C. L. R., 140
James, George, 49
jazz heads, 99, 100, 106, 109, 116–20, 137
jazz music, 98–100, 106
Jefferson, Thomas, 86
Jim Crow, 9, 11, 35, 74, 96, 135, 153
John Edgar Wideman: The European Response, xi, xix
Johnson, Jack, 154
Johnson, James Weldon, 7
John XXIII, Pope, 141, 142
Jones, Gayle, 62, 103
Jones, Leroi. *See* Baraka, Amiri
Jones, Margaret, 62, 103
Jordan, Edward "Kidd", viii
Jordan, Michael, viii

Journalists, Framing, and Discourse about Race Relations (Domke), 35–36
Joyce, James, 10
Julien, Claude, x, xi

Karenga, Ron, xvii, 9, 19, 20
Kate's story, 83–87, 129
Kerner, Michael, 124
King, Martin Luther, 50
Kinnamon, Keneth, 147
Kongo cosmology, 5, 29–31, 39, 46, 140, 144

lack Atlantic craft, 30
Lacy, Steve, 99, 100
La Tête d'obsidienne (*Picasso's Mask*, Malraux), 15, 25
Leaphart, Vincent, 58, 89, 98
Lemann, Nicholas, 33
Lemon, Stanley, 56
Leperlier, Antoine, 157
Les Demoiselles d'Avignon (Picasso), 15, 26, 40
Liam's story, 76–81, 86, 97, 98, 104, 130, 143
The Life and Work of John Edgar Wideman (Byerman), 9, 23
likeness, 122, 131
"Literary Publishing After Nigerian Independence: Mbari as Celebration" (Currey), 20
loa (*lwa*), 143
Lock, Graham, 160–63
Lodge, David, 45
Lott, Eric, 56, 57
"The Louis Till File", 135, 136, 141, 144, 145, 149, 154, 156
"Love and Theft: The Racial Unconscious of Blackface Minstrelsy" (Lott), 56
Lumière, Aguste, 41
Lumière, Louis, 42
The Lynchers (Wideman), 8, 12, 13
Lyotard, Jean Francois, 53

Mackey, Nathaniel, viii
Malcolm X, 42, 91, 94, 96, 154
Malraux, André, 15, 25
mass incarceration, 3, 5, 11, 36, 43, 70, 74, 80, 81, 141
Matisse, Pierre, 104
Matthews, Donald, 161
Mbalia, Doreatha Drummond, xii, xiv
McKay, Claude, 145
Mifflin, Houghton, 122
Miller, Ivor L., 144, 149
"Mimesis and diegesis in modern fiction" (Lodge), 45
Mingus, Charles, 99
minstrel show, 56, 57
misterios, xxii, 134, 136, 142, 143
Monk, Thelonious, xviii, 27, 92, 99, 100, 103, 105; Zombie music, 105–7, 109
moral panic, 56–58
morgues, 49, 115, 145, 148
Morrison, Toni, viii, ix, xi, xxii, 1, 6, 31, 32, 50, 53, 85, 140, 154; discredited knowledge, 18, 19, 72, 116, 159
MOVE group, 52–54, 59, 61, 62, 143; bombing, 96; tragedy, 53–56, 58
Mulvey, Laura, 126–28
Mumbo Jumbo (1972, Reads), 7, 42, 94, 145
Murphy, Eddie, 7
musical ritual, 99–100
Muybridge, Eadweard, 40–41, 47, 58

Napier, Winston, xiv, xvi
narrative modes, 47, 52, 54, 159, 161, 163
narratological re-enslavement, fetish of, 53–57
Native American genocide, 141
"Native Fathers" (Clausen), 62
Native Son (1940, Wright), 12–13, 135, 145–48, 154, 156
Naylor, Gloria, vii
necromancy, 49, 77, 116, 120, 121, 123, 125, 131, 145, 148

Negritude, 19–21, 25
Negroes, 25, 135, 146
Neo-Hodoo aesthetic, 123
Nerone, John, 37
Neroni, Hilary, 124
"Newborn is Thrown in trash and Dies", 49, 64
The New Jim Crow (Alexander), 8–9, 11, 15, 43, 62, 63, 73–74
News for All the People: The Epic Story of Race and the American Media (Torres and Gonzalez), 36
newspapers, 36–38
Nielson, Aldon, xiii, 61
nigger murder, 151, 153
nkisi (pl: *minkisi*), 30–32, 39, 45–47, 60, 61, 76, 102, 107, 109, 140; of Black Atlantic bundle, 70, 72; of Black Power, 57–58; *Philadelphia Fire* (1990, Wideman), 48–52
nkpulu chi, 131
non-Black, 17
Nongqawuse, 81, 82
non-white races, 36, 54
Norton Anthology of African American Literature (Gates), xiv, 3, 6, 18, 43, 52, 82
Norton Anthology of American Literature, 14
Norton Anthology of Contemporary African American Poetry (Rowell), 6
nyama, xxii, 78–79
nyamakala, xxii, 78
nzo a nkisi, xviii; secular, 5, 25, 26, 30, 39–42

Obama, Barak, 114
Okri, Ben, 121
Okunoye, Oyeniyi, 20
Ong, Walter, x, 130, 150
"On Repetition in Black Culture" (Snead), 18

pacquets congos of Haiti, 30, 140

Padilioni, James, 142–44
Pan Africanism, 112
Papa Legba, 89, 95, 97, 139, 144
Parker, Charlie, 99
Pentcheva, Bissera V., 135
Persuasions and Performances: The Play of Tropes in Culture (Fernandez), 54–55
Petro and *Rada,* 156
Philadelphia, 79–80, 109
Philadelphia Fire (1990, Wideman), viii, 4–5, 21, 29, 43–48, 53–54, 70, 76, 80, 98, 103, 108, 129, 143, 161, 163; capture and fetish of narratological re-enslavement, 53–57; extracted children, 59–61; extracted expression, 61–63; extracted identity, 63–66; historical extraction, 58–59; *minkisi* and, 48–52, 57–58
Picasso, Pablo, 15, 19, 21, 25, 26, 36, 40, 41
Pinckney, Darryl, 24, 44
Pisan Cantos (Pound), 150–54
Pittsburgh, 44, 50, 80, 81, 91, 92, 109
Playing in the Dark (Morrison), 85
poetry anthology, 6–7
A Portrait of the Artist as a Young Man (Joyce), 10
possessed texts, 5, 144, 145, 154, 156, 157
post-9/11, 112, 114, 116, 119, 125
The Postmodern Condition (Lyotard), 53
postmodernism, 24–26, 45–46
Pound, Saint Ezra, 150–54
"Prayer to the masks" (Senghor), 20
prenda, 30–31
"principle of word magic", 15
Prokopow, Michael, 72
The Promised Land (Lemann), 33
prophecy, 87–88
Pryor, Richard, viii
Puckett, John, 98
punto de segurar of Cuba, 30, 140

quilted narrative, 74–76

Ra, Sun, viii, 19, 160–62
races, 36
Race: The History of an Idea (Gossett), 36
racial allegory, 147
racial caste system, 11
racial expropriation, 56
racialized narratives, 74, 81
racial solidarity, 4
racism, xi–xii, 4, 5, 13, 15, 36, 37, 39, 75, 112, 142, 152; American media in, 36; intuitional, 12
radical groups, 9
Rampersad, Arnold, xiv
Ray, Michael, viii
Reagan, Ronald, 2–3, 8, 33, 43; drug war, 73; War on Drugs, 12
Reed, Ishmael, 6, 7, 42, 48, 49, 94, 116, 123, 140, 145
religion, 140
Renaissance space, 128
representation, 46, 47
Reuben (1987, Wideman), xviii, 4, 5, 15–19, 21, 24–29, 46–51, 61, 70, 76, 80, 103, 107, 108, 139; African Motherland, 31; ancestral figures, 31–33; disintegrating communities, 33–35; dominant written fetishes, 35–39; Kongo cosmology, 5, 29–31, 39, 46; secular *nzo a nkisi*, 39–42
reverse photography, 125, 131
revolutionary effects, 52
Reynolds, David, 5
Rhodes, Jane, 57
Ricoeur, Paul, xvi
ritualistic spiritualization, 131
"the Robert Nixon" case, 146–48
Romare Bearden's collages, 102, 109, 127, 128
"Rootedness: The Ancestor as Foundation" (Morrison), 18
Rowell, Charles Henry, 6–8

Sahelian Africa, *griot*s of, 76, 78
Samuels, Wilfred, 14
Santeria, 44, 142, 143; cosmology of, 144
Sartre, Jean Paul, 104, 117, 127, 132
Saturday Night Live (Murphy), 7
Schmidt, Klaus, xii, 16, 29
secular *nzo a nkisi*, xviii, 5, 25–26, 30, 39–42, 46, 65
self-inscription, xi, xix
Senghor, Leopold, 9, 20, 78
Sent for You Yesterday (*Wideman*), 101, 119
Senufo, 19
sex crime, 147
Seymour, Gene, 75
Shakur, Assata, 143
The Signifying Monkey (Gates), 28
silence, 149–50
slavery narrative, xix, 8, 70–73, 75, 82, 83, 85, 103
The Slave's Narrative: Texts and Contexts (Gates), 68
Smith, Julia M. H., 134
Smith, Rachel J. D., 135
Smith, Valerie, 3, 96
Snead, James, 18
social Darwinism, 36
social death, 17, 19, 21, 161
social justice, 142, 143
sorcerer, 10–21, 26, 59
southern lynch law, 145
Soyinka, Wole, 152
spirit embodying material, 30, 58, 109, 110, 140
spiritualization, 116–22, 125, 132
Stamelman, Richard, 104, 105
Staub, Michael, 56, 57
Stepto, Robert Burns, 30, 71, 75
Stowe, Harriet Beecher, 83
strategized profanity, 62
stubborn silence, 154
subjective mystification, xvi
supernaturalism, 142, 143

superstition, 17
supreme disorderly conduct, 57
survivance theory, xx
The System of Dante's Hell (Baraka), xx, 106

Taylor, Cecil, xvii, xx, 106, 107
Things Fall Apart (Achebe), xi, 38–39
Thomas, Saint Bigger, 145–48, 154
Thompson, Robert Farris, xxii, 21, 30, 39, 45–47, 72, 91–92, 97, 103, 107, 139, 140, 144, 162; secular *nzo a nkisi,* xviii, 5, 25–26, 39–42, 46, 65
Till, Emmett, 95, 96, 117, 135, 137, 138, 140, 155
Till, Mamie, 155
Till, Saint Louis, xiii, 38, 117, 133, 135–40, 144–56, 163
To Be or Not to Bop (1979, Gillespie), 99
Tomahawk, 141, 142
Torres, Joseph, 36, 54
torture, 124–25
torture porn, 123
transubstantiation, 156–57
Troupe, Margaret Porter, viii
Troupe, Quincy, viii
The Truly Disadvantaged (Wilson), 10–11, 35, 51
Turé, Kwame, 51, 143
TuSmith, Bonnie, xxi, 164
Two Cities (1998, Wideman), xviii, 4, 5, 21, 27, 40, 61, 89–92, 99–101, 108, 109, 119, 120, 124, 126, 130, 143; John Africa, 89–93, 99, 100, 106, 161; Kassima, 93–97, 107–10, 164; letters of Mr. Mallory to Giacometti, Alberto, 101–9; Liam of, 104, 130; Martin Mallory, 90–93, 95–99, 101–10, 164; plot, 93–95; Robert Jones, 93–95, 107; second line, 95–98

Uncle Tom's Cabin (Stowe), 83
underclass, 11

Understanding the New Black Poetry (Henderson), 9
utopian dreams, 80
Uzukwu, Elochukwu, 121

"Visual Pleasure and Narrative Cinema" (Mulvey), 126
Vizenor, Gerald, xx
Vodun, 44, 156
Voodoo, 139, 140

Wagner-Pacifici, Robin, 43, 54, 55
Wahlman, Maude Southwell, 72
Walker, Alice, vii, ix, 1, 73, 82, 102
Walker, Margaret, 146
Wall, Cheryl A., xiv, 6, 9
Wallace, Michelle, 62, 74, 80
War on Drugs, 3, 12
The Water Cure (Everett), 124
West, Cornell, 73
White, 18; identity, 37; race, 36; supremacy, 56, 145, 147–48
Wideman, Bette A., 122
Wideman, John Edgar, vii, viii, 1, 03–10, 12–15, 18, 20, 21, 23–29, 32, 34, 39–40, 42, 43, 46, 48–50, 53, 59–64, 67–68, 75, 76, 78, 85, 86, 91–96, 98–102, 104, 105, 107, 108, 111–14, 117, 120–22, 124, 126–30, 132–41, 144, 145, 155, 157, 161–64; Black postmodernism, 16–18, 25; ceremonial acumen, xxii–xxiii; criticism, neglected writer, ix–xi; deculturation, xxi–xxii; functional art, xiii–xv; ideal poetic truth and reality, xv–xvii; poetics, xix; real and imagined, xi–xiii; self-inscription, xi; words and, xvii–xviii
Wideman, Robert, 4, 13, 14, 23, 32, 137; "death by incarceration", 4, 14, 32, 39
Wilderson, Frank, 17, 47, 54, 117, 159
Williams, Mary Lou, 106
Wilson, William Julius, 10–11, 13, 35, 51

Wise, Christopher, 78
Wolfe, Tom, 57
The Women of Brewster Place (Naylor), vii
The Wretched of the Earth (Sartre), 124, 129, 132, 161
Wright, Richard, 12, 135, 145–48
Writing Blackness (Coleman), xx
Writing to Save a Life: The Louis Till File (2016, Wideman), xiii, xvii–xviii, xix–xx, 4, 5, 19, 21, 27, 32, 38, 41, 95, 133–39; de Porres, Saint Martin (*see* de Porres, Saint Martin); family Saints, 154–56; lives of the Saints, 139–41; Pound, Saint Ezra, 150–54; Thomas, Saint Bigger, 145–48, 154; Till, Saint Louis, 38, 117, 133, 135–40, 144–56, 163; transubstantiation, 156–57
written English, 129–30

Xhosa cattle killing, 68, 70, 81–82

"yeast" (*le levain,* Senghor), 20

Zeus, 151, 152
Zombie music, 105–7, 109
Zoning (Williams), 106

About the Author

Stephen Casmier is an associate professor in the Department of English at Saint Louis University. Casmier is a native of St. Louis, Missouri, and his work has appeared in Ishmael Reed's *Conch Magazine, African American Review, Callaloo, Multi-Ethnic Literature of the United States, The Moving Image, Literature and Theology,* and critical collections on John Edgar Wideman, Walter Ong, S. J., American multiculturalism, and film.